Understanding Customers

The Marketing Series is one of the most comprehensive collections of books in marketing and sales available from the UK today.

Published by Butterworth-Heinemann on behalf of The Chartered Institute of Marketing, the series is divided into three distinct groups: *Student* (fulfilling the needs of those taking the Institute's certificate and diploma qualifications; *Professional Development* (for those on formal or self-study vocational training programmes); and *Practitioner* (presented in a more informal, motivating and highly practical manner for the busy marketer).

Formed in 1911, The Chartered Institute of Marketing is now the largest professional marketing management body in Europe with over 60,000 members located worldwide. Its primary objectives are focused on the development of awareness and understanding of marketing throughout UK industry and commerce and in the raising of standards of professionalism in the education, training and practice of this key business discipline.

D0552871

Titles in the series

Behavioural Aspects of Marketing
K. C. Williams

Cases in Marketing Financial Services
Edited by Chris Ennew, Trevor Watkins and Mike Wright

The CIM Piploma Case Study Book 1995–96
David Pearson and Paul Fifield

Economic Theory and Marketing Practice
Angela Hatton and Mike Oldroyd

Effective Sales Management
John Strafford and Colin Grant

Financial Aspects of Marketing
Keith Ward

The Fundamentals of Advertising
John Wilmshurst

The Fundamentals and Practice of Marketing
John Wilmshurst

International Marketing
Stanley J. Paliwoda

Marketing Financial Services
Edited by Chris Ennew, Trevor Watkins and Mike Wright

Strategic Marketing Management
R. M. S. Wilson and C. T. Gilligan

Understanding Customers
Second edition

Chris Rice

Published on behalf of
The Chartered Institute of Marketing

Butterworth-Heinemann
Linacre House, Jordan Hill, Oxford OX2 8DP
A division of Reed Educational and Professional Publishing Ltd

℞ A member of the Reed Elsevier plc group

OXFORD   BOSTON   JOHANNESBURG
MELBOURNE   NEW DELHI   SINGAPORE

First published as *Consumer Behaviour* 1993
Reprinted 1994
Second edition 1997

British Library Cataloguing in Publication Data
A catalogue record for this book is available from the British Library

ISBN 0 7506 2322 5

Typeset by Avocet Typeset, Brill, Aylesbury, Bucks
Printed and bound in Great Britain by
Biddles Ltd, Guildford and King's Lynn

Contents

Foreword

If there were prizes for writing textbooks which combine up-to-date information with reader-friendliness and even a soupcon of style and wit, then Chris Rice would walk away with an armful of them. We all know that students find preparing for examinations to be work of a peculiarly unforgiving, implacable and unpleasant kind, especially as so many textbooks seem to be written as if their authors were trying to emulate the tedium of Kennedy's *Latin Primer*. Anyone approaching *Understanding Customers* with such depressing expectations cannot fail to be jolted with warm shocks and pleasant surprises as they read about (for example) the wonders of cat-food preparation and the elegant delicacy of the Rice PV/PPS model of consumer decision making.

This new edition has been revised, partly because of recent developments in the investigation of consumer behaviour, and partly because of new syllabus requirements initiated by The Chartered Institute of Marketing. It is even more comprehensive than before, yet remains firmly focused on the instrumental demands of students. It can be picked up voluntarily and read for pleasure. Few technical publications justify such an accolade (apart from sex manuals), yet in Rice's case it is well deserved.

Dr Ted Johns
CIM Senior Examiner, Understanding Customers

Preface

Four years ago, when writing *Consumer Behaviour*, I put forward some ideas about control and its problems. In the process I discussed 'Sod's Law' – the idea that if something can go wrong, it will. As the book was published, The Chartered Institute of Marketing announced a change of syllabus to the new 'Understanding Customers' programme at Certificate level. So Sod's Law had struck.

This new edition has some six new chapters and much material which reflects the new syllabus.

The subject remains as fascinating as ever and we have seen a continued growth in the use of influencing techniques well beyond the area of 'shopping'. Vast efforts are now expended to convince us of the need to vote in favour of particular political parties, to conserve the environment, to support charities and other, similar, 'non-commercial' ideals. The basic element of influencing other people remains at the core, however, and it is this process which forms the main thread of the ideas within this text.

The book has been designed to meet the requirements of The Chartered Institute of Marketing professional education scheme, but will also be of immediate relevance to undergraduate and Higher National business studies courses. In a field which has such a rapid rate of change it was decided, as a matter of policy, to encourage the reader to look around to find current examples. This has the advantage that reading newspapers and watching television may now be counted as 'coursework'!

My objective in writing this book has been to produce something which is 'user-friendly'. The aim was to attempt to reproduce the processes which make a 'good' class when teaching – involvement of teacher and students, exchange of ideas, activity, thought and, above all, fun.

My thanks to all those who wrote giving such positive feedback on *Consumer Behaviour* and the style in which it was produced. In other places, I have referred to 'the loneliness of the long-distance learner' – the problems experienced by the solitary student (whether as a long-term experience or because of missing a session at college). It is hoped that, by emphasizing some of the discussion points in this way, some of the difficulties may be reduced. For those who are study-ing in a group, the 'Think' exercises have no 'right' answers, so comparisons of opinions and subsequent arguments are not only common, but are to be welcomed.

A special note of thanks to Ted Johns for his encouragement at the start of the project and his insights at the end. Lastly, my thanks to all the students who have been the experimental proving ground for so much of my work and enjoyment.

Chris Rice
Nottingham

Part One   Identifying the Customer

Introduction

This section introduces ideas and concepts which can be used throughout the programme of study. It attempts to review different stages in marketing development, and looks at some contributions from wider organization/management studies to set a context for the more specific study of aspects of consumer behaviour. Thus many of the ideas in this first section should continue to be considered as part of the background to most of the remainder of the book.

At the end of this section the reader should be familiar with the following concepts (and the associated language) and should be able to relate them to marketing situations and activities:

- Historical perspective – differing marketing orientations
- Customers and users
- Decision Making Units (DMUs)
- Segmentation
- Dependency theory
- Stakeholders in the business/enterprise
- Demographic changes
- Competition
- Ethical issues
  - Deontological/transcendental and utilitarian perspectives
- Total Quality Management
- Customer care
- Organizations as customers
  - Similarities and differences between individual, family and organization buying situations
  - Roles in the organizational buying process
  - Different levels of complexity of buying decisions
  - Decision Making Units (DMUs) and the associated roles (again)
  - American Marketing Association 4-cell model
- Perception as a crucial concept which runs throughout the whole book:
  - The senses, sensation, awareness thresholds
  - Weber's Law
  - Selectivity of perception – external and internal factors affecting perception
  - Habituation
  - Awareness sets
  - Communication

1 'Marketing, management, customers, competitive advantage and the meaning of life!'

A historical perspective

Introduction

The American Marketing Association in 1985 defined marketing as:

> The process of planning and executing the conception, pricing, promotion and distribution of ideas, goods and services to create exchange and satisfy individual and organizational objectives

In the UK The Chartered Institute of Marketing defines it as:

> the management process responsible for identifying, anticipating and satisfying customer requirements profitably

Some of the key words in both definitions identify the concern with satisfying the individual customer, and this is commonly tackled by the idea of the 'marketing mix' – one of the most common formulations of which is that of the 4 Ps:

- **Product**
- **Pricing**
- **Place**
- **Promotion.**

This has been the basis of most thinking about marketing over the last thirty years. Kotler has suggested adding

- **Politics**
- **Public relations**

to make the 6 Ps

whereas Cowell has suggested adding:

- **People**
- **Physical evidence**
- **Process**

when considering the marketing of services, creating an alternative 7 Ps model.

But central to the whole function is the concept of the customer, and the aim is his or her satisfaction.

Marketing is an integral part of the process of managing a business enterprise. Within that context its significance has changed over time. In the early years following the Industrial Revolution, the shortage of products and the demand generated by a population earning cash as the means of exchange led to a situation where many products 'sold themselves'. The development of the assembly line led to a standardization of product – but given a high level of demand, the customer was not necessarily a critical part of the process, as is witnessed by Henry Ford's well-known assertion that '… they can have any colour they like – as long as it is black'.

The growth of the mass communication systems in the middle part of the century led to a growing move towards 'selling' the product to the population via an emphasis on advertising. The latter part of the century saw an increasing awareness of the need to satisfy the customer's needs – once again changing the focus of marketing efforts.

The current situation is one which is influenced by the convergence of a number of trends:

- Growing international competition
- Very rapid and comprehensive channels of communication
- Technological improvements leading to very reliable products
- The growth of the 'quality' movement, further enhancing reliability.

The logic of such a situation is that there is likely to be little significant difference between many competing products within a market. It seems likely that future marketing efforts will focus increasingly on aspects of customer care as a way of creating a differential between products, as suggested by Johns (1994). It also seems likely that ever more effort will go into the process of creating 'emotional value' as a way of distinguishing an organization's product from those of its competitors. As writers such as Tom Peters have argued, the growing competition means that we may need to move beyond consumer satisfaction and aim to 'delight' the customer.

Another possibility is that some markets may move even further towards satisfying the customer by aiming to satisfy needs specifically and directly. It has been asserted that 'Customers do not want choice – they want exactly what they want'. This approach has given rise to a movement which some have called 'mass customization' – a process whereby the organization does not manufacture a product until it has been ordered. In these early stages this would appear to be operating within markets which have an expert customer base and who are prepared to specify exactly what it is that they wish to purchase. Examples of this include Dell Computers, who manufacture to order – but with a very short timelag to delivery. Another example is Raleigh Bicycles, where, if you wish to buy a specialist bike, you can discuss the precise specification with the factory and it will then build your special machine to order (but normally using standard parts). Clearly, this may not be applicable to many markets which will continue to sell and advertise, but such initiatives may well point the way to the future of marketing.

We are also currently seeing the early stages of a new approach which is sometimes called 'relationship marketing'. Here the organization attempts to get close to the customer, developing the relationship so that the customer's behaviours and needs are fully understood. In some cases this can be seen as a further step on from the TQM idea; in others the main driver appears to be the emergence of electronic methods for recording purchasing patterns which can then be used to 'understand the customer' and personalize the marketing effort.

Another prediction is that we will see a continuing growth in the area of 'social marketing' as described by both Kotler and Roberto (1989) and Foxall (1990). Here the emphasis lies on changing social behaviour and is commonly initiated by governments, political parties or other pressure groups wishing to change the awareness, values and behaviour of the population. This is likely to raise significant ethical issues for marketing professionals, as discussed by authors such as Bowie and Duska (1990) and Cannon (1994).

So an important point to remember throughout the course of study is that:

- Different societies may be at different points of marketing development
- Different cultures may have different beliefs, values, economic systems and ethics
- Different markets may have reached different levels of sophistication
- Different organizations may have reached different levels of marketing orientation

> **Think** – At what phase of marketing development/orientation is the market in which you operate?
> – At what phase of marketing development/orientation is your organization?
> – At what phase of marketing development/orientation is your society?

However, in all foreseeable scenarios the understanding of consumer behaviour would appear to be of ever growing importance.

Customers and users

In his book *Perfect Customer Care* (1994), Ted Johns raises the issue of customers and users as a powerful distinction for marketers to make when developing marketing strategy. The case that is made is so relevant that it is well worth examining at the very beginning of a book called *Understanding Customers*.

Definitions

Customers are people who use our services and pay for them, while,
Users are individuals who are affected by or who affect the product that we supply. Users are often people who use the product but do not pay for it.

Implications

Examples abound of situations where there is a clear distinction between the two sets of individuals. Children do not buy toys; parents, relatives and friends of the family do. Similarly, in the petfood market, it is rare to see a cat or dog paying at the checkout!!

Where this is the case, we have to realize that the people we are trying to satisfy and delight are the parents, relatives and friends who part with their money. Thus it may be valuable to focus our attention on the interests, motivations and emotional values attached to toys (or catfood) by these groups.

When purchasing our products, these groups may be thought to be attempting to purchase love or peace! Granny buying a teddy bear for a grandchild is wanting the child to fall in love with the bear and to express delight and love in return. This is likely to be a major motivation for many 'givers'.

An alternative scenario is where a child has pestered a parent mercilessly to get a skateboard. The parent, driven to distraction, finally gives in. In this case the payoff is peace and an absence of demands. In this second set-up we will be concerned with satisfying the child – but only as a means of satisfying the real, paying customer.

If we stick with the child/adult situation there may be a number of alternatives:

- Some presents may be purchased by customers who never had one as a child and can now fulfil the dream – we have all heard of the stereotypical train set for the child which is played with by the father, the mother who buys the child ballet lessons or a pony as a vicarious fulfilment of her own dream.
- Another possibility is where the child demands a computer on which to play games, but which the parent finds interesting and starts using as an aid to domestic administration.

The clear comparison for marketing purposes is with the Decision Making Unit (DMU) favoured in organizational buying. The children are likely to be the key influencers, with the added factor of the emotional influence that a child can wield over the significant adults (our customers).

Some criticisms of the customer/user model have been made, but these have focused mainly on situations where the users were not very influential – one of the quoted examples being the prison service, where it may not be sensible to view the inmates as important influencing users who will directly affect the real customer (i.e. the government which ultimately and directly pays for the service). Even in that extreme case, conditions and facilities have been improved following prison riots.

In the context of the toy industry the distinction between customer and user seems well made. The child will still remain a significant target for marketing messages as the key influencer in the social DMU – so advertising can continue to be directed at the children. However, the major insight of the analysis is the need to centre attention on the paying customer. It may therefore be necessary to undertake market research to explore the motivation and emotional values which adults attach to the process of giving presents to children. This insight could give us a significant competitive edge over the organization that thinks that its customer is the child.

A similar analysis can be applied to the catfood example where, the customer is the cat or dog owner. Petfood manufacturers go to considerable lengths to ensure that the product is acceptable to humans – hence an emphasis on making the smells acceptable, and also ensuring that the fatty jelly is not immediately evident when the tin is opened. Try opening a tin from the bottom and discover how unattractive it can be if you see brownish jelly/gunge rather than the more acceptable 'meaty chunks'.

Think – Who are the customers and users for perfumes?
          expensive lingerie?
          cut flowers?
          charities such as Oxfam, etc?
     – What other examples can you identify where customers
          and users may be different?

This idea of targeting the marketing message at the 'right' person leads quite neatly into another idea which may help develop our framework for analysing purchasing decisions.

Segmentation

The advent of the mass market posed problems about whether universal messages and products were appropriate. The idea developed of segmenting the market. Market segmentation involves the breakdown of the total broad and varied market into groups. The aim of the process is to identify groups whose constituent members have characteristics in common – in this way messages and products can be tailored specifically to address the needs and wants of the group. Successful segmentation also produces groups (segments) which are significantly different from one another in their requirements. It also hopes to identify segments which are:

- accessible
- stable
- large enough to make marketing worthwhile and profitable.

We shall look at segmentation in more detail in later sections of the book.

Dependency Theory

Yet another notion which may be of use in making suitably sceptical sense of our world is that of dependency theory. This was proposed by Douglas McGregor (1960), who suggested that there is a relationship between the amount of authority or power which you can exert over a person or an organization and the degree to which that person or organization is dependent upon you. He illustrates the relationship diagrammatically (see Figure 1.1).

One interesting offshoot of this idea is that it can be applied globally, nationally or individually.

McGregor used the notion to explain how authoritarian organizations had come to be accepted as standard (and were effective) by considering the social conditions at the time at which they were being created.

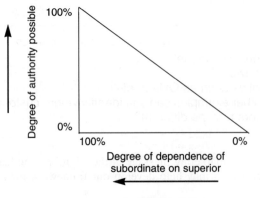

Figure 1.1

In the latter part of the nineteenth century unions were very weak, there was virtually no legislation for the protection of workers, unemployment levels were high and there was no Welfare State – a potent mix for the employee to experience high levels of dependency upon the employing organization or individual. McGregor argues that this allowed high levels of autocracy to be both accepted and appropriate. This may be contrasted with the position in the 1960s, when we had a Welfare State system, legislation to protect employees, strong and powerful trade unions and what, in retrospect, was 'over-full' employment. Here the response of managements was to move sharply towards consultative and participative styles of management. At the time this was regarded as being 'enlightened', but realistically they may well have had little option but to 'be nice to staff'. The 1990s have seen an erosion of employees' rights, a reduction in welfare benefits and high levels of unemployment – managements have also become more 'authoritarian'.

A similar analysis may be applied to changes in power/authority relationships at an individual level. New-born children are highly dependent, and hence high levels of authority may be used. As the child begins to learn to move it becomes less dependent on the parents – as a result, furniture and ornaments are repositioned to ensure that they are out of reach. However, until the little one learns to master the door handle it is prone to being left in one (relatively safe) location. The next move towards independence comes with the ability to open a closed door. This poses a major problem for the parent as the child may begin experiments with climbing (and falling down) stairs – so the parent erects gates to stop such adventuring. The following years are characterized by the child being dependent on the parents for cash. While shopping it is not uncommon to hear small children asking loudly for things to be bought. While the parent holds the purse strings control can be exercised over purchases, clothing, appearance, etc. However, once the child (perhaps now a teenager) obtains an independent source of income via a paper round or a Saturday job, the parent may well have lost the ability to control things such as the purchase of clothes or CDs.

In terms of this introductory stage we can allow that dependency may be:

- physical
- financial, or
- emotional

and, additionally, that it can have 'knock-on' benefits for others – an example might be someone hoping to impress a loved one (and hence dependent on their goodwill) who does some voluntary social service in order to get into his or her good books. The action may benefit the recipient of the social service as a by-product of another dependency.

Let us move on to look at some of the Parties with an interest in the business or enterprise.

Any organization has a number of significant stakeholders. Usually these will be groups such as:

- the shareholders/owners/banks
- employees
- other businesses
- the environment (or, more accurately, environmental pressure groups)
- the government
- customers.

The process of managing an enterprise can be seen as one of balancing the competing demands of the different stakeholder groups. This idea is sometimes shown in the form of a *Stakeholder map* (Figure 1.2).

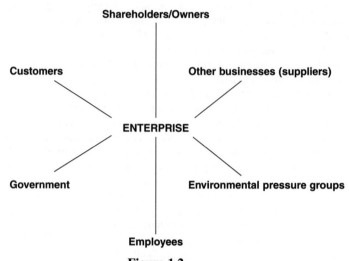

Figure 1.2

The implication of this view is that at various times management may become very concerned with satisfying the demands of the different groups – government when tax demands fall due, the environmental lobby when protesters are picketing their offices, shareholders when the Annual General Meeting is due, employees when there is an industrial dispute, etc.

In this way management can be seen as somewhat reactive – the image of managers as jugglers springs to mind. The different groups are likely to have different interests and to place different demands on the organization:

- *Owners/shareholders* are likely to demand profit, income, interest and return on capital from the enterprise. In the case of the public sector it may be expressed the other way round, in that we may be asked to produce the maximum levels of service from a limited budget.
- *Other businesses* and suppliers have an interest and expectation that the enterprise will honour its contracts, pay its bills and deliver the promised products or services according to the agreements made.
- *The environment* has become increasingly significant over the last few years as the public has become ever more aware of pollution in all its various forms.
- *Employees* seek a fair wage, security, a safe place of work and a degree of confidentiality from the organization.
- *The government* is concerned that enterprises obey the laws of the land, pay their taxes and conform to charters and codes of practice which may have been applied.
- Finally, *customers* are interested in honesty in advertising, value for money, product/service quality and safety.

It is clearly desirable for management to become proactive in running the business.

So we could restate our stakeholder map emphasizing the wants/needs/ interests/demands of the various groups, as in Figure 1.3.

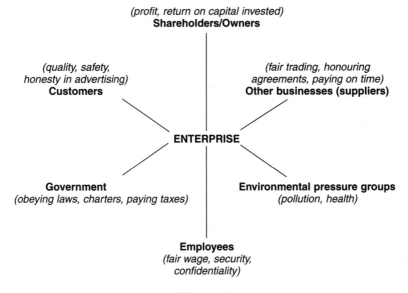

Figure 1.3

Using our ideas from Dependency Theory (above) we could predict that the influence of the different groups *at any point in time* will be a direct function of the degree to which the organization (or the management/decision makers) are dependent on that particular group. As we observed earlier, we can sometimes respond to one dependency to satisfy others. Examples could be organizations adopting 'green' policies and products due to a dependency on the environmental groups and (perhaps) the government – thus retaining their market share, producing profit and satisfying another primary stakeholder, the owners/shareholders. Similarly, our earlier example of government and prison inmates could be explained using such a model – if the government is approaching an election, or has a very slender majority, it may be highly dependent on the goodwill of the general public. In such a case the behaviour of prison inmates could well influence policy decisions as a means of satisfying both the electorate and/or the government's own backbenchers/supporters.

The Competitive Environment

Marketing is essentially a competitive process which aims to deliver needed goods and services for consumption at a profit. The type of economy in which the business is attempting to operate will be an important factor in determining marketing activities. The UK operates an economic system which aims to be competitive. Indeed, the governmental policies of the 1980s and 1990s have been directed specifically and openly towards making the UK economy more competitive. We may identify three broad categories which typify different types of market:

1 *Free enterprise (private sector) markets*, where economic decisions are taken through the mechanism of the market place. The forces of supply and demand are key concepts, and the important feature for marketers is that a dissatisfied customer can switch to another supplier in order to gain satisfaction. In terms of our earlier analysis, the business becomes very dependent on the customer and therefore 'the customer is king'. The USA is probably the clearest example we have of this type of economy.
2 *Collectivist (public sector) economies*, where all business activity is state-owned or controlled. Decisions are taken centrally by the government or its agencies. These were seen in the old Communist bloc dominated by the USSR during the post-war period. Currently China and Cuba are the closest examples, although some developing countries with authoritarian (but not necessarily Communist) governments may tend to follow policies of this type due to the difficulties of shortage of resources.
3 *Mixed economies* exist in a wide variety of countries. While government may play a key role in some sectors, such as power, welfare, health, transport or defence, the activity may well be split between the public and private sectors. This phenomenon has been seen in the UK, with the creation of 'market forces' in the heath service being a good example.

It can be argued that society itself is an economic organization – the type of economy which is operated will directly affect the business and the practice of marketing. The notion of competition has a number of elements which may be worth developing at this point:

● *The degree of captivity of the market* – this refers to the extent to which consumers have to buy from suppliers or the extent to which the market is totally fluid – where anyone can supply and consumers are free to go to whomsoever they choose for their products or services. Clearly this will vary from market to market – we can think of examples where the market is fluid and others where the customers are captive.

Think – Where on the fluid–captive continuum would you place the market for:
● Dental treatment
● Butter
● Water
● Sports clothes
● Electricity
● Professional marketing education
● Your own industry or product/service sector?

- Another dimension of the competitive market is the idea that markets can be *static, expanding, declining* or *stagnant*. Such judgements can be made on a number of criteria, such as in terms of sales turnover, range of product offered, demand, or even reputation.
- Competition also occurs within the society as a whole and, as such, is bound and limited by its rules and norms of behaviour. This may include *ethical considerations* which may be determined by religious, political and legal frameworks.
- Market competition will be influenced by *the difficulty of entering the market*. If factors such as the level of capital investment or technology are very high, the result will be that it becomes very difficult for new enterprises to enter a market. This can result in what is sometimes called an 'oligopoly', where a whole market is dominated by a handful of players, such as we have in the petroleum-refining industry in the UK. Here we see a situation where half a dozen companies control the supply of petrol via outlets, and there are sometimes suspicions that the industry could become something of a 'cosy club' in which the best interests of the consumers may not be sought. In the UK, bodies such as the Monopolies Commission exist to review such situations and report on the public interests involved.

In this market economy context the objectives of the business are to make a profit and survive.

Control

Most management activity may be viewed as being concerned with coping with, and controlling, an uncertain environment.

The basic ideas of control theory come from engineering, and centre on the concept known as *feedback*. This may best be described by reference to Figure 1.4.

This cycle is perhaps most easily explained by using an example such as a refrigerator. Here the situation to be controlled is the temperature of the container.

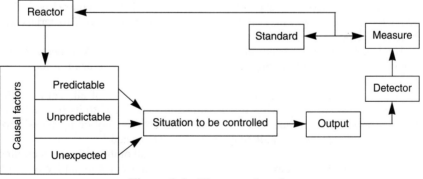

Figure 1.4 The control cycle

The output is temperature, and the machine must be able to detect this output. We will also need to measure the level of the temperature, and this can then be compared with the standard that we have set via the 'warmest/coldest' dial. This comparison tells us whether we are on target or whether it is necessary for the system to react in some way in order to achieve the standard desired. Reaction will be through what we are calling 'causal factors'. In the fridge the motor is triggered when the temperature rises above the desired limit so that the temperature is reduced. When the lower level is reached, the system reacts by switching off so that the container slowly warms up. In this way we control the temperature inside the machine within the limits set.

Causal factors are any factors which affect the situation to be controlled, and fall into the three categories set out below.

Predictable factors are those which affect the situation and whose effects can be accurately and consistently predicted. Many of the physical laws fall into this category, e.g. materials expand by predictable amounts with rises in temperature and water boils at 100°C.

Unpredictable factors are those things that we know have an effect on the situation, but these effects cannot be accurately or consistently predicted. Having a puncture will affect the performance of my bicycle, but the detailed effect is likely to be a function of many other things, such as whether it is in the front or back tyre, whether I am moving fast, moving slowly, whether it is a slow puncture overnight and the road conditions obtaining at the particular point in time.

Unexpected factors are those factors that you have not thought of. Generally these are occurrences which have not yet happened. Once they have happened they will no longer be unexpected and will therefore be reclassified as predictable or unpredictable.

At the risk of appearing sexist, the traditional view of management is that it is the manipulation of the five 'Ms' in the interests of the objectives of the organization – the five 'Ms' being money, materials, machines, men and markets.

If these are the basic elements of the managerial situation, it follows that we could examine them as causal factors to the situation to be controlled (the enterprise).

Money is not predictable – future interest rates, exchange rates, credit-worthiness, etc. are all clearly open to question – so we must consider it to be an unpredictable factor.

Materials run into similar problems – is quality what we require?, will they arrive on schedule?, will they arrive at all? So again, it looks as if materials will have to be considered as an unpredictable factor.

Machines look rather better at first sight – but then we look at breakdowns. They do happen, usually at the worst possible time – so once again it looks like an unpredictable factor.

Men (and women) are perhaps the most erratic resource of all. They are the ones with minds of their own – the resource that can vote with its feet, work to rule, come up with productivity-enhancing suggestions, buy competitors' products. At best, they are unpredictable; at worst, unexpected!!

Markets are also made up of people, so they share all of the problems identified above – but in addition they are prone to interference from external factors such as the level of unemployment, interest rates, wars and the like.

At first it may appear that we have shown that management is impossible! The reality is that management is about coping with unpredictable factors in an uncertain world. It is difficult – this is what makes it rewarding and well paid. If the factors were not unpredictable we would not need managers, only planners and doers – i.e. in a 'better' world my cat could manage ICI!

Rather than prove that management is impossible, I think we have explained the phenomenon sometimes known as Sod's Law (also attributed to Murphy on occasion). This is not a true law, but a joke which has enough truth in it to make it funny. Sod's Law comes in many forms, but at its most general it claims that:

> if something can go wrong, it will – but only at the most inconvenient and unexpected times.

Thus it is often used to explain why buttered bread falls butter side down (except when we are conducting an experiment to prove Sod's Law!). Another formulation of the same idea emerges as:

> when you have found the answer, they change the question.

Its applicability comes from the fact that we tend to notice things that go wrong more than we recognize that something has gone according to plan.

It is quite possible to perceive management as activities designed to minimize the effect of Sod's Law – in fact, much managerial activity is devoted to making the various factors more predictable.

Money is made more predictable by establishing borrowing capacity in advance of need, borrowing at fixed rates of interest and, above all, by budgeting for income and expenditure.

Materials are subjected to goods inwards inspection to ensure that substandard materials are not allowed into the system, which can lead to enormous expense if work is carried out only to be subsequently scrapped. Carrying adequate stocks of necessary materials is one way of minimizing the risks associated with running short of crucial inputs to the organization.

Machines are made more predictable through maintenance. This extends the time during which they work effectively, but may still leave us with a problem of sudden breakdown. This can be minimized by preventative maintenance, where items are replaced before they are able to affect the whole machine. Predictability of machine systems may also be improved by avoiding dependence on single units.

The human factor is made more predictable by a series of devices associated with the personnel function – manpower planning, recruitment and selection, reward systems, training, rules, appraisal, job descriptions.

Markets are made more predictable through the activity of advertising after suitable market research – the aim being to create and control demand for our product.

This view is therefore a useful focus for our study of customers and our attempt to understand them: i.e. how does what we are doing illuminate or assist us in this central problem of controlling that prime aspect of the organization – its market, both existing and potential?

> **Think** – How do you feel regarding the manipulation of the
> behaviour of staff, colleagues and the public?

These ideas of controlling others, managing the conflicting demands of the stakeholders and generally viewing business as a balancing or juggling act implies that life may be full of dilemmas. These quandaries, which characterize many management decisions, may have ethical implications. Let us try some examples.

> **Think** – You discover an addictive (but not banned) substance
> which is tasteless and appears to have no side-
> effects. You manufacture instant coffee, and realize
> that adding a little of ingredient X could ensure
> product loyalty:
>
> a) Is it ethical to do it?
> b) If you manufactured pet food, would it be any more
> acceptable/less acceptable/different?

There are two contrasting perspectives on ethical thinking:

1 *Deontological or Transcendental ethics* are based on clear and absolute beliefs about what is right and wrong, and on universal standards of goodness and justice. Consequences of actions are not the primary considerations in deciding what ought to be done. Obligations, responsibilities and considerations of justice and fairness take precedence. This can be a relatively clear-cut framework, although it is not always comfortable as people of this value system will do things because they are right rather than because they are comfortable. Deontologists will claim that 'the ends do *not* justify the means'. This viewpoint is often associated with firm religious or political convictions.
2 *Utilitarian ethics*, where the consequences of an action are the prime determinant of whether an action is right or not. Utilitarians will argue strongly that 'the ends *do* justify the means'. Perhaps the key issue for the utilitarians is the question of whose ends we are talking about. At the wider level, seeking 'good' outcomes for the mass of the population is laudable, but seeking 'good' outcomes for the individual may be perceived as being selfish.

It is also clear that different societies will develop different rules and ethical systems depending on their beliefs and history. This leads us to problems as to whether what is 'right' in one society may not be viewed as 'right' in another.

Other marketing issues can be problematic.

> **Think** – You are the marketing manager for a firm which distributes 'health foods'. Recent research has cast doubt on the safety of one of the products you handle – 'Steroidal', a preparation for bodybuilders. The government has just announced a ban on its sale in the UK. The firm holds considerable stocks of the preparation and your MD asks you to explore the possibility of selling the stock abroad to a country which does not ban the substance.
>
> a) What would you do?
> b) Is it different if you are offered a sizeable bonus for disposing of the preparation?
> c) Is it different if failure to do so could result in the closure of the company, with the loss of fifty jobs?

Customer care and Total Quality Management (TQM)

As we saw at the start of this chapter, marketing has developed over time through a number of phases. Our explorations so far may have given some insight into the reasons underlying such changes and helped to explain why things do not operate in identical fashion throughout the world. We commented that under our present competitive conditions the customer has moved to become the central figure of marketing.

Customers matter. This seems to be self-evident – but it was not always so (and still is not in some countries). However, the behaviour of some organizations suggests that customers are not valued.

> **Think** – What examples can you think of when you did not feel valued as a customer?
> – What examples can you think of when you did feel valued?
> – What can you learn from your experiences?

Johns' *Perfect Customer Care* (1994) has a chapter headed 'Why does customer care matter?'. He says that the first reaction may be that this is a daft question, since if you do not care for your customers, you will surely go out of business. However, he identifies some possible exceptions:

- You may be competing with other organizations who don't care about their customers either
- You may be able to compete on factors other than customer care, such as price
- You may not need to compete at all if you are a monopoly
- You may be a solitary genius, offering products or services which are in great

demand and which nobody else is yet in a position to imitate.

The problem with these exceptions is that they are only likely to be temporary conditions if we are operating in a competitive environment.

In the first exception all is well until one of your competitors decides to go for a competitive advantage by improving customer service.

In the second case the comfort zone exists on the assumption that price is the sole or dominant factor in the purchasing decision (whether this be organizations or individuals) and, unfortunately for the individual operating under this assumption, this is very rarely true. The overwhelming majority of surveys of consumer motivation find that issues such as value for money, quality, availability and service rank higher with the customer than pure price. This is consistent with the 'marketing mix' approach to marketing strategy.

The third scenario may be true in some cases – but the reality in most Western economies is that the 'traditional' monopolies of the nationalized industries are being privatized. Even where they continue to exist (e.g. the National Health Service in the UK) they are being opened up to competitive pressures. The NHS has developed the idea of fundholding general practitioners who will have purchasing power to buy health services for their patients from the hospital sector. Other examples from the public sector are the moves towards compulsory competitive tendering for services and functions.

The last option, that of the in-demand genius, is fine so long as the demand for the genius continues. Our everyday experiences confirm the old truism that value is defined by the purchaser (think of selling a car or a house). The demand for the expertise is likely to be a fashion, and fashions change. Even if they do not alter drastically, the very nature of competition means that others will eventually cotton on to the demand and offer alternative services – which are likely to include more sensitivity to customer needs.

So we can argue that customers must matter in the long run, and that the needs and wants of the consumer must be considered by organizations.

One of the approaches which encompasses this notion is that of *Total Quality Management* (TQM). TQM puts the customer centre stage. Satisfying the customer is the fundamental principle of TQM, since this approach to business assumes that customers are the guarantee of the organization's profitability and continued existence.

One of the most spectacular transformations of the last fifty years has been that of Japan, from the despair following the 1939–45 war to the dominant economic and producing nation of the world. In the immediate post-war phase the country was looked upon as a supplier of inferior goods, and during the late 1950s company-wide quality control systems started to be introduced as a way of combating the situation. This quality movement led to the *quality circles approach* of involving staff in quality issues which became popular during the 1960s and which has been popularized by writers such as Ishikawa.

Another important leader of the quality movement has been Juran, who introduced the concept of managing quality as opposed to just controlling it. Juran also gave us the definition of quality which is 'fitness for purpose' and placed the responsibility for quality firmly on management. As he observes, 'quality does not happen by accident, it must be planned'. He also introduced the idea that quality goes beyond planning and control to encompass the notion of continuous improvement. He noted that 'normal' management involves operating within boundaries set by history. Only when performance deteriorates significantly does action result in order to return the performance to the norm. Juran aims for 'breakthrough', where the norm itself is improved – thus making progress a standard.

The third 'guru' of quality is Deming, who again made his name through his work in Japan. His contribution was in developing a systematic approach towards operations, identifying causes of variability and proposing the notion of TQM.

There are three basic principles which underpin customer–supplier relationships under TQM. They are:

1 The recognition and acceptance of the strategic importance of customers and suppliers, *both internal and external.*
2 The development of win–win alliances between customers and suppliers rather than exploitative relationships.
3 The establishment of a supplier–customer relationship based on trust.

These principles are translated into practice by:

● continually collecting information on customer needs, reactions and attitudes
● feeding back this information widely throughout the organization
● using this information to improve the design, production and delivery of the organization's products and services.

Customer satisfaction (internal as well as external) is a key objective (indeed, it could be argued that customer satisfaction, in essence, defines quality).

It has been claimed by writers such as Tom Peters that the aim is to 'delight' the customer by delivering more than was expected. This is sometimes referred to as 'added value' – the extra that makes your product/service special. As we achieve ever higher levels of technical and procedural excellence via benchmarking, the 'something special' that the customer perceives is likely to lie in the area of customer care and quality.

In order to be effective, TQM programmes require the following conditions to be fulfilled:

1 *Commitment from top management.* Top management needs to ensure that the programme is delivered and also that it provides the cash payoff from improved quality in customer service.
2 *Defining customer requirements and obligations.* From the viewpoint of an organization, customers can be thought of as a collection of requirements and obligations. Customers may be external consumers, employees (internal consumers), shareholders, top management, government and so on. Requirements will be fitted to resource constraints and the objectives of the organization and must be realistic and obtainable. Obligations need to be clearly defined and requirements need to be quantified and accepted by both sides as reasonable. If a customer care programme is to be effective, the relations must be clearly specified on both sides.

3 *Customer orientation*. Each internal group in the quality chain comprises a customer and/or supplier to other internal groups and, in some cases, to the market. Although programmes can start at any point in this chain, even if the quality of the goods from a supplier is low, the group should aim to build up its own quality before addressing the shortcomings of its supplier. TQM programmes therefore stress the importance of departments within organizations regarding each other as internal customers.

4 *Total staff involvement*. A cultural (and sometimes an equivalent structural) change is essential for the achievement of a quality programme. These schemes can be presented as a 'total way of thinking' or even 'a philosophy of life' rather than just another technique or fad for management. It is a peculiar feature of these systems that they can sometimes have a religious passion: advocates are spoken of as 'evangelists' or 'gurus'.

   For this system to work, however, it is important that all staff are involved and subscribe to the values and attitudes. The key people in terms of making quality work are the people who actually carry out the processes which are involved in delivering products or services. In addition, particular quality improvements will constantly face the problems created by those parts of the system which have not been reformed ('converted'), when one group of staff are trying to improve the quality of what they deliver to customers and are having to deal with other groups who do not see the importance of quality. The need for training in terms of both skills and, particularly, attitudes is very clear.

5 *Measurement*. This is extremely important for any quality programme and, so far as customer care is concerned, measurements must be continuous and all-embracing. Required performance needs to be clearly specified in terms which can be measured, and mechanisms must be instituted which provide clear indicators that these have been achieved. These must be in place before programmes are instigated. Customer care programmes will require survey data on internal and external customers, on customer behaviour and on the degree to which customer needs are being satisfied. These should permit the application of techniques such as trend analysis, and fit into a cycle of assessment, planning, implementation and monitoring.

6 *Standard processes and procedures*. Processes and procedures which are developed and specified as an end product of a TQM customer care programme are intended to be followed. Such directions are intended to reproduce proven consistent quality and should specify administered processes, timing, responsibility and areas of expertise, gathering feedback data and so on. When these procedures are adhered to, the output remains consistent, processes are appropriately monitored and the data provides the basis for learning and consistent improvement.

7 *Paying customer objectives*. The end product of any programme must be to satisfy the needs of the paying customer in order to accomplish particular commercial, financial or strategic objectives. To that end, all analysis within customer care programmes, and the development of any processes and procedures within such programmes, must relate to those objectives.

   The mission of the organization, and the corporate values which underlie it, must always be clearly and directly related to the formulation of such objectives. If they are not, then TQM programmes will not tie in with the strategic direction which has been agreed.

TQM is more than a management technique – it is a comprehensive approach which runs through all aspects of the organization, both internally and in its relationships with outsiders. It is sometimes shown diagrammatically (see Figure 1.5).

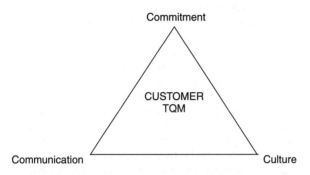

Figure 1.5   Key elements of Total Quality Management

There are a number of approaches to management which are complementary to customer care and which are commonly part of any comprehensive customer care initiative.

- *Business process re-engineering* (BPR) is the expression currently fashionable to describe reorganizing the business according to the processes it performs rather than the function performed. This enables concepts such as TQM to be built into the very structure of individual jobs.
- *Empowerment* allows individuals in the organization, particularly front-line sales staff in the context of customer care, to decide how to do the necessary work, using the skills they possess and acquiring new skills as necessary; with power comes responsibility, so individuals become personally responsible for what they do. This increases motivation, accountability and identification with customer satisfaction.
- *Performance related pay* (PRP) emphasizes the individual's performance and contribution to the organizational goal. In this sense it is a direct incentive to staff to achieve targets, including those encompassing the area of customer care.

In summary, TQM is a total approach for the organization which places customers and their care at the very centre of the organization's activities. It affects internal and external relationships and is not a simple, 'bolt-on', technique.

TQM: and criticisms

We noted earlier that marketing is an evolving and ever-changing activity, with different organizations operating at different stages. This is a comment which can be applied to management in general. There is an argument that TQM has already 'had its day' as a management 'tool'. This is not to deny that there are many organizations who need to take quality on board and make the whole organization more 'customer facing'. Wilson (1992) reports that some of those who have experienced TQM programmes have voiced a number of criticisms, which can be grouped as:

- *Sectional interests* – TQM can create 'evangelists' (managers who are seen as fanatical supporters) and this can be divisive within a management team.
- *Questionable benefits* – there is a great deal of activity involved in a TQM programme, but it is often difficult to measure and identify benefits other than the award of the ISO 'label'. The achievement of the standard is seen by some to be a process of 'jumping through hoops' in order to get a certificate. In some instances this may be a prerequisite to entering some markets, but it cannot then be said to give a competitive edge if all competitors have the same certification.
- *Customers define success* – not internal processes.
- *Re-creating the rigid organization* – achieving the standard can lead to complacency and a plateauing of effort which can render future change more difficult.
- *Claiming too much* – TQM can be such an all-embracing cultural activity for the organization that there may be a tendency to think that all organizational problems and ills can be solved by it. In some cases TQM may be unable to deal with a specific problem so there is a danger of judging the programme to have failed, despite using inappropriate evaluation criteria.
- *Lack of evidence* – there is a general lack of satisfactory empirical evidence about the effectiveness of TQM and, in particular, there can be difficulties with the apparent rigidity of the systems, especially in the ability to adapt to differences in international operations.
- *Means vs ends* – TQM can become an end in itself, particularly when the scheme demands sequential steps and one stage needs to be completed before the next can begin. As a result, the real purpose of the exercise can be lost.
- *It can make things worse* – such programmes require the organization to be in a reasonably healthy state. There should be enough slack in the system to allow space for the scheme to work. If the enterprise is already in crisis, TQM may 'finish it off', as the costs of such programmes are significant and the payoffs may be longer-term.

These criticisms do not invalidate the case for quality and quality management, but they do emphasize that there is no universal, simple, 'off the peg' solution to business problems. The danger of most fashionable management 'fads' is that they rapidly deteriorate into unwieldy bureaucratic systems which do not deliver the original promise. A key concept of business success is competitive advantage. Once we have reached a situation where all organizations competing in a market have taken on board the quality message, quality no longer becomes a significant discriminator for the consumer. The successful manager will move on to other areas to obtain 'the edge'.

Throughout the course of study you are following it is worth remembering that some customers may be organizations. It is therefore worth taking a brief look at the notion of organizations as buyers.

Organizations as buyers

> **Think** – How does your organization make purchasing
> decisions?

Organizations, like individuals and families, make purchases. In some cases the buying decisions are completely routine – replacing envelope stocks or re-ordering cleaning materials; while other decisions may be new, complex, technical and very expensive. Such decisions may need careful problem definition (often by specialists), extensive research, a sometimes lengthy evaluation process, negotiated purchase and long periods of post-purchase evaluation. Sometimes a decision is individual; at other times it is very formalized, with defined guidelines at every stage.

In the words of Hawkins, Best and Coney (1989):

The stereotype of organisational buying behaviour is one of a cold, efficient, economically rational process. Computers rather than humans could easily, and perhaps preferably, fulfil this function. Fortunately, nothing could be further from the truth. In fact, organisational buying behaviour is at least as 'human' as individual or household buying behaviour.

Organisations pay price premiums for well-known brands and for prestige brands. They avoid risk and fail to properly evaluate products and brands both before and after purchase. Individual members of organisations use the purchasing process as a political arena and attempt to increase their personal, departmental or functional power through purchasing. Marketing communications are perceived and misperceived by individual organisation members. Likewise, organisations and individual members of organisations learn correct and incorrect information about the world in which they operate.

Organisational decisions take place in situations with varying degrees of time pressure, importance and newness. They typically involve more people and criteria than do individual or household decisions. Thus, the study of organisational buying behaviour is a rich and fun-filled activity. (page 713)

> **Think** – In the previous exercise, thinking of the purchasing
> activities of your own organization, did you conclude
> that they were a 'cold, efficient, economically rational
> process' or did you analyse the situation as one of
> greater complexity?

There are a number of areas of similarity between family decision making and the activities of an organizational decision-making unit:
- They are both commonly made by groups of individuals
- They both have clearly identifiable roles within the process, such as Gate-keeper, Influencer, User, Buyer, Preparer
- Both situations may be characterized by decisions being made within constrained budgets.

There are, however, some significant differences:

- The market is smaller in the sense that there are fewer organizations than members of the general public
- The market is clearly segmented – a supplier may know all potential customers and a potential buyer may know all potential suppliers. This knowledge can allow marketing efforts to be tightly targeted
- Some large organizations (including governments) have enormous purchasing power
- Organizations are more likely to employ specialists, who could have a significant impact on the decision process
- The phenomenon called *reciprocal buying* may exist. Here Company A agrees to buy the products of Company B on condition that Company B reciprocates by purchasing Company A's products
- Much of the purchasing is done on the basis of history and tradition. Long-term relationships can develop between a supplier and a purchaser this can lead to repeat orders on the grounds of the supplier being a 'known' quantity in terms of quality, reliability and continuity.

The fact that industrial purchases are made by people not for their own consumption but for the good of the organization should imply that their buying behaviour would be more rational and less emotional than that which applies in the broader field of consumer behaviour. It is also likely that a much wider range of criteria will be used to judge 'good value'. These criteria could include:

Price/Discounts
Technical advantage and advancement
Quality
After-sales service and maintenance   Note: the ranking of these
Reliability and continuity of supply   factors will vary from
Back-up advisory services   situation to situation
Credit facilities offered

In addition, the decision could be influenced by other historical relationships between the two organizations – misbilling, difficulty in communication, personal friction or personality clashes in the past can be held in some sort of 'corporate memory' and militate against the errant supplier.

It is common to draw a distinction between different types of industrial purchasing decision based on the complexity of the behaviours involved which relate to the complexity of the decisions to be made. We identify three types which form a continuum.

At the simplest end we have:

1 *Routinized buyer behaviour* or *straight re-buy*, where buyers know both their own requirements and the products on offer. The items tend to be regular purchases, and the process is usually repeated frequently. In this case, history is likely to be a very significant factor, as there is an inertia about such decision making which tends to reward the current supplier – 'better the devil you know'. It is often difficult for another supplier to break into such a market – price cutting is often the only way in.
2 *Limited problem solving* or *modified re-buy*. Into this category would fall the purchase of either a new product or service from an existing or known supplier, or the purchase of an existing product from a new supplier. As the title suggests, the process is characterized by limited problem-solving behaviours and investigations.
3 *Extensive problem solving* or *new buy* is the name given to the category that involves the purchase of new, unfamiliar products or services from previously unknown suppliers. Such processes can be very lengthy, as the criteria by which the purchase will be judged will need to be developed from scratch.

This categorization is very similar to the distinction made by some authorities who categorize individual consumer buying into *low-involvement* and *high-involvement purchases*.

Internal processes of the Decision Making Unit (DMU)

In the context of industrial or organizational marketing the *Decision Making Unit* or DMU is the expression used to describe the group of people who make the buying decision. The DMU can be defined as 'all the people who have influence, whether positive or negative, at one or more stages of the purchasing process'.

In many larger organizations this will centre on the Purchasing Department or the role of Buyer, but may extend way beyond the official professional limits.

If we make a comparison with family purchasing decisions, we might conclude that one of the main differences between the two situations is the formality of the organizational decisions – the need is identified, requisitions are completed, countersigned by more senior staff and passed to Purchasing before the 'buying' process officially starts.

The roles usually associated with organizational buying are as follows:

The *gatekeeper* controls the flow of information. Such a role may be at a senior level or it may simply be the secretary who controls the Buyer's diary. Many salespeople have found that getting past a receptionist to see the Buyer is as big a challenge as selling the product. However, in this situation the gatekeeper could be a specialist who can feed relevant information into the rest of the DMU, and so there may be some overlap with the next role.

The *influencers* are particularly important in the technical and problem-solving type of decisions. Who they are and where they are located within the organization are key facts for the supplier to determine. It is likely that the patterns of influence will also be a function of the culture and the orientation of the organization. For instance, in a company which prides itself on its technical advancement and excellence, the engineers are likely to be significant players in any large-scale purchasing decisions. In contrast, engineers may not be so influential in organizations which do not share the value systems and technical orientation. In some organizations the accountants may be the dominant personalities, and it may be found that price becomes the crucial criterion. In yet other circumstances it may be the case that large-scale purchases will need approval from the whole Board of Directors, thus adding still more influencers to be considered. Some organizations will employ a number of Buyers; the degree of their independence and/or limitation by overall policy will need to be ascertained.

The *user* or *preparer*, in the industrial situation, may also be a significant influencer of the decision. Senior managers may heed the experience and opinions of the people actually doing the job, either via direct communication or by such means as method study reports. Users and preparers may also have very high levels of technical expertise, and so their opinions can influence both the identification of the need and the required specification.

The *buyer* in this context is commonly a role carried out by an individual rather than an activity carried out by a busy, multi-roled parent. This has the effect of professionalizing the process, and, to some extent, removing extraneous elements from the decision. However, the point must be made that the buyer may not make the final decision – indeed, in some cases the role can become solely administrative.

The *decider* is obviously the crucial role, as this is where the whole purchase decision stands or falls. As noted above, the decider can be at a relatively mundane level for routinized decisions, but may involve the Board of Directors for major projects and expenditures.

See Figure 1.6.

The foregoing discussion implies that the process is much more complex than just selling the product to the buyer. Hence one of the major problems facing the potential supplier is identifying the individual influencers and decision makers within the target organization. Only when this has been done can the supplier plan the campaign to inform and persuade the key persons within the DMU.

As these people are likely to have different roles, specialisms and professions, a multi-pronged attack may well be necessary, involving direct mail and personal contact as well as the use of technical, trade and professional press and other promotional channels.

A final input to this collection of ideas pre-empts Chapter 10, where we examine models of consumer behaviour. As we will see, models are the underlying assumptions about the way people behave as customers, and they attempt to define these assumptions so that we can improve our understanding of the processes involved. In simplified terms, we can identify three separate underlying approaches to understanding customers:

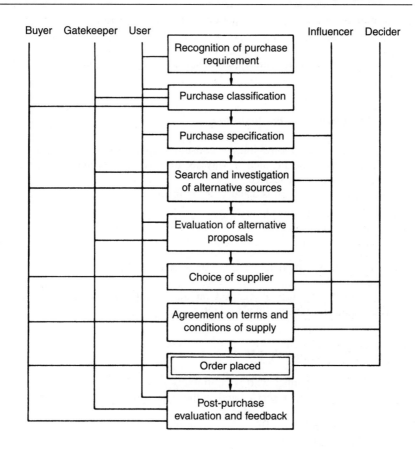

Figure 1.6 A decision process model of industrial purchase behaviour
Source: Behavioural Aspects of Marketing (BPP, 1991)

1 The 'wanting' customer

This is summed up by the common marketing AIDA version of consumer behaviour. This assumes that the process gone through is:

Awareness → Interest → Desire → Action

So this assumption about customers focuses on making them aware of the product or service, generating interest in it, making them want it enough to take action by buying whatever it is that is our product.

A slightly more elaborate version, but one which is based on similar assumptions is:-

Awareness → Interest → Evaluation → Trial → Adoption → Post-purchase
evaluation

So this model gives a clear indication of some of the steps we shall be considering
in the book.

2 The 'problem-solving' customer

In this case the assumption is that the consumer reacts to a perceived problem and
will direct behaviour in such a way as to solve the problem – ideally by
purchasing our product/service.

The sequence proposed is usually of the form:

Problem recognition → Information search → Evaluation of alternatives →
Decision

As in the previous model, the final stage may be followed by post-purchase
evaluation.

So the marketing task is centred on identifying consumers' problems and
offering them solutions via our product.

3 The 'perceiving' customer

This assumes a consumer who is continually making judgements as to the perceived value of a good or service and, at the same time, estimating the probability
that purchase will provide satisfaction.

Thus, in practical terms this model identifies two key objectives of marketing
effort and communication:

- to raise the perceived value of the outcomes of purchase
- to raise the perceived probability of satisfaction following purchase.

Given these views of consumer behaviour, we might conclude that selling to
organizations may not be that different from selling to individuals!

2 'There's more to this than meets the eye...!'

Perception

Introduction

As we saw at the end of the previous chapter, the perceived value and the perceived probability of satisfaction may be viewed as the key factors in determining customer behaviour. Implicit in this view of consumers is the importance of their perceptions and the fact that it is fundamental to much of what we call marketing practice and anything which might be titled 'understanding customers'.

Perception is the term used to cover those processes which give coherence, unity and meaning to a person's sensory input. It involves all those processes that we use to select, sort, organize and interpret sensory data to make a meaningful and coherent picture of 'our world'.

Here is a very old sensory input:

Do you see a woman's face?
Is she young or old?
Can you see both?

Figure 2.1

This immediately raises an important point. Although subject to the same sensory input, different people may perceive quite different things.

As individuals we are continually subject to stimuli from our environment. These stimuli impinge on us via our senses, and it is the way that we interpret these sensory signals that determines the way we see our world. It is generally accepted that our perception of the world is not an absolute, determined by the physical stimulation received, but is both organized and dependent on a variety of other factors.

Clearly, we need to consider the sensory channels, as they are the source of perception. We are all aware of the five senses:

- Hearing
- Sight
- Smell
- Taste
- Touch

but it is usual for physiologists to point out that we do, in fact, possess a number of other senses, with pain being an obvious one, while other internal senses identify variations in temperature and the state of some of our internal organs (e.g. heartbeat). Another is our sense of balance, which is sometimes referred to as the vestibular sense, stemming from the position of the head and determined by the operation of the inner ear.

Marketers will often attempt to involve all of the five primary senses in order to influence consumer behaviour. Supermarkets commonly put vegetables just inside the entrance and light them with 'daylight' tubes. Here the aim is to get the customer actively involved in the buying process by touching, picking up and choosing produce right at the beginning of the shopping visit. Products are displayed in attractive packaging designed to catch the eye, so they utilize sight. Tempo-controlled music is sometimes played – interspersed with announcements drawing the customer's attention to special offers or groups of products (hearing is thus involved). Taste can be brought into play by offering customers 'tasters' of food products, while smell has proved a most potent weapon since the development of in-store bakeries. There would seem to be considerable potential for further expansion using other smells in appropriate areas of the store.

There is a need for the consumer to be aware of a stimulus. This involves the notion of sensory thresholds. Psychologists draw a distinction between different types of threshold:

1 *The absolute threshold.* This is the level of stimulation at which the individual begins to experience sensation – i.e. it is the lowest level of stimulus that can be detected.
2 *The differential threshold.* This is the point at which the magnitude of the difference between two stimuli is sufficient for the individual to perceive that the two are, in fact, different – i.e. it is the lowest level of difference between stimuli that can be detected.
3 *Dual thresholds.* This term refers to the fact that some senses appear to have two separate thresholds. An example is that people can commonly identify the

presence of an odour at one threshold, but have a second, higher threshold at which they can identify what the smell is.

One obvious problem for the marketer is that the efficiency of people's senses may vary widely. We are all aware of people with hearing difficulties and of those who need glasses or contact lenses to see adequately. It therefore becomes clear that the same stimulus will be received differently by different individuals, thus leading to different perceptions, even before we consider the internal processing of the signals received.

Sensation may also be relative. At junior school you may have done the experiment where you have three bowls of water. One bowl contains hot water (hand-hot, not scalding), the second contains cold water, while the third has a tepid mixture halfway between. You place one hand in the hot water and the other in the cold and leave them there for 30 seconds or so – time enough for you to adjust. Both hands are then placed in the tepid water. If you have not done this, do try it because the experience is fascinating – the tepid water feels hot to the hand that was in the cold water and cold to the hand that had been placed in the hot. So we have 'first-hand' evidence that the same stimulus can feel different to different parts of our own body.

On the other hand, people have the ability to 'adjust' their perception to produce the phenomenon called 'constancy'. This refers to the tendency for our perceptual world to remain 'the same' despite significant alterations in the sensory input – e.g. a saucer or plate seen from any angle (other than directly above or below) is still perceived as being round, although the image received by the eye is an ellipse. This, of course, raises the issue of how much of perception is innate and how much is learned through experience. The opposite situation is also of some significance – the extent to which learning can function to modify our perceptions – and this will be discussed later.

One interesting aspect of our senses is the way in which high-intensity inputs appear to dull the senses (reduce our sensitivity), while low levels of input may increase our sensitivity. Actors (and sometimes teachers) say that one way to get people's attention is to speak more softly – it makes them concentrate and gets them 'on the edge of their seats'. Another, more extreme, example is the way in which people who suffer from impaired sight, for example, will often seem to compensate for this by developing other senses, e.g. hearing, to high levels of sensitivity.

Another complicating factor is that we seem to respond best to changes in our environment. We can 'get used to' noises such as the flow of water through a radiator or the ticking of a clock.

Exercise – Stop reading and sit silently for a minute. Close your eyes and concentrate on the sounds in the room.
– What can you hear?
– What sounds were you unaware of before you did this exercise?

This illustrates the phenomenon of *habituation*. There are some sounds which we filter out of our consciousness. Not all of them are quiet (like the clock ticking); it is possible to work in very noisy environments and 'not hear' the noise most of the time.

On a quiet night we can hear clearly sound which would be lost during the noisier daylight hours. If we are away from our usual home base we sometimes claim that these sounds keep us awake at night. Similarly, the absence of the sounds to which we are habituated can disturb our sleeping routines.

Another example of habituation is the hot bath. Getting in can be quite a painful experience, yet after only a short while all feelings of discomfort can vanish as we get used to the temperature of the water.

Think – Habituation can mean that consumers get used to our advertising and cease to be aware of it. How can we combat this tendency?

An important contribution to our understanding of sensation is Weber's Law. This was developed by the German physiologist Ernst Weber (1795–1878) and concerns a phenomenon called the *just noticeable difference*. Formally, it states that the just noticeable differences in stimuli are proportional to the magnitude of the original stimulus. In mathematical terms:

$$\frac{\delta I}{I} = k$$

where δI is the increment in intensity that is just detectable, I is the intensity of the comparison stimulus and k is a constant.

Weber's Law is of interest to marketers when they seek to establish their product as being 'different' from either the competition or an earlier version. The ideas of 'new, improved' products imply and demand that the consumer can detect the difference from the old product. Weber's Law points out that the notion of 'noticeable difference' is proportional. The addition of a small amount of salt will be noticeable in a bland, unseasoned soup, but that same amount of salt would go unnoticed if added to a highly spiced and already well salted dish. Similarly, we will notice the difference if we upgrade the lightbulb in our lamp from 30 to 60 watts. What we notice is the doubling of the light power rather than the addition of 30 watts. If we have a 100-watt bulb in the lamp, we would need to go to 200 watts to get the same effect – moving to 130 watts would have a lot less impact.

It is likely that consumers will see price increases in much the same way – a 10p increase in the price of a packet of cigarettes may be seen as much more significant than putting up the price of a car by £100.

Thus marketers may be concerned to initiate changes which are above the just noticeable difference in some circumstances and just below that level in others.

> Think – What is the just noticeable difference for products that you are concerned with?
> – What other examples can you identify of marketers using this idea?

Selectivity of perception

Attention. Before we can perceive an event or object, it is necessary that we notice it. A problem that we then run into is that attention is selective – attending to one stimulus (awareness, focusing, processing) tends to reduce the attention paid to others. Generally, selectivity functions so that, at any instant, a person focuses on a certain feature of his or her environment to the (relative) exclusion of other features.

> Exercise – 1 Find someone who wears an analogue wristwatch (one with a dial and hands rather than a digital read-out).
> 2 Ask them what form the figure '6' takes on their watch dial – without looking.
> 3 Having got an answer, invite them to check whether they are correct or not.
> 4 Then say 'Without looking at your watch again, what is the time?'

When trying this out in practice we find that the majority of people cannot say what the time is, despite having just looked at their watch. They have clearly looked at the watch dial, they must have observed the position of the hands, but because they were not looking for that information they did not 'see' it.

Attention may be *conscious* (we make a conscious decision to concentrate on one element of the total input); alternatively, and quite commonly, it is *unconscious* in that something 'catches our attention' and we find ourselves attending to it, although we are not explicitly aware of the factors which caused us to perceive only that small part of the total stimulus array. One interesting phenomenon is sometimes called the 'cocktail party effect', where most people find it possible to concentrate on (or attend selectively to) one person's speech when surrounded by the competing speech of many others. At the same time, we appear to be able to monitor other incoming messages so that our attention can switch to another topic or person almost instantly. We can therefore focus on one activity at any given moment, but that may, in turn, become peripheral in the next moment. This gives rise to the notion of *attention span*.

The evidence suggests that the attention span of students in lectures is very short – however, individuals can develop longer attention spans when they practise some activity in which they are interested. An example might be listening to music, where there seems to be a need to develop listening skills in order to attend to longer pieces of music. Advertisements are short partly because of cost, but also because there is a fear of boring the receiver – a fact noted by many politicians, who practise shortening their messages to create short, sharp 'soundbites'.

Marketers are very concerned that their messages attract the attention of potential consumers. Initially their targets may not be aware of the product or the message, so the factors which direct our attention are of obvious importance. The broad classifications are of external and internal elements: external factors relate to the physical characteristics of the stimulus; internal factors relate to our feelings, motives, interests and expectations.

External factors influencing attention

Size

Generally we notice larger, rather than smaller, stimuli. The size element suggests that the sensory input to the system is proportional to the size, although it is possible to imagine situations where a small, bright object is highlighted against a large, dull background, and is by far the more eye-catching. Increasing the size of an advertisement will increase the chances of it being noticed. Similar relationships appear to hold good for the size of the illustrations or pictures within an advertisement.

Intensity

Perhaps even more significant, as pointed out above, is the idea that the intensity of a stimulus may be the very facet that catches the attention. Bright, primary colours can be dominant features of packaging or visual advertising material. An interesting 'new' development has been the emergence of advertisements which feature sounds that have been 'over-recorded' and the natural sound boosted and intensified. Lucozade used this idea when the opening of a can in the grandstand was enough to cause a false start in the athletics race.

Position

Stimuli may be more noticeable simply because of their location. Supermarkets place products that they wish to move at eye-level on shelves – the so-called 'hot spot'. Similarly, impulse items such as sweets and chocolate are often placed next to the checkout. In print media there has been work to indicate that right-hand rather than left-hand pages get more attention, as do the covers, both inside and out. The same work suggested that the front of a magazine is the best part of the journal in which to place material, but it would seem that this must be a function of the ways and patterns adopted by readers when flipping through the magazine. Depending on the target population, placing material among the sports pages is likely to attract the attention of a different set of readers from those advertisements positioned among the arts pages. Similarly, the choice of which slots feature in the midst of which television programmes will determine who sees your advertisement.

Contrast

As noted above, much of our attention is relative to norms or standards. The phenomenon of habituation has been discussed above. Our attention is grabbed by changes in the stimulus. Thus our attention can be attracted as much by a sudden silence as by a sharp, unexpected noise. Black and white pictures can stand out when surrounded by colour (and vice versa). Main points and headings are picked out in this text by making them look different:

heavier type,
italic type,
<u>underlining</u> or
<u>***all three***</u>.

In effect, contrast can create an apparent intensity of stimulus without utilizing size, loudness or colour. The contrast can be thought of in two dimensions. First, it needs to be different from its specific context – hence the idea of styles, whether of advertisement or packaging or product, passing through phases of unusual, fashionable, standard, old-fashioned and ready to be overtaken by the next wave. Secondly, there is a need for advertisements, packaging or products to offer a contrast to their competitors – thus giving an identity and, hopefully, a competitive edge. The presentation of stimuli which are inconsistent or contrast with one another creates a perceptual conflict which attracts attention.

Novelty

The unusual or unexpected attracts attention. Here the problem centres on whose view of unusual is taken, and for how long a stimulus remains unexpected. In this sense it is very similar to the contrast element discussed above. There is also some sort of parallel with jokes, in that there is nothing so attractive as a new joke and nothing quite so boring as the joke you have already heard!

Repetition

As mentioned earlier, our attention continually switches from one stimulus to another, and it seems logical to assume that a stimulus that is repeated has an improved chance of catching our attention. This does need some words of warning, however, as repetition is the route to habituation and loss of attention. The art is to get enough repetition to reinforce the message, but not so much as to 'switch off' the receivers.

Movement

Stimuli in motion attract greater attention than static stimuli. Skilful artwork which gives the illusion of movement may enhance the awareness factor of stationary material. The development of billboards which 'roll over' to display a sequence of different posters is an example of how eye-catching movement can be. Sometimes watching the advertisements change can be more interesting than the football match which is supposed to be the focus of our attention when watching television.

Think – List some current advertising campaigns.
– What external factors do they employ to attract our attention?

Internal factors influencing attention

There are internal factors which affect our awareness of stimuli:

Motivation

Hungry people are commonly more aware of food stimuli – the moral being to eat before you visit the supermarket for your groceries! Similarly, the motivation associated with undertaking this course of study is likely to increase your awareness of advertising messages and media.

Interest

We tend to be more aware of things in which we are interested. The soccer fan can tell you which clubs play in which colours, the film buff can recite appearances by actors, the keen cook can remember recipes apparently without effort.

Need

If we need to replace our trainers we may well become much more aware of sports shoe shops and what others are wearing.

Think – Using your list of current advertising campaigns, what internal factors do they employ to attract our attention?

Awareness Sets

Howard and Sheth (1969) point out that consumers can only select products from those of which they are aware. So they draw a distinction between those brands within a market that the consumer is aware of. They call this the *awareness set*. They call the remainder of the available brands the *unawareness set*. They argue that consumers, in order to simplify the process of choice, will make their final choice from a limited range of brands drawn from the awareness set. These are the brands about which the consumer has positive feelings. This group is called the *evoked set*. The important fact is that, for a product to be chosen, it is not enough for the consumers to be aware of it – they must think well enough of it to place it in their evoked set.

These ideas were further developed by Narayana and Markin (1975), who suggested that those brands which did not feature in a consumer's evoked set could be subdivided into an *inert set* (those that the consumer was aware of but whose feelings for the brands were neutral – neither positive nor negative) and an *inept set* (those that the consumer was aware of but whose feelings for the brands was negative).

This is commonly represented diagrammatically as, in Figure 2.2.

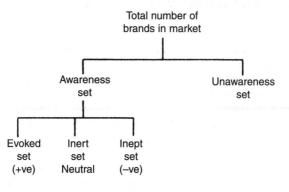

Figure 2.2

The message for marketers from these ideas may be highly significant, as it can help determine the advertising objectives and strategy that should be adopted. Should market research indicate that the brand is in the unawareness set for a large proportion of the population, then the task is to raise awareness in order to get it into the awareness set. Thus widespread media campaigns are indicated, with the aim of getting the brand known. An example might be Cornhill Insurance raising their profile by sponsoring Test cricket.

If the brand is found to be in the evoked set, the promotional strategy would be defensive reinforcement, whereas, should it appear in the inert or inept sets, positive attempts will be made to change consumers' perceptions and attitudes towards the brand.

> **Think** – What advertising/promotion examples can you think of
> for each of these awareness set situations?

Earlier we explored some of the factors, both internal and external, that influence selective attention. One hazard in the path of the marketer who is seeking to design strategies for advertising and promotion is that consumers may not select our message to attend to. The other side of this coin is the idea of *selective exposure*. Here we will seek out inputs which we find rewarding/ interesting/satisfying and avoid those which are the opposite. The soccer fan purchases and reads the sports pages of the daily newspapers, the theatre buff is likely to read the programmes of the shows he or she attends, while the keen cook may choose to switch on the television to watch a cookery programme.

> **Think** – What newspapers do you read?
> – Why do you choose them as opposed to others?
> – How does this choice affect the stimuli to which you
>   are subjected?

This is an obvious way to target specific market segments. If you have a clear idea of the people you are trying to reach with your advertising message, the special interest publication, programme or medium is likely to be a useful way of getting your message across. However, to some extent this approach is preaching to the converted, and there may be even more problems emerging as the habits of 'zapping' (changing channels during advertisements in the middle of television programmes) and 'zipping' (fast-forwarding through the advertisements on a recording of a television show) become ever more established and possible with the advent of the remote control device for television sets. These habits reduce or even eliminate the advertising process so carefully and expensively developed by the marketer.

An even more interesting challenge is how we might attract new customers. Here we may look to what Peter and Olson (1990) have christened *accidental exposure*. This refers to the advertisements on such things as posters, buses and tube trains. Here the target is not selected by some process of segmentation, but is offered up to the population at large, and so may attract the attention of those who would not normally select such a stimulus for themselves.

Expectation is another crucial determinant of what we perceive. Indeed, it may not be unreasonable to claim that people often perceive what they expect to perceive rather than the message that they do receive. A well-worn example is shown in Figure 2.3.

Most people coming across this for the first time read it as 'Paris in the spring' rather than what is actually printed – 'Paris in the the spring'. Here the human brain seems to process the stimulus and jump to the wrong conclusion – thus it may be an accelerated form of closure (described below).

The phenomenon seems to be quite widespread in everyday life. It seems that many of us will sit down to watch a comedy programme on TV and expect to laugh. The stars of such shows have won more than half the battle before they even start, because we are looking for them to be funny!

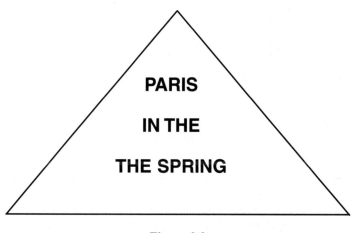

PARIS

IN THE

THE SPRING

Figure 2.3

Think – How do your expectations affect the way you watch party political broadcasts?

Another phenomenon is *closure* – the tendency of people to perceive incomplete objects as complete, to close up or fill in gaps in sensory inputs and to view asymmetric and unbalanced stimuli as symmetric and balanced.

Marketers have used the idea of closure in such classic advertising messages as 'Schh... You know who', which has worked well for the Schweppes organization for many years. The observer completes the message on behalf of the advertiser, thus involving mental processing or elaboration which, in turn, is likely to imprint the message.

Another example of closure which saves the advertiser money is the short version of the longer advertisement on television. Here we seem to relish the process of spotting the advert on minimal input – and then completing it in our own minds! Very economical, given the cost of TV slots!

Communication

While we are considering the problems and issues surrounding perception, it is useful to look briefly at the process of communication. We may define this as the process whereby ideas, information and instructions are transmitted from one brain to another.

Figure 2.4 gives a representation of the channels which might be followed when one person is talking to another.

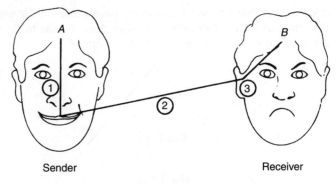

Sender   Receiver

Figure 2.4

First, there is a clear implication that there will be a message of some sort. This will be transmitted by the sender and taken in by the receiver (stage 2). However, in order for the communication to be effective, we must also consider the stages at which A decides what sounds to make and which words to use (stage 1), and the sense that B makes of the message that has been received (stage 3).

So we can say that the communication process has three basic stages:

Encoding ⇒ Transmission ⇒ Decoding

Once this sequence has been understood, it becomes clear that the effectiveness of communication can only be measured at the receiver's end of the process. In other words, effective communication depends on the perceptions of the message received being the same as the perceptions of what the sender thought was sent.

Once the idea of coding and decoding messages has been absorbed, we can see the importance of language. Clearly, it is necessary for both the sender and the receiver to be using the same code, language or system. If I send you the following message:

'yjod dysyr,rmy od om vpfr'

you will find it difficult to read unless you understand the code which has been used (in this case the message was typed shifting one letter to the right of the 'true' message on my keyboard). Given this information, a typewriter and sufficient interest and motivation, it is possible to decode it as:

'this statement is in code'

(was it worth the effort?). You may have used codes as a child to pass messages to a friend in what you hoped was complete secrecy.

An interesting aspect of communication is that if you do receive a message such as:

'yjod dysyr,rmy od om vpfr'

the readers are likely to realize that they do not understand the message and may therefore decide to take further action to clarify what was meant.

Perhaps a more difficult situation arises when I send a message such as:

'you are requested to scan the contents of this book'.

Think – What are you going to do?

The answer that you give to that question is likely to depend on your decoding of the verb 'scan'.

Many people (certainly most managers and students) decode it to mean 'have a quick look through', 'cast an eye over the main headings', or 'get a rough idea of what it is about'.

However, the *Concise Oxford Dictionary* defines the verb 'to scan' as:

'to look intently at all parts successively' (among other meanings)

so if the sender intends the message to mean 'study carefully' and the receiver interprets the message as 'cast a quick eye over' (or vice versa) we have poor communication in the sense that the perceptions of the sender and the receiver do not coincide. Perhaps the most important aspect of this example is that in this case the receiver did not realize that there was a misunderstanding.

This brings us on to the idea of words – perhaps the most common medium of communication in our society. The key point to realize is that the meaning of a word is relatively arbitrary – if we move to another country we rapidly discover that common objects are called by different words. We may also discover that even within our own country local words exist for objects which are not understood in other localities. Even more odd is the occurrence of the same word being applied to different objects in different places. The author has been told, apparently in all good faith, that the word 'moggie' is used in parts of Scotland to mean a mouse, in other parts of the UK it commonly means a cat, while others claim it is the word used for a Morris Minor car!

One interesting aspect of this is that words mean what people and society decide they mean. Despite complaints from those who wish to 'prove' that standards of English are declining, it must be realized that language is a developing thing. If people in general use the word 'scan' to mean 'cast a quick eye over something', then the dictionary definition will have to change.

Emotional meanings. As well as the dictionary definition, it is useful to examine the emotional or affective associations of words.

Request   Ask   Demand

are all verbs meaning similar things.

> **Think** – Which is the most aggressive?
> – Which is the most neutral?
> – Which is the most gentle?

It takes little analysis to understand that, while the cognitive definition might be similar, the emotional meaning is clearly different. Thus an important part of any message may be the affective content of the words and the emotional perceptions that are created in the receiver.

As an aside, it is an interesting piece of social conditioning that, in the field of industrial relations, trade unions make 'demands' while managements make 'offers' – an emotional distinction which seems rather loaded.

Similarly, advertisers will be careful to create the emotional overtones they feel are appropriate for their product. Many washing powders use words such as 'soft', 'gentle' and 'delicate' in their copy, usually accompanying pastel-shaded images. In contrast, Radion used very strong 'dayglo' colours and slogans such as 'Radion dismantles dirt' (this last with a very powerful visual image of a spanner clamping onto the 'd' in the word 'dirt').

> **Think** – Motor manufacturers spend a great deal of money on
> selecting the names for their products. What are the
> emotional overtones of:
>
> – 'Fiesta'?
> – 'Cavalier'?
> – '480 ES'?
> – 'Probe'?

Other products use words such as 'natural', 'fresh', 'countryside' alongside rural visual images to create the emotional message they seek to transmit.

> **Think** – What other 'emotional' messages can you think of in
> current advertisements?

We have already mentioned the use of colour in advertisements to create an appropriate atmosphere, and it is perhaps worth mentioning the increasing use of music to form associations and set 'moods' for products. Much use is currently made of music which has 'transferred' from other areas, most notably pop music. At present, some advertisers are using classical themes (Carmina Burana for aftershave), while many others are utilizing pop classics from some years ago (jeans, building societies). Here the thinking may be to re-create the feelings and wants of youth in the minds of people who are both older and better off in material terms and thus better able to afford the product. These ideas are explored in more detail when we consider attitudes and attitude change.

As marketers communication is our business, and the majority of the media we use is one-way. This suggests that we may be opting for the quick, cheap but inaccurate message.

> **Think** – How can we improve the efficiency of our communication?

A key concept in communication studies is that messages need to be tailored to the audience to which they are addressed. Marketing messages are no different, as a single department may need to communicate with:

- potential customers
- existing customers
- wholesalers
- retailers
- competitors
- suppliers
- government
- shareholders
- employees
- the public at large.

> **Think** – In what ways might messages need to be tailored for each of these groups of receivers?

Key learning points from Part One

Historical perspective
Marketing has developed through production, selling, advertising phases to the current emphasis on customer care, quality and meeting customer needs. An emerging trend may be 'relationship marketing'.

Customers and users is a key concept.

Decision Making Units (DMUs) – decider, purchaser, influencer, user, etc.

Segmentation
A way of breaking down the total market into sub-groups (segments) which have significantly different wants and needs, but which are large enough to make it profitable to develop separate marketing or product strategies.

Dependency theory and **Stakeholders** in the business/enterprise.

Demographic changes
May be key influencers of markets.

Competition – captivity/fluidity of markets.

Ethics
Deontological/Transcendental – clear view of right and wrong – the ends do *not* justify the means
Utilitarian – the outcome is what is important – the ends *do* justify the means.

Total Quality Management and Customer Care
TQM slogans are 'right first time' and 'continuous improvement'. It seeks win–win alliances between customers and suppliers, with an implied high level of trust. Its focus (as well as on quality) is on customer care (customers define quality) and feedback. The conditions needed are usually:

- commitment from the top
- defining customer requirements
- customer orientation
- total staff involvement.

It also encompasses the idea of internal as well as external customers.

Organizations as customers
There may be a tendency to concentrate solely on marketing to individuals – remember that much marketing activity goes on in the business to business sector. So work on:

- Similarities and differences between individual, family and organization buying situations
- Roles in the organizational buying process
- Different levels of complexity of buying decisions
- Decision Making Units (DMUs) and the associated roles (again).

Perception
This is a crucial concept which runs throughout any attempt to understand customers, as it is believed that our behaviour may be governed by a combination of the perceived value of a good, service or action together with our perception of the probability of satisfaction.

- The senses, sensation, awareness thresholds
- Selectivity of perception
    External factors:
    - Intensity and size
    - Position
    - Contrast
    - Novelty
    - Repetition

    – Movement
Internal factors:
    – Interests
    – Needs
    – Motives
    – Expectations
- Habituation – the danger of our messages getting stale
- Awareness, evoked, inert and inept sets.

Part Two Understanding Customer Behaviour

Introduction

This section seeks to introduce key concepts from the behavioural sciences – economics, sociology and psychology – which are relevant to the understanding of the ways in which consumers behave. It introduces ideas such as:

- Utility
- Opportunity cost
- Price elasticity
- Trade cycle
- Culture
- Cross-cultural marketing
- Socialization
- Family
- Groups
- Categories of group
- Influence of groups
- Roles, norms, inter-role conflict, intra-role conflict
- Family
- Family life cycle
- Attitudes
- Relationship between attitudes and behaviour
- Functions of attitudes
- Consistency theories
- Compensation theories
- Motivation theories

3 'What I need is a one-armed economist...'

Ideas from economics

Introduction

Economics plays a large part in influencing both individuals and organizations with regard to their buying decisions and behaviours. It might be viewed as the broad background against which more personal and individual decisions are taken. Traditionally a distinction is drawn between *micro-economics*, which affects individuals, and *macro-economics*, which is concerned with the whole economy.

Trade

If we start with the broad picture, one of the key concepts is that of trade. Here the fundamental point is that an economy (country) aims to grow in terms of its economic activity. This is measured in terms of the total amount of business that is transacted. The implications are that, as a whole, the nation becomes more wealthy. More business is conducted, so more tax is available to the government to provide appropriate services. More profit is made by companies and individuals which, in turn, cascades down by their making more purchases and investments which creates more business...and so on.

It is possible to consider whole countries as businesses which trade with one another. This gives us the concept of *exports* and *imports* and the resultant *balance of trade*. So we can use the idea of a nation selling more than it buys and hence having a positive balance of trade with the rest of the world (and so we might even consider that the country was 'making a profit'). In other circumstances, a country might be importing more than it exports and so generating a negative balance of trade (or making a loss). The overall level of trade in an economy may be rising, static or declining, thus identifying the concept of *economic growth*.

Governments are concerned with growth, as it allows an increase in what we know as the *standard of living*. This in turn makes the voters happy, and so the government gets returned to power and influence when election time comes round – they are seen as 'good managers of the economy'.

However, everything is not always so simple and straightforward. Within even this desirable scenario of growth there are variations, which have come to be known as the trade cycles.

The trade cycle

The *trade cycle* is a function of the total economy of a country and, as such, affects the individuals within that economy. It influences the levels of money available for spending on goods and services and, most importantly, *consumer confidence* and the 'feelgood factor'.

The trade cycle (sometimes also called the *business cycle*) is the pattern of the overall national income and reflects the level of economic and business activity within the economy. The levels of activity tend to follow a pattern, and it is the pattern which defines the cycle. There are a number of phases through which the economy progresses, which may be illustrated diagrammatically as in Figure 3.1.

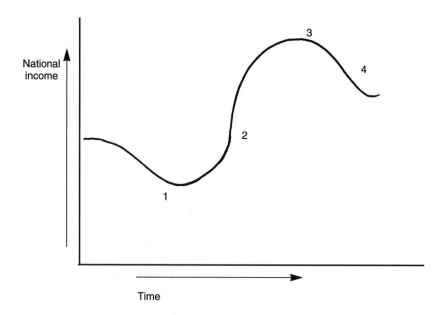

Figure 3.1

1 *Depression.* This is when the levels of activity within the economy are relatively low. As a result, staff are laid off and there are high levels of unemployment. This means less earnings to be spent, less income for the government and overall there is low consumer demand. This, in turn, means over-capacity for production and low levels of business profits. In an attempt

to retain sales it is common for companies to keep prices relatively stable, and these may, in some cases, actually fall as companies try to keep orders coming in. As a result of this combination of factors, business confidence is low. However, there may be a silver lining to such a situation. As the economy is not doing well, the value of the currency on the international market falls. This increases the cost of imported goods and makes home produce look relatively cheaper. This can be a significant factor in introducing the next phase.

2 *Recovery.* The recession, with its low profit margins, will tend to depress the stock market. Eventually companies will start to look relatively underpriced and people will look to invest in the next stage of growth. So after a while investment picks up. Companies build new factories, buy new equipment, etc. Unemployment begins to drop as more jobs are created and so, with more people in work and earning, consumer spending begins to rise. The increased level of activity leads to an increase in company profits and, given the relative improvement, companies do not feel the need to increase prices too quickly. As a result of all these factors, business confidence begins to grow. The next phase is...

3 *Boom.* Here we have a situation where consumer spending begins to rise quickly and businesses increase production until they reach the limit of their capacity. We get close to full employment. Labour shortages begin to become a problem. Output can only be pushed up by investment in new equipment, so investment is high. At the same time, because the economy is doing well, the value of the currency on the international exchange markets goes up – the pound looks 'strong'. This means that, to customers in other countries, our goods begin to look expensive. Conversely, a strong pound means that goods made in other countries begin to look relatively cheap, or certainly better value. This, together with the high levels of demand and limited output, tends to increase imports from abroad, cause problems with the balance of payments and push up prices generally. Profits are high, but inevitably the situation cannot last and the economy moves into...

4 *Recession.* Consumption levels out and then begins to fall off. The investments begin to look less certain and new investment drops. Production levels decline and staff begin to get laid off. Profit levels decline and businesses fail and stop trading. More unemployment, less income, less demand, more unemployment, less demand....

Think – What stage is the economy in at the present time?
– How do you know?
– What impact does the stage of the economy have on your business?
– On other businesses?

Some industries are highly sensitive to this trade cycle, others less so.

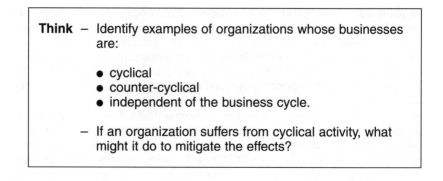

Disposable income

This is a crucial concept for the marketer as it describes the amount of cash which individuals or households have available to exchange for goods and services. In other words, it describes the size of the cash pool which is 'up for grabs'.

The different stages of the trade cycle have different characteristics so far as disposable income is concerned:

- Recession means a cutback in jobs, overtime and a reduction of disposable income
- Depression takes this even further, with less disposable income reducing the market
- Recovery sees an increase in employment and disposable income increases
- Boom raises the prospect of very high levels of disposable income – often with people wanting to invest their money while they have it and before the good times come to an end.

Linked to this macro concept is the notion of confidence or the famous 'feelgood factor' so beloved of politicians. This reflects consumers' willingness to commit themselves to high, long-term expenditures such as mortgages or hire purchase agreements. As in many things in consumer behaviour, it may all be inside the head!

> **Think** – What is the current level of the 'feelgood factor' or
> consumer confidence?
> – How do you know?

Impact on consumer behaviour

At first sight there may seem to be little obvious connection between the macro level observations on the nation's economy and the behaviour of individual consumers. But the truth is that they are inextricably linked – the first point being that the individual consumers are the elements that make up the economy and the second focusing on the impact which the overall economy has on consumers' levels of confidence.

The confidence factor is crucial, as it permeates all of life. If you as an individual are low on confidence – say there are rumours of redundancies at work and you feel that you may shortly lose your job – then this will affect all of your purchasing decisions. You may well decide to cancel the holiday to be on the safe side, you may defer changing the car, you may decide to cut back expenditure on items that might be considered luxuries (even if they are relatively basic, such as food and drink).

One of the areas which has an enormous effect is that of the housing market. You are less likely under these circumstances to move house. You might consider that moving would not be rational, as you may have to move later if you are forced to change job and the thought of getting locked into a new, larger, 25-year financial commitment may seem crazy when you fear you are about to lose your job. The lack of movement in the housing market has significant knock-on effects – fewer kitchens get fitted, fewer gas cookers are sold, less furniture, curtains, paint and wallpaper. Fewer housewarming parties are held. House prices stagnate or fall; the dreaded 'negative equity' strikes: 'we must never get caught like this again!'

This may seem to be overstated, but the atmosphere of confidence is a very real and all-pervasive phenomenon. The difference when house prices are rising ('we could sell this place and make ten grand profit!'), the firm has a strong order book and there is the prospect of salary increases and promotion is dramatic. In this scenario the consumer feels that anything is possible – confidence is high, the risks are *perceived* to be less.

So we may conclude that the trade cycle and consumer behaviour are closely linked – primarily via the factors of confidence and disposable income. This 'feelgood factor' is of crucial importance to expenditure patterns, which is why it is so important to marketers (and politicians!).

Scarcity

This refers to the lack of availability of a good or service which prevents the would-be customer from making the perfect purchase. In economic terms, the scarcity could be of the product/service or it could be concerned with the scarcity of cash with which to purchase.

Scarcity leads the consumer to seek a substitute, and may also reflect in the *opportunity cost* when the buyers realize what they have gone without in order to buy the particular good.

In some markets scarcity is not an important factor. In the case of purchasing cars, scarcity is unlikely to occur except at the very top end of the car market where, for example, the new Ferrari was only available to previous Ferrari buyers.

In contrast, some markets are dominated by scarcity – any items which are collected are likely to have scarcity as an important characteristic, whether it be stamps or antiques. In some markets the items are extremely scarce; Old Master paintings, for instance, are, by definition, scarce. There are only a limited number in existence, there is no current production of the product and there is unlikely to be any significant increase in the total number in existence. An additional scarcity arises in that they only rarely come onto the market. The scarcity in such examples raises the status of the goods and also their value – to such an extent that it is not uncommon for items to appear on news bulletins about the latest record price paid for a particular artist's work. We tend to find such items interesting even if we are never likely to be able to afford one ourselves.

The scarcity notion leads quite well into the concept of supply and demand.

Supply and demand

Here the underlying concept is that *the more of a good or service that there is on the market, the lower will be the price/value.* Conversely (as mentioned above), *when less is available, the value will rise.* This could cause some organizations to limit output in a conscious effort to 'keep prices up'.

The examples used in the previous section on scarcity apply equally well in this refinement of the idea.

Elastic and inelastic demand

This extends the idea expressed above by considering whether changes in price have a greater or lesser effect than we might expect.

Technically, the price elasticity of demand (PED) is expressed by the equation:

$$PED = \frac{\text{change in demand (quantity) as a \% of demand}}{\text{change in price as a \% of price}}$$

So, if the price elasticity of demand is equal to 1, then raising the price of the product by 10 per cent will result in a drop of sales of 10 per cent.

Not all products are so neatly balanced – there are some goods where increasing the price by 10 per cent will result in a fall in demand that is *less* than 10 per cent. If we look back at the equation, the price elasticity of demand is less than 1. When this situation arises, economists call the demand *inelastic.*

This could also be shown graphically, as in Figure 3.2.

A closer look at the graph shows that if we increase our price from 5 to 7 (an increase of 40 per cent), the demand would drop from 10 to 9 (a decrease of 10 per cent). Another way of saying the same thing is to call this product *price-insensitive.*

> **Think** – What goods or services can you identify which have this characteristic?
> Make a list of them.
> – What do they have in common that might account for their inelasticity?

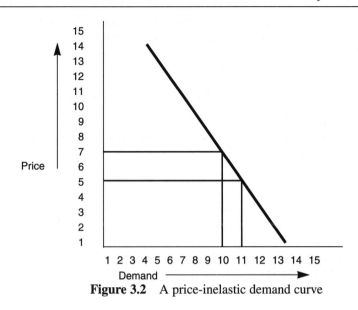

Figure 3.2   A price-inelastic demand curve

A contrary example – price elasticity or price sensitivity – is the opposite – when increasing the price by 10 per cent will result in a fall in demand that is <u>more</u> than 10 per cent, i.e. the price elasticity of demand is more than 1. When this situation arises economists call the demand *elastic*. Again, this could be shown graphically, as in Figure 3.3.

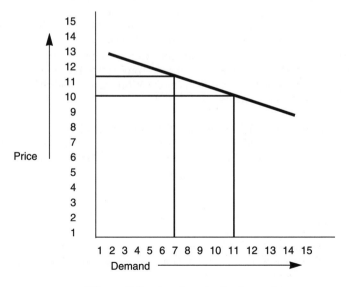

Figure 3.3   A price-elastic demand curve

In this instance increasing the cost from 10 to 11 (10 per cent) leads to a drop in demand from 10 to 6 (40 per cent). So in this case the price elasticity of demand is 40/10 = 4. We can also see that this good is *price-sensitive*.

Think – What goods or services can you identify which have this characteristic?
Make a list of them.
– What do they have in common that might account for their elasticity?

---

then,

Think – How do your reasons for elasticity and inelasticity compare?
– As a marketer, which kind of product would you prefer to handle?
– Why?

The usual response to the last 'Think' exercise is that people would rather handle goods and services which are *inelastic* or *price-insensitive*. The response to the 'Why?' question normally revolves around such concepts as basic needs, addictive substances and goods where there are no substitutes.

The notion of inelastic demand helps to explain why governments tax certain goods highly – particularly alcohol and tobacco. Putting the price up through increasing tax levels will cause some distress, but is unlikely to result in a large reduction in demand. In this way the government increases its total take from the tax revenues. If it were to tax price-sensitive goods, the reduction in demand would more than wipe out the income from the higher taxes.

These ideas give rise to a view of marketing which could be summed up by considering the question 'How can we make our products/services more price-inelastic?' Again, the responses can influence our priorities and objectives within the marketing mix. We may hope to:

● encourage and develop brand loyalty as a form of 'addiction'
● work to develop the perception that our luxury items are, in fact, necessities
● aim to emphasize our brands' unique characteristics – which has the effect of reducing the volume of direct (or close) substitutes.

Exceptions

There are some goods which do not appear to follow the normal rules of supply and demand. Some demand curves seem to slope in the opposite direction so that demand increases as the price rises (see Figure 3.4).

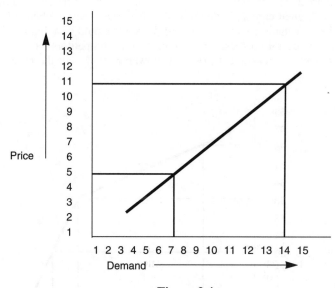

Figure 3.4

This seems to occur when we look at goods where status or value is judged by price. Examples would include very expensive items which are high on what Rogers called 'observability'. These are the overt 'status symbols' of a society, and might include such disparate 'goods of ostentation' as a Rolls Royce car, a desirable location for a house or flat, or even items such as Perrier water.

So we might add another option to the list of strategies for shifting to price insensitivity above:

● consider moving the goods to the category of 'goods of ostentation'.

Price wars and other oddities

There are some situations where economists predict and observe conditions where the competitive patterns create some interesting and unusual positions on price sensitivity. The most common scenario is where we have a few major players in a market. This is not monopoly (a single player) and is far from perfect competition, due often to the difficulty of entering a particular market. This situation is called an *oligopoly* by economists, and is perhaps best typified by the market for petrol in the UK. Here we have a relatively small number of producers and sellers of petrol. There are rather more sellers than producers, as the 'independents' buy their petrol from the major producers and are therefore not truly 'independent' (indeed, if we look back to our earlier discussion of Dependency Theory, we might conclude that they are highly dependent). Each of the main organizations (BP, Shell, etc.) are large enough and influential enough to affect the market. This means that each firm monitors the prices charged by the competition with great care and attention. This is perhaps best explained by the notion of a 'bent' demand curve (Figure 3.5). Here we would have highly elastic demand if prices are raised (customers going to our competitors); matched by immediate competitive reaction if prices are lowered (if we cut the others will follow).

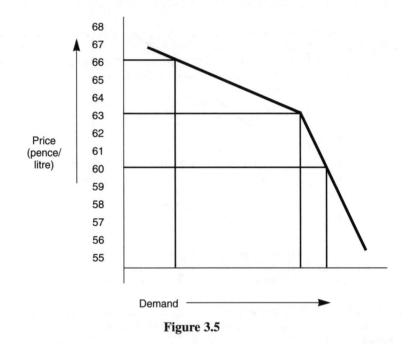

Figure 3.5

Here we see the effect of the powerful competition – a rise of 3p/litre results in a sharp drop in demand, but a reduction of 3p/litre is likely to spark off an immediate 'retaliation' by competitors and results in only a small gain in market share and a likely drop in total revenue (for all of the players). This situation is what the media commonly calls 'price wars'.

Think – How descriptive of the retail grocery trade is this model?
– How descriptive of the financial services industry is this model?
– What other examples of a 'bent' demand curve can you think of?

Price, volume and profit

The aim of the whole of a marketing exercise is to make a profit – so we may need to look at how supply and demand affect the 'bottom line'. Here we will look at a concept borrowed from accountancy called the 'break-even chart'.

Our main concern is with expenditure and income associated with different levels of output or activity. Expenditure falls into two broad categories:

1 *Fixed costs* – these are costs which exist and are not dependent on the levels of output, sales or activity. These costs could include items such as rent, rates and basic administration to enable the enterprise to exist. In graphical form, fixed costs are represented by a straight, horizontal line (Figure 3.6).

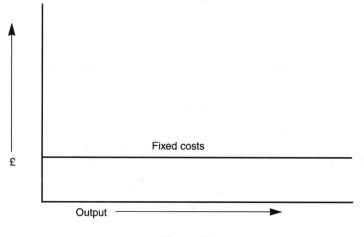

Figure 3.6

In contrast:

2 *Variable costs* are those which depend on the level of output – in this case, raw materials, manufacturing labour would fall into the variable cost category, as might electricity costs and selling costs. These variable costs are usually thought of as £x/unit produced, and so we have a different straight line to represent these (not horizontal this time) (Figure 3.7).

We can now add the two elements together to generate our *total costs* (Figure 3.8).

Income or *revenue*, on the other hand, will be variable depending on the number sold. So we will have another straight line through the origin (Figure 3.9).

We can now put the total costs and income curves onto the same graph and produce a *break-even chart*. The *break-even point* is determined by where the total costs line intersects with the income curve. To the right of this point is the *profit* area, where income exceeds costs, and the profit is measured by the size of the gap between the income and total costs lines. To the left we have the area of *loss,* determined by the gap between total costs and income (Figure 3.10).

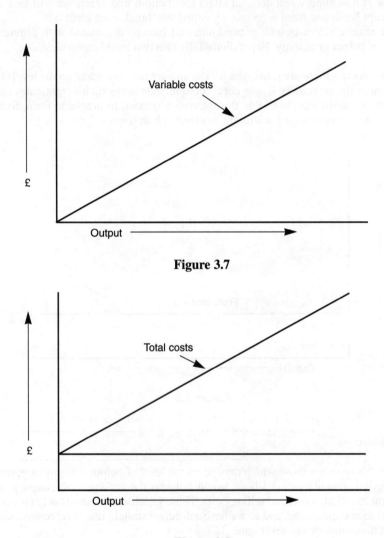

Figure 3.7

Figure 3.8

Calculating the break-even point for a product or service can be an important step in managing the product and will identify whether profit is a realistic prospect. In some instances it may be necessary to determine price by such considerations.

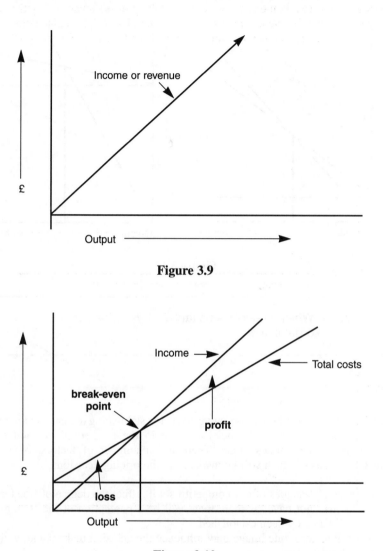

Figure 3.9

Figure 3.10

It is interesting to consider the difference between the situation where there are very high fixed costs (e.g. where there is considerable investment in expensive equipment or property) and where the fixed costs are relatively low. This affects the angle at which the costs and income lines intersect and hence the rate at which profit accumulates once the break-even point is passed (Figure 3.11).

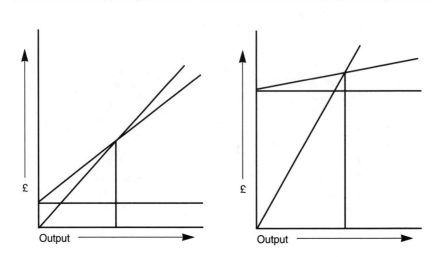

Figure 3.11

Think – Which break-even chart best describes your organization?

Pricing

We have already seen how important price is to establishing demand and potential profit. However, price is a crucial element in the marketing mix and is not determined by economics alone. There are a number of factors, other than demand and costs, which will be involved in the pricing decision:

● The pricing strategies of our competitors will affect the degree of freedom we may or may not have, as there may well be a perception of the 'going rate' which has already been established
● The desired corporate image may influence the decision makers and, with it,
● Product positioning
● The stage of the product life cycle may be a determining factor
● The prices of other company products in the marketplace
● Our corporate objectives may be a crucial influence, especially if we are seeking to gain market share rather than maximize profit in the short term.

So we could represent this diagrammatically, as in Figure 3.12.

Economists have also contributed to our understanding of behaviour. They have suggested that there may exist a number of economic theories of motivation.

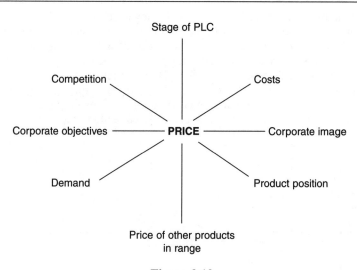

Figure 3.12

Economic theories of motivation

It is often proposed that there are four styles of consumer buyer behaviour:

- *Economic Man* – rational, logical, analysing all information in order to be satisfied with the purchase
- *Passive Man* – irrational, impulsive, easily swayed by marketing promotions
- *Cognitive Man* – learned, shrewd and relatively risk-averse, so will consider purchases in the light of physiological, psychological, sociological, economic and time aspects
- *Emotional Man* – will purchase on a whim or for immediate gratification depending on moods and emotions.

The example of purchasing a new car might well illustrate the different buying styles quite elegantly. The process would be very much as described above, and the actual choice might be inferred from the descriptions, i.e. Economic Man would buy a reliable, economical, cheap-to-insure vehicle which is very practical. Passive Man may well be influenced by a 'hot' promotion. Cognitive Man would have complex and plentiful criteria, while Emotional Man may well go for the flash status symbol.

It also leads us on to the concept called *Utility Theory*. This refers to an idea that most people recognize as 'satisfaction'. The theory concerns the feeling consumers experience when they buy a product or service. If the purchase has been 'successful', it should provide satisfaction, and this should lead to further repeat purchases. *Marginal utility* is the satisfaction gained from one additional purchase or consumption of a product. It is linked to the *Law of Diminishing Marginal Utility*, which suggests that the satisfaction gained from the purchase of an additional unit is less than the satisfaction gained from the previous purchase.

The Cumulative satisfaction rises – but more slowly (Figure 3.13).

It could be speculated that most people would get more satisfaction from their first car than they would from the purchase of a second (or even third) vehicle. The theory works particularly well with products such as cups of coffee or chocolate bars – the first may be ecstasy, but after a few in quick succession the consumer may feel very sick! However, it may not work quite so well with the Old Master example, as one could envisage a collector gaining increased satisfaction (utility) from acquiring a more complete collection of a particular artist's work.

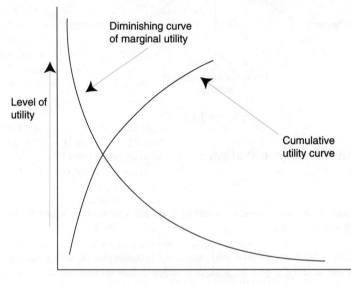

Figure 3.13

Implicit in these speculations is the idea of a decision-making process, which, as we saw in Chapter 1, in the marketing context is usually remembered via the mnemonic AIDA:

● awareness,
● interest,
● desire,
● action.

It has a number of components – the first of which is problem recognition, the second is generating alternatives, the third is evaluating the alternatives and the final stage is the decision. It also implies a degree of *rationality*, which comes into play throughout the sequence, but particularly in the decision stage. Rationality is based on the assumption that people will act in such a way as to maximize the utility (satisfaction, benefits or usefulness) of goods and services obtained within a limited budget. Here we come face-to-face with the concept of *scarcity of resources*. Most people would like to have more – a better car, a new kitchen, a new pair of shoes, a new house, a house! These commodities are the goods and services of the marketing process which are consumed by the customers for these goods and services. Since resources are scarce and there are not enough goods and services to satisfy the total potential demand, choices must be made. Choice is necessary because resources are scarce. So consumers must choose what goods and services they will expend their scarce financial resources on; and producers must choose how to use their available resources and what to produce with them.

This gives rise to the notion of opportunity cost already mentioned above. Choice involves sacrifice – if there is a choice between having books and having beer, and a person chooses to have books, they will be giving up beer to have the books. The cost of having books can therefore be regarded as the sacrifice of not being able to have beer. They are giving up the opportunity to have some beer, and the 'benefits' that the beer would have provided.

The cost of an item measured in terms of the alternatives forgone is called its *opportunity cost*. Thus the opportunity cost of buying a loaf of bread can be measured as the two pints of milk or the one bus ride that could have been bought instead. Similarly, at a national level the opportunity cost of a country having a nuclear missile could be measured in terms of the number of hospitals that could have been built and staffed with the same amount of resources.

Returning to our concept of rationality, the decision is assumed to be rational in the sense that the consumer will attempt to maximize the benefits from a purchase of the product or service and assess whether the benefits of purchase exceed the benefits of purchasing alternative goods or services – i.e. we assume that rational consumers consider the opportunity costs.

The concept of *rationality* appears both relevant and plausible. However, for marketers there are a few problems – the principal one being that individual consumers will have different *perceptions* of the benefits, satisfaction and usefulness (utility) of a good or service. Complications arise when we realize that many products will have an emotional value to the consumer as well as an economic one. This emotional value is, in many cases, the determinant of specialness which leads people to purchase 'up-market' items when comparable goods may be found cheaper. Much of our marketing effort goes into attaching emotional value to what is otherwise a standard product.

Another aspect is the reality of the 'impulse buy'. Here we have what could be called *time-limited rationality* – it seemed like a good idea at the time! We must have thought it rational (worth it) at the moment when we weakened. We have all had experience of buying something which, in retrospect, could not be called a 'good idea'.

To add to the confusion, consumers are not always consistent. The same consumer can have different values for the same item at different times – for instance, the value of a hamburger when one is very hungry is very much higher than when one has just eaten a Sunday dinner.

Overall, we seem to have a situation where the general principle seems right, but the ability to predict behaviour may be less than we might hope. At one level it could be asserted that we all behave rationally – it is just that our concept of rationality may differ with our perceptions, attitudes, values and situation.

Let us look at the relationship between some of these ideas. We have already introduced the notions of rationality and utility – both ideas used by economists. By *rational* they assume that consumers will act rationally and will seek to get the maximum total utility possible from their limited resources. By *utility* they mean the satisfaction or benefit derived by a person from the consumption of goods. Other relevant notions are those of *total utility* (the total satisfaction derived by an individual from spending income and consuming goods) and *marginal utility* (the satisfaction gained from consuming an additional unit of a good).

Rationality theory assumes that generally the consumer prefers more goods to less, and that the consumer is willing to substitute one good for another (provided its price is right).

Acting rationally means that consumers attempt to maximize their total utility within a limited income. This, in turn, suggests that consumers consciously seek 'value for money'. This is clearly a perceptual issue – what is good value in my eyes may not be in yours – so we must centre our discussion on how marketers can affect this perception.

Perception of 'value'

The principal way in which marketers tackle the problem is to concentrate on the *benefits* of the product and the associated *customer satisfaction*. Finding out which benefits will provide the greatest utility will help firms to gain the greatest competitive advantage. The idea of perceived value also brings in the material from the previous chapter on perception.

The first stage in influencing the consumers' perceptions is to ensure that the product falls into their *awareness set*. Only when they are aware of the product can it form part of the option set for purchasing decisions.

The next problem is to shift the product into their *evoked set* (i.e. among the products which are viewed positively). This is done via a variety of strategies. As mentioned above, concentrating on benefits is an obvious way to enhance perceptions of value. We may also attack the problem by attaching *emotional value* to the product. This can be done by using suitable advertising material and enhancing the status of the product.

Throughout the campaign we will use our knowledge of perceptual processes to attract attention by making use of the external factors influencing perception – *size, novelty, position, intensity, contrast, repetition* and *movement*. We will undertake research to establish the *interests, needs* and *motivation* of selected market segments. We will use the four Ps of the marketing mix to enhance the perceived value of the product. Our advertisements will introduce and reinforce the emotional value that we identified earlier.

One of the crucial 'Ps' is *price*. It is clear from our knowledge of consumers that decisions are not made on price alone but on:

<u>Marginal utility</u>
Price

Lowering price may improve the ratio, but it is not the only strategy open to the marketer. There are also ways in which consumers' perceptions of the utility of a good may be increased. Not all of these ways involve changing attitudes to products. For example, if a product is made more convenient to buy, a consumer will derive more net utility from consuming it.

So utility and rationality both exist within the consumer's head. Our task as marketers is to ensure:

- that our product or service is in with a chance of being chosen through the consumer being aware of its existence
- that our product is in with a good chance of being chosen due to the benefits which we have identified it as bringing the purchaser
- that we emphasize not only the 'economic' benefits (cheaper, more efficient, etc.) but also the 'emotional' benefits (feeling good, well regarded, stylish, 'with it', etc.).

We will do this via a co-ordinated series of marketing strategies involving tailoring messages that will get noticed and will be relevant to the selected market segment.

Some other ideas which stem from economics and which may have value for the marketer are:

- *Interest rates* – in the UK these are fixed by the Bank of England and, in turn, this figure influences the rates of interest we pay on our mortgages, overdrafts, credit card accounts and bank loans. The higher rates of interest mean that the cost of borrowing (and hence the cost of goods and services) is increased. On high-cost items such as houses or cars, the price which it is possible to afford may be fixed by the level of repayments which the lender allows. When big items are involved, an increase in the interest rate means that the residual disposable income is reduced, thus limiting the purchasing power of the individual/household. The government and the Bank of England use interest rates as a way of stimulating (by lowering the rate, increasing disposable income, boosting confidence) or depressing (by raising the interest rates, decreasing the disposable income and 'tightening the belt') the economy. It is one of the principal levers for exercising some control over the economy.
- *Cost of living* – this is commonly measured by the Retail Price Index. It is a relatively easily understood concept which measures the cost of a represent-ative 'basket' of goods and services. It measures the change in prices over a period of time. There are eleven main categories of items in the basket:

  - Alcoholic drink
  - Food
  - Housing
  - Tobacco
  - Fuel and lighting

- Durable household goods
- Clothing and footwear
- Transport and vehicles
- Miscellaneous food
- Services
- Meals bought and consumed outside the home.

There is a vast range of items – of the order of 350 are selected each month for investigation. Basically, a sample of prices is taken from different areas and different types of stores. The figure is given as an index based on the prices at a given point in time, and it allows a comparison to be drawn with prices historically.

- *Inflation* – this is the name we give to the increase in prices over those of a year ago expressed as a percentage. So we have some readily understandable notions, such as 5 per cent inflation means that things are costing 5 per cent more now than they were one year ago. During the 1970s the UK experienced some high inflation figures, and it became one of the key indices for establishing pay demands. As politicians regularly remind us, inflation is particularly hard on retired people, whose savings have, in effect, decreased by the level of inflation over the year in question.
- *Exchange rates* – these are established by the value of one currency in terms of another. The value is commonly influenced by factors such as the balance of trade (our earlier notion of how 'profitable' an economy is – the more profitable the higher will be the value ascribed to the currency), and the levels of interest being charged within the system. The importance to marketers is that changes in the exchange rate affect our costings when we import items from abroad, and our prices when we are selling in other countries. If the pound declines in value, our products will look relatively 'cheap' to buy by overseas customers, but importing goods from abroad will be relatively more expensive. If the pound gains in value, then imports look cheaper, but our exports will begin to look expensive.

4 'So you want to be a social climber?'

Marketing aspects of sociology

Introduction

In this chapter we examine some of the influences which stem from membership of a wider society. This is a huge field of study – so, once again, we are dealing with 'edited highlights' and attempting to look at them from a marketing perspective.

This is another subject area that is all around us – we are all part of society and both influence and are influenced by it. The newspapers regularly carry interesting material of the 'Is this the end of society/the world as we know it?' kind. Keep an eye open, as such material often indicates a general area of interest or concern.

The first 'edited highlight' we shall look at is the broad concept of culture.

Culture

Raymond Williams (1976) maintains that culture is one of the most complicated words in the English language due to its historical development and the fact that it is a word used for important concepts in several different intellectual disciplines. We use the word to describe high art (classical music, theatre, painting and sculpture) and it is often used to contrast these forms with popular taste. It is used by biologists who produce cultures of bacteria on petri dishes. Farmers are part of the agriculture industry, gardeners practise horticulture and so forth.

In the context of this book we consider it as an important area of sociology which is concerned with what we might describe as the 'way of life' adopted by groups of people. It is important to marketers in that it both affects and describes human behaviour. A good way of thinking about culture may be in terms of its usage in words such as agriculture and horticulture, as it can be thought of as describing the human environment in which behaviour is developed.

So, for the purposes of studying consumer behaviour, culture can be defined as:

The values, attitudes, beliefs, ideas, artefacts and other meaningful symbols represented in the pattern of life adopted by people that help them interpret, evaluate and communicate as members of a society.

This is a wide-ranging definition for a very wide-ranging concept which includes codes of manners, dress, language, rituals, norms of behaviour and systems of belief. It is an all-embracing concept which examines the institutions developed by a society and the ways in which these interact to define and determine acceptable behaviour.

Culture has a number of characteristics:

1 It is a *social characteristic of people*, and its purpose is to serve the needs of the people making up the society.
2 It is *learned* by the members of the society through the processes of socialization, and it defines the behaviours that are acceptable within the society. As we will see later, one of the basic requirements of membership of any group is conformity with its norms and acceptance of its values.
3 It is *cumulative*, in the sense that it is passed from generation to generation and often has historical justification. However, this is not to say that culture remains constant.
4 It is *adaptive*. When we look at Figure 4.1, we can see that few of the institutions or elements are absolute – values, religion, politics, laws and so forth can all change in response to the needs of the society. Each and all of these changes influence the culture, customs and rituals of the society.

We could represent culture as shown in Figure 4.1.

In a very real sense culture is exhibited by the customs and rituals of a society, so it is worth examining these ideas in more detail:

1 *Customs*. These are the established patterns of behaviour adopted within the society or community. They regulate and regularize social practices and define which behaviours are acceptable. Williams (1981) defined four classes of custom which constitute a continuum of customs from the least to the most serious, in as much as the response to non-adherence becomes noticeably more emphatic as we progress from a) to d):
   a) *Folkways* – these are the everyday customs of the community. Shaking hands would be a typical example; here the general pattern is defined and regarded as being appropriate, it is widely accepted behaviour when meeting people, but, significantly, it is not insisted upon and failing to shake hands is not normally punished. If it is noticed, the 'punishment' is likely to be a comment rather than punitive action. This also serves to highlight cultural differences, as many Europeans are more likely to use a kiss as a greeting.
   b) *Conventions* – these are folkways which have become hallowed by time and usage. Thus they are slightly 'stronger' than folkways and are often concerned with behaviours which the society considers polite. Taking a gift of chocolates, flowers or wine when visiting friends for a meal or a party would fit neatly into the convention category. Again, it is to be noted that

the 'penalties' for non-compliance are not severe, but perhaps a little more serious than for flouting folkways.

c) *Mores* are the accepted and strongly prescribed forms of behaviour within the society and cover the more significant social norms. Issues such as murder, theft, incest, monogamy and so forth are covered by mores in the UK. Some societies might include other areas, such as honouring your elders. In this category failure to comply results in significant reaction and punishment.

d) *Laws* represent the formalized recognition of mores which the society as a whole deems necessary for its well-being. Laws carry penalties which are imposed on those caught breaking the law. Most societies have processes for revising and reviewing laws in the light of the beliefs and values obtaining at any given time. Thus they are not absolute, but reflect the society at a given point in time, and existing laws can be altered when the society feels it is necessary so to do.

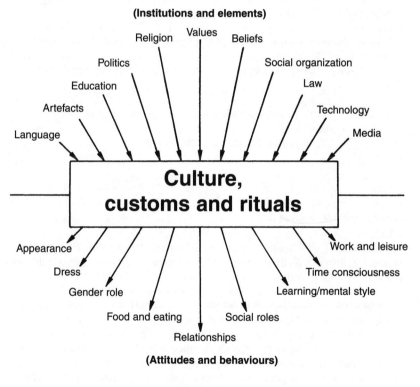

Figure 4.1

2 *Ritual.* This has two meanings in the behavioural sciences. One is the idea of a routine activity characterized by its ordinariness – you may have particular rituals which you follow before going to bed, shaving, getting undressed and

so forth. Students commonly go through quite complex rituals to ensure 'good luck' in examinations!

More significant in this context is the ritual which has symbolic significance – such rituals are commonly formal, ceremonial and public. An example might be the degree/diploma/certificate graduation ceremony run by your college. Other examples of ritual behaviour include religious services, weddings, funerals and many sporting events. Sociologists also refer to rituals which constitute the rites of passage within a society. These commonly accompany a change of status which occurs in the course of the life cycle. Examples include the acknowledgement of the arrival of a new child through ceremonies such as christenings (or the equivalent in religions other than Christianity), the attainment of adulthood, which in the UK is often marked by the 18th birthday party, marriage ceremonies and retirement. These rituals are a means of drawing attention to changes in status and social identity, and also offer a way to manage some of the tensions that such changes may involve, e.g. the linking of two families, the acknowledgement of an offspring's independence, or the end of a working life.

These rituals enable the individual to publicly subscribe to the values of the culture; they often involve the conspicuous expenditure of resources and may offer significant marketing opportunities for the sale of appropriate symbols.

Think – What significant rites of passage have you
experienced?
– What expenditure was involved?

Figure 4.1 highlights culture emerging from a number of elements and institutions associated with living within a large group or society. Some of these will repay further examination:

1 *Values, beliefs and religion.* Sociologists such as Parsons have emphasized 'shared values' as playing a key role in the integration of a society or group. While it can be argued that a similar effect may be obtained via the use of raw power (as in some military dictatorships), most analysts accept that such societies tend to be less stable. So culture is, in part, a reflection of the ethical ideals accepted by the people making up that group and, as such, is concerned with what the society believes ought to happen and how it sees itself. This is reflected in the attitudes of individuals, the rules and enforcement processes it employs, and in the customs embraced by the society. Clearly, religious beliefs will fall into this category, as religion is often the determinant of values, and belief is fundamental to religion. From such beliefs stem ideas which are held as important within the British culture, such as the right of free speech, or involvement in decision making via the democratic process. Other societies with different religions, beliefs and values may develop different, but no less valid, cultures.

2 *Language and communication.* The fact that different cultures speak different

languages is an obvious means of distinguishing between large groups of people. Language is itself a fascinating field of study, as it has a long history, examination of which emphasizes the fact that language itself is a changing entity. New words are invented, meanings of words change over time and, as we noted earlier, language is particularly rich in communicating feelings and emotions as well as facts.

A specific problem can arise when products (or marketing messages) are expected to cross cultural/language barriers. On occasion, a word in one language may also exist in another but mean something very different. For instance, an Italian walking through a UK shopping centre may see a poster saying 'Sale' in a shop window. This means 'salt' in Italian and thus has the potential to confuse. The problem may be even greater for the visitor from France, to whom the 'sale' sign means 'dirty'! Examples of such confusion in naming products which cross language barriers can give rise to humorous situations (but only if you are not the person responsible for the product). Colgate attempted to use the name 'Cue' in France, only to find that it was an obscene slang expression. The Vauxhall Nova tends not to be popular in Spanish-speaking areas where 'no va' translates into 'does not go'! Another example is the Toyota MR2 sports car. 'MR2', when said in French, emerges as 'MR deux', which sounds remarkably like another French word 'merde' – needless to say, Toyota changed the name for the French market.

Because of such dangers, consultancies now exist to check out possible product or brand names to ensure that such mistakes do not occur. It is claimed that the up-market ice-cream Häagen-Dazs brand name was invented by such a consultancy, and was adopted specifically because it had no known meaning or association (it also has the advantage of being different and hence noticeable (as discussed in the chapter on perception) due to the double 'a', the umlaut and the 'z').

Think – What examples can you think of where language is a marketing problem?

---

3 *Politics, law, social organization and education.* The *political* system adopted by a nation will be an important determinant of the culture – and will do so in a relatively formal manner. The political system will allocate power and influence to certain groups of individuals and this will, in turn, directly affect 'the way things are done'.

Laws logically follow as the formalized statements of acceptable behaviour as discussed above, and will set the limits of tolerated conduct.

Social organization will be considered later, as notions of social class and status are acknowledged to be important ways of viewing social stratification.

Education plays an important part in the whole socialization process, affecting language, values and learned behaviour as well as linking to social class.

4 *Artefacts and technology.* In the holiday brochure, culture is often linked to historical artefacts. In modern society, technology directly influences the way

in which people live. The explosion in mass communication in some parts of the world has had an enormous impact on whole societies, and the rate of social change has been accelerated by having live news reports beamed into our living rooms. In a similar way, transport systems within an area will affect the way of life, social interaction and shopping patterns.

5 *Media*. Culture will influence many important behaviours and attitudes, and some of these behaviours may affect us in the activities associated with marketing.

It is worthwhile looking at some of these areas in a little more detail.

- *Appearance and dress* – any visit to another country will highlight the different appearance and dress of other peoples. To some extent this may be a reflection of affluence and fashion, but cultures may differ significantly in their views on issues such as whether adult males should shave their beards. There are also very different views and standards about the extent to which females may expose their skin. Compare the different cultural values which are represented by female members of some Muslim sects who dress so that only the eyes are uncovered with the scantily clad females who appear in photographs from the Cannes Film Festival. Even within a larger society the various micro-cultures exert strong influence over their members, as witnessed by the pinstriped suit of the stereotypical businessman and the apparel of the football fans turning up for the match. One oddity of culture in the UK is the wearing of ties on important occasions – the tie seems to represent one of the least useful elements of clothing ever devised, and yet it remains essential for many people and would normally be worn for significant encounters such as job interviews.

> **Think** – How might this aspect of culture affect marketing and advertising?

By its very nature appearance becomes highly influential in determining the behaviour of those people within the cultural group, and thus becomes a field of great interest in marketing terms.

Examples of the influence of culture might be basic items such as clothing or food. In its original form clothing was a means of covering our bodies in order to protect against the weather – but fairly rapidly it became a symbol of many other social and personal characteristics. Clothes became a statement about the identity of the person wearing them. The statement could include issues such as gender, modesty, affluence, status, religion, race, age and so forth. From humble initial beginnings clothing has become a complex badge of membership of both society and the groups that make up the society.

Similarly, food was initially a means to sustain life – but, again, we have imbued many foods with symbolic meanings. We may eat certain things as special treats, or at specific times (the 'traditional' Christmas dinner would be one example). Food can be an example of family bonding, with recipes being handed down from one generation to the next. It can also be a symbol of racial or ethnic identity. In extreme cases certain foods can become religious icons, eaten as part of specific religious ceremonies.

Think – What foods are significant to you?
– Why?
– What defines a Sunday dinner for you?
– How does this meal differ from other meals in the week?

As we have observed, culture is a wide-ranging concept. Part of its significance is that it is the system that provides people with an understanding of acceptable and expected behaviour within the society. This, in turn, will go some way towards providing people with a sense of identity.

- *Sense of gender roles* – different cultures have different expectations and rules governing the roles of men and women. Traditionally in the UK women have been looked on as the homebuilders and nurturers while men have been expected to fulfil the breadwinner role. However, the rise of feminism and the growing value attached to equal opportunities within the society has shifted some of these expectations. A typical example of the use of the expected roles of men and women in advertising material might be the long-running Oxo advertisements which showed the wife as the provider of meals for the hungry males of the family. Later versions have portrayed her as rather more independent – but still carrying out the caring role by the use of Oxo! In contrast, other societies may allocate rather different roles to the genders and enforce those expectations with varying degrees of sanctions.

Think – What other marketing examples can you think of which involve 'usual' gender roles?
– What examples can you think of which attract attention by using 'unusual' roles?

- *Food and eating habits* – as mentioned above, this is a basic activity which is likely to be affected by culture. It is often regarded as a communal activity where the individuals take meals with their primary groups, so, in addition to fulfilling physiological needs, it may be an important mechanism for social bonding. Again, food can have symbolic and ritualistic elements.

Think – What are the ritualistic elements required of:
- a wedding breakfast?
- Christmas dinner?
- a working lunch?

Another aspect of food and culture may arise from the importance of beliefs and religion. Some religious groups will not eat pork, others will not eat beef, still others will not eat meat of any sort, some will not drink alcohol, others will take no stimulants of any kind. Clearly, such beliefs will affect buying behaviour with regard to foodstuffs.

● *Relationships* may be defined by the culture within which the individuals are operating. Expectations of children by parents (and of parents by children) may vary from society to society.

> **Think** – What obligations do you think children have towards
> supporting their ageing parents?
> – Why?

● *Mental processing and learning styles* may vary from culture to culture. Many anthropologists will argue that so-called 'primitive' cultures possess knowledge which more 'advanced' societies have lost. Western societies tend to be dominated by logic and proof in terms of mental processing. Other societies may have different approaches – this is often cited as a problem for Western businesspeople visiting Eastern societies.

> **Think** – What examples can you think of where people have
> adopted different mental processes and learning
> styles?

● *Time and time consciousness* can vary markedly from culture to culture. Western perspectives of time can seem very short in comparison with other cultures. We go on time management courses, have electronic notebooks that act as alarm clocks for appointments and generally live in a 'hurry, hurry' environment. Yet, in contrast, we like to holiday in places where the pace of life is slower, and this is sold to us strongly in holiday advertisements.

> **Think** – What examples can you identify of different time
> consciousness?

● *The place and importance of work* in our lives can vary dramatically. In the UK, asking someone what they are usually results in an answer which involves a job title. We have developed a system where the job a person does fulfils a number of different functions. Our job is:

– the source of income and, hence, economic stability, status and power
– an important determinant of how we spend our time

- a source of social contact and friendship
- a significant factor in the way our place in society is determined
- a crucial determinant of our own self-image.

It is for these reasons that redundancy or unemployment can be so psychologically damaging for those who experience it.

Originally the concept of culture was applied to whole societies such as nations, but increasingly it has become clear that it is a useful framework to adopt when analysing different sizes of societies and also significant groupings within the set we think of as a society. So it is now applied in a variety of settings:

- *Macro-cultures* refer to large groupings, such as whole continents (e.g. the idea of European or North American cultures), or
- individual nations (e.g. contrasting English and French cultures).
- *Micro-cultures* refer either to significant groupings within a society, such as classes (e.g. comparing 'upper' and 'working classes), or
- other micro-cultures, such as religious groupings, racial groups, specific age groups, or even as 'micro' as followers of a particular football club.
- Increasingly the expression is used to describe the style adopted within a business or company, and this is referred to as *organizational culture*.

While many of the points that are raised have a degree of validity, there is a danger of oversimplification due to the assumption of national stereotypes. However, examination of the world in which we live seems not to support such a view. In the UK it seems rash to claim 'sameness' for the different regions of the country – the inner cities and rural areas; Protestants, Catholics, Muslims, Sikhs and Rastafarians; Asian, Afro-Caribbean and Anglo-Saxon races and so forth. The reality seems to be that society is made up of a series of micro-cultures, many of which are significantly different. Far from being a handicap, such a view may help us to segment the society into targetable markets.

It is sometimes suggested that the six prime micro-cultures within our society are based on:

1 *Geography*. This reflects regional differences in patterns of speech (accents) and some stereotyped assumptions about eating, drinking and consumption patterns. Such variations have a strong historical basis, as the different communities developed differently due to the economic and geographical factors influencing the area. However, the advent of mass media has had the effect of reducing some of the variance – the standardization of speech patterns around some notional BBC norm would be an example, although such evening out is opposed by those who wish to keep to the old traditions and maintain separate, distinct cultures.

2 *Ethnicity*. Historically, for obvious economic reasons, ethnic groupings have tended to develop in certain areas. This has the advantage of enabling the original cultures of the immigrants to be maintained. An example of this would be in the author's home town, where a significant Polish population has settled within a specific locality. The result of such concentration is that children can be taught the Polish language, the customs and rituals of the 'old country' can

be emphasized and maintained, and a number of Polish clubs can exist in the city where the expatriates can meet and retain their Polishness. Clearly, such a situation suggests that marketing opportunities exist to cater for the needs of such micro-cultures. Similar examples from other ethnic groups can be found in most large conurbations. In the past, marketers have not targeted ethnic groups for most products – there seems to have been an assumption that mass marketing would, by definition, reach all members of the society. However, we are beginning to see advertising aimed at specific ethnic groups in product areas such as beauty and grooming.

3 *Religion*. For those who subscribe to a religious creed, the belief and membership of the religious community is likely to be a major influence on their attitudes, lifestyle and behaviour.

4 *Age*. Later we will look at the family life cycle and discuss the segmentation of markets according to the prime interests and levels of disposable income, and the various stages of the cycle could have many of the characteristics of micro-cultures. Perhaps the most significant of these is the so-called 'youth culture'. As a market segment this came to the fore in the 1960s when the combination of the immediate post-war baby boom and increasing affluence led to a sizeable market opportunity. The market was identified by such things as choice of music and clothes. For the first time there was a situation where a very young age group had high disposable income, and this led to a massive growth in items such as records and fashion. More recently, the emergence of the 'yuppie' has had a major impact on product development, the notion of style and the identification of a clear market segment. In the UK at the present time, the 'grey' market is becoming increasingly important. Here we have a growing number of older people, some of whom have inherited considerable sums of money following the spectacular rise in property values during the 1980s and so have very great discretionary spending power. There is evidence that this group does not perceive itself as being old and is maintaining high levels of market activity. Given their numbers and relative wealth, the 'greys' form a very attractive market segment. The recent growth of television situation comedies which centre on older characters (e.g. *'Til Death Us Do Part, Waiting For God, One Foot In The Grave, The Golden Girls* being the current crop) reflects its influence and potential.

5 *Gender*. The roles of the sexes are often defined by the family setting and may well determine the location of a number of purchasing decisions. The marketing implications of a micro-culture based on gender are based on the assumption that men or women have beliefs and values which make them different. Here we might have basic examples such as shaving equipment for men or sanitary protection for women. Beyond these physiological sets we are likely to be concerned with notions of male and female roles within the society. Here we have seen changes over the last decade with the emergence of the career woman and the 'new man', both powerful social images which have developed market segments based on these micro-cultures.

At the simplest level, culture is concerned with 'how we do things here'. So the variations may be viewed as different perceptions of who 'we' are, and where

'here' is. Perhaps even more significant is the opportunity that cultural analysis offers the marketer in terms of giving opportunities to segment the market.

Socialization

We commented in our earlier discussion of culture that it was both learned and passed from one generation to another. This learning process is called *socialization* and we can define it as:

> the process by which the culture of a society is transmitted to children and succeeding generations so that they absorb all of its values and symbols and become able to function effectively within it.

Socialization is concerned with the ways in which an individual's behaviour is modified from infancy to conform to the demands of the social system. It involves learning the expectations associated with various roles within the society, but, given the nature of human beings, it does not just produce clones – there is another significant element, which is about the individuals and the development of their separate identities.

The socialization process is concerned with preparing individuals for the roles that may be required of them and also with the continuation and development of the culture itself. Thus it focuses on relationships between the individual and society. In this sense the study of this concept bridges the disciplines of sociology and psychology.

Much of our social behaviour is learned via connectionist principles, which we will expand on later. Children learn family rituals and how to respond in different situations, and much of this learning may continue into adulthood. The author has an unfortunate linkage from his childhood, which is that being addressed by his full given forename 'Christopher' still leads to a conditioned response of 'what have I done wrong?' Similarly, the process of growing up will lead to experiments with various behaviours and learning which ones lead to reward and positive reinforcement and which ones lead to punishment. Reflection may lead us on to the conclusion that such conditioning does not only occur in childhood; a significant part of adult life can be viewed in these terms – not least the ways in which our employers may attempt to condition our work behaviours by offering rewards for behaviours they define as 'good' and negative reinforcement for those they define as undesirable. Further reflection may lead us to conclude that such conditioning is conducted in adult life by others in our lives, including our partners, friends and even governments.

Think – What social conditioning are you aware of in your own development?

The process of watching other people, absorbing the roles, specific behaviours and making judgements about their appropriateness is likely to result in storing the knowledge for recall at some later point in time. In addition, we may well indulge in imitation. This, in turn, may lead to reactions (positive or negative) which help us to decide whether to adopt the behaviour as part of our 'normal' repertoire.

Implicit in the idea of imitation is the concept of the *role model* – the individual's perceived ideal which he or she seeks to emulate. Identification takes the process even deeper, with the person taking on the perceived attitudes and values of the role model, i.e. attempting to become exactly like the ideal. Once these values and attitudes have been adopted, the 'learned' behaviour emerges when the situation is perceived as being appropriate.

> **Think** – Who are your role models?
> – How have they affected your behaviour?

Role-play is another mechanism of learning which fits into the socialization process and involves consciously 'trying out' roles. This is a common experience of childhood ('let's play doctors and nurses/mummies and daddies/cops and robbers, etc.') and is increasingly being used in management training. The practice of playing a role allows experimentation, and repetition leads to the imprinting of particular (but necessarily appropriate) behaviours. This can be a valuable device for developing the skills needed for unaccustomed roles.

> **Think** – Have you ever role-played being the applicant before going for a job interview?
> – What did you learn from the experience?

As has been hinted at in the above section, learning and socialization takes place via a number of agencies:

1 *Family.* Much of the discussion has centred on children learning, as this process of passing on from one generation to another has been defined as one of the prime characteristics and aims of culture. The child is particularly susceptible to the learning because of its dependence on the family and its very high involvement with family members and family activities.

   In particular, the child is likely to be exposed to experiences which will fundamentally affect the perception and expectations associated with roles such as 'husband', 'wife', 'mother', 'father'. Embedded in these roles will be values, attitudes, relationships, specific behaviours and decision-making patterns. Experience suggests that much of this early learning is carried over into adult life, and many problems experienced by people may be diagnosed as a re-enactment of early experiences.

> **Think** – What values, attitudes and behaviours have you
> carried from your childhood?

2 *School*. Again, this is influential in that it can initiate behaviours, values and attitudes while the individual is both dependent and impressionable. Schools ostensibly teach knowledge and skills to pupils, but few of us would deny that it is a period in life where cultural values are both introduced and reinforced. The phenomenon of unexpected learning may occur, as, for instance, when a pupil is asked to come out in front of the class and work through a long division problem on the board. This experience may not teach the individual anything about mathematics, but a great deal about humiliation (and teachers) may be learned! Similarly, most schools place great emphasis on honesty and ideas such as 'good citizenship', but we also learn that there is a strong, unwritten code which demands that one does not 'tell tales' about other classmates.

> **Think** – What values, attitudes and behaviours have you
> carried from your schooldays?

3 *Peer groups*. In the next chapter we shall see evidence of the influence of our informal social groups. The power of such groups is their ability to control a person's personal and emotional satisfactions. The 'ultimate deterrent' may be the threat of being isolated or 'sent to Coventry' by one's friends. We often find that peer group pressure is more influential than the expectations of the family. Part of the process of growing up is resolving the potential conflicts between the values, attitudes and behaviours demanded by one's peer group and those expected by the family. This process is commonly a source of tension within families as children progress through adolescence. Both the family and the individual are attempting to come to terms with changing status and independence. However, peer groups continue to be important throughout our lives, and may generate significant changes in behaviour, particularly if the peer group changes (as may happen when couples form a partnership and each is introduced to the other's group of friends).

> **Think** – Which of your values, attitudes and behaviours have
> been influenced by friends, colleagues and peer
> group?
> – What peer group pressures have you rejected?

4 *Mass media*. Exposure to the mass media has a significant impact on our view of the world. In Chapter 2 the ideas of selective perception and selective exposure were explored, and we can see the way in which reading a particular newspaper may reinforce political beliefs and value systems. However, the

media is now virtually all-pervasive, and few of us can escape images and inputs from television, radio, magazines and newspapers. Inevitably, these will give a particular vision of reality, and it seems unrealistic to suppose that people's perceptions will not be affected. Repetition of specific messages gradually 'sinks in' to the cultural subconscious – so that the values and assumptions of things such as the 'enterprise culture' of the 1980s influenced the majority of the population. Similarly, single images may live in the mind and affect our perceptions in the longer term. Here the picture of the solitary student standing in front of the advancing tanks in Beijing might be an illustration. As students of marketing processes we may also need to consider the cumulative influence of the advertising images that our trade puts before the public. The continual presentation of images of wealth, prosperity, power, gender roles, sexual attractiveness and racial characteristics seems likely to produce expectations in the population at large which at best may be motivating, but which may also give rise to frustration, anger, resentment or distress.

Think – How has the mass media affected your values, attitudes and behaviours?

Much of the foregoing discussion has centred on the idea of individuals learning behaviour appropriate to the different roles they play. It is worthwhile to spend a little more time exploring some of the ideas surrounding the notion of a role.

Role

Engel, Blackwell and Miniard (1990) define a role as:

What the typical occupant of a given position is expected to do in that position in a particular social context

In other words, it is used in very much the same way as it is used by actors. You may have a role which is 'assistant product manager' and there will be behaviours which the person holding that role will be expected to exhibit.

We each belong to many groups, both formal and informal. Each of these may allocate us one or more roles to play. So an individual may have roles such as husband or wife, friend, son or daughter, member of a political party, football fan or churchgoer, in addition to the work roles of 'assistant product manager' and general 'rising star'.

Inevitably, a person cannot comfortably exhibit all of the appropriate behaviours at the same time – wearing the tribal warpaint of the football fan is more relevant to match days than formal meetings at work. Indeed, it is interesting to note that several roles within our society demand a specific appearance or uniform (milk and post deliverers, railway guards, bus drivers, clergy). In a less formal sense there may be a 'uniform' for managers or marketing specialists.

Think – Which of the roles that you play involve any form of uniform?

In many situations the 'uniform' is an important role sign. Examples such as weddings (being a bride or groom, or even a wedding guest) and funerals demand an expected appearance, while attending an exercise class certainly involves considerable expenditure on 'suitable' clothing. This means considerable opportunities for marketing products which could be seen as role signs – briefcases, organizers, 'executive toys' and even motor cars are typical examples of merchandise which may be sold in order to reinforce a person's perceived role.

Roles will often define a relationship quite specifically – here the role of teacher or tutor would be a good example, with the expectations that the teacher will transmit information and the student will accept it. The other individuals who relate to an individual in their specific roles are referred to as the *role set*. The membership of such role sets will change according to the roles being played – e.g. the home role set would consist of family members, the work role set would be made up of colleagues, superiors, subordinates, customers and so forth. Behaviour is likely to change in as much as few families can tolerate a teacher lecturing them over breakfast, while management students may even be expected to manage when at work.

Once again, the core issues appear to centre on the *perceptions* of the role by both other people and the person carrying it out along with a more generalized expectation of the 'rules' of behaviour associated with the role (i.e. the norms established by society).

If all parties share the same perception, things are relatively straightforward, but if there is any degree of mismatch then accommodations will have to be made. See Figure 4.2.

Given that much of role theory depends on the perceptions of the individuals concerned, it is likely that some discrepancies will occur. The problems associated with differing expectations can be classified into:

1 *Role ambiguity* – this is where the expectations are not clearly defined, either for the role player or the associated role set. Thus the problem can centre on
   - *the individual's uncertainty about what is expected in the role*. Examples could include 'finding one's feet' on appointment to a new job, or uncertainty about the full implications of changing marital status or becoming a parent.
   - *the role set's uncertainty about what is expected in the role*. Examples could include your class 'negotiating' an acceptable style with the tutor, couples working hard in the early days of a relationship to clarify role specializations within the household, or a department faced with a new manager showing uncertainty as to whether the boss will maintain the status quo or become a 'new broom'.

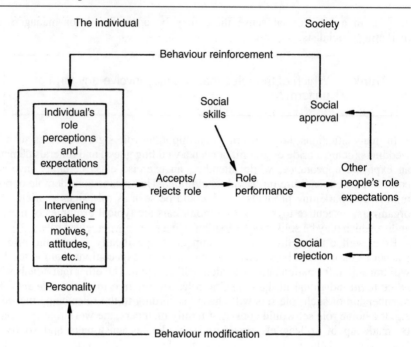

Figure 4.2　The effect of role on the learning of social behaviour (adapted from Williams, *Behavioural Aspects of Marketing*, 1981)

2 *Role conflict* – again subdivided into:
  ● *inter-role conflict*, where the conflict occurs between roles. An example might be the conflict between the individual being asked to work overtime on a rush job having to decide whether the demands of the employment outweigh missing an offspring's scheduled birthday party. In this case the conflict is between the expectations associated with the 'conscientious employee' role ('of course I will work extra') and the demands of the 'loving parent' role ('of course I'll be back for the party'). Women face particular problems due to expectations that they will fulfil the caring/nurturing roles within families, thus setting up immediate conflicts with employment expectations. Many convenience foods slant their advertising material towards bridging the gap by showing how use of the product will create the space to be a successful career woman and feed the family nourishing meals. Such advertising offers a solution to the cognitive dissonance which often arises from inter-role conflict.
  ● *intra-role conflict*, where the conflict arises from different aspects of the same role. For instance in the parental role, the caring and loving elements may at times be in conflict with the need to discipline a child.
  As we have noted earlier, conflicts or problems often offer marketing opportunities in as much as the solution to the problem (or the resolution of the conflict) may be the true product being sold.

> **Think** – What examples can you identify where a product is
> sold as a solution to an inter-role conflict?

Social class, status and other forms of market segmentation

> **Think** – What class are you?
> – On what basis do you make that judgement?

The concept of class is a very complex one which is important in sociology. It has a number of similar and interlinked usages and meanings. Some of the key ideas associated with class are:

- the notion of *hierarchical distinction*, which also finds itself expressed in ideas such as social stratification – hence the ideas of upper class, middle class, lower class, working class and so forth
- the use of census data to provide descriptive categories such as those used by the Registrar General in dividing up the population of the United Kingdom
- the use of occupations to identify what are sometimes referred to as socio-economic status groups, such as manual and non-manual, or white-collar and blue-collar occupations
- the description of a society in terms of the degree of social mobility that is possible. This leads directly to classifications such as *open societies* (social mobility and movement from one class to another being possible) and *closed societies* (social class being defined and fixed at and by birth, as in caste systems). Ideas of inherited wealth, influence and position, such as is implied in the existence of the aristocracy in the UK, would indicate a relatively closed system in parts of the society, as wealth does not entitle the individual to move into a group such as the aristocracy
- the ideas of Marx, which centred on ownership and non-ownership of property and resources and which give rise to the classifications of bourgeoisie and proletariat as the dominant classes in capitalist societies
- Weber's use of similar analysis focused on the subdivisions of property that might be the basis of distinctions. Property could thus include ideas such as knowledge or education.

> **Think** – Which of these ideas were part of your analysis of
> your own social class?

Within the marketing context the importance of such ideas is that they offer the possibility of segmenting the population into groups which might have similar beliefs, attitudes and values which are reflected in their behaviour. This would enable suitable marketing messages to be designed and sent specifically to influence the buying behaviour of the group.

We use ideas such as class to help us find groups which are collections of individuals who are of sufficiently similar status to give them the same sort of command over goods and services and to share belief systems, aspirations and values.

Class is essentially an objective means of classifying people according to criteria such as occupation, education, lifestyle, place of residence and income. It implies (and as marketers we seek) an awareness of class consciousness within the group, a degree of uniformity of lifestyle and social interaction so that processes of group conformity can operate.

Status, on the other hand, is essentially a subjective phenomenon which is the result of a judgement of the social position that a person occupies. Here the distinction from class becomes somewhat blurred, as the judgement is usually also based on factors such as power, wealth and occupation.

It is possible to identify three forms of status:

1 *Ascribed status* – this is similar to the ideas of ascribed groups described in the previous chapter. This status is something that the individual has little control over, as it covers the status accorded by the society to classifications such as gender (male/female) and race/colour. So far as any person is concerned, this is primarily defined by the 'accident of birth' and is, by and large, permanent. It is an interesting aspect that, while ascribed status is outside the control of the individual, it is not necessarily fixed, in as much as it is possible to chart the changes in status of, say, women over a period of time within a given society.
2 *Achieved status* – in contrast, this has been acquired by individuals through such things as their occupation, place of residence and lifestyle. Once again, this is subjective and open to change as the values of a society alter. It is often assumed that status is linked to spending power, but it is possible to find groups of people who enjoy relatively high status but relatively low income. The clergy, nurses and even teachers might fall into such a category, but, as with ascribed status, the valuation of occupations (or residential areas) can change. Recent events and publicity seem to have dented the reputation (and status) of groups such as social workers, and the property boom of the 1980s led to disaffection for estate agents.

Think – Which occupations can you think of which are 'on the
    way up'?
  – Which do you think are 'on the way down'?
  – Why?

---

3 *Desired status* – this is the social position an individual wishes to attain. The assumption is that status is actively sought by the individual who seeks to acquire and conform to the desired roles. In this case it is something over which the individual can exercise some control, and is identical to the

important notion of ego or status motivation as proposed by Maslow (see Chapter 6).

For marketers the key to influencing consumers in this way depends on the concept of the open society. The idea that individuals can improve their lot and rise in the hierarchy of class and status leads to the strategy of placing the product in such a setting that it appeals to the target segment/class/status group and implies that adoption will lend credence to their aspirations to be seen as a member of the next higher group.

5 'Here we go, here we go, here we go...'

People in groups

Introduction

Groups are a basic part of human life. We all come from some sort of family background, we have friends, we work in departments or sections. Another aspect of group membership is that it usually involves a degree of give-and-take in behavioural terms. We compromise to keep the others happy, or go along with the wishes of the rest when we do not feel strongly about something. In this way groups affect our behaviour.

We will start our review of the subject by considering some of the classic experiments which have highlighted some of the elements of group behaviour.

Elton Mayo and the Hawthorne Experiments

The famous Hawthorne Experiments were conducted by Professor Elton Mayo at the Western Electric Company in Chicago during the period 1927–32. There were three main studies which are of interest in our quest to understand customers:

1 *The Drawing Office experiment* – here the problem lay in low morale, which was blamed on the lighting. Mayo split the department into two – the first group was the experimental group, the second group acted as the control group, whose lighting remained unaltered throughout the experiment. When the intensity of the lighting of the experimental group was increased, the expected improvement in morale and output occurred. What was unexpected was that the morale and output of the control group rose in exactly the same way. This puzzled Mayo, who proceeded to reduce the intensity for the experimental group – output of both groups again rose! His conclusion was that the changed behaviour was nothing to do with the intensity of the lighting, but was a group phenomenon.
2 *The Relay Assembly Room experiment* – here a self-selected group of six operators was used. The job consisted of assembling some forty components to produce the small but intricate relay. The production rates of the women were known, and it was thought that the level of production would give a measure of

the effectiveness of the changes planned. Throughout this experiment an observer sat with the group, noting all that happened, keeping the women informed, asking for advice and information and listening to their complaints. Each change was run for a test period of 4–12 weeks. The results are summarized below:

a) Under normal conditions (48-hour week, including Saturdays, no rest pauses) the operatives averaged 2400 relays/week each
b) Put on piecework for 8 weeks: output rose
c) Two 5-minute rest pauses, am and pm, introduced for 5-week period: output rose again
d) Rest pauses increased to 10 minutes: output rose sharply
e) 6 x 5-minute rest pauses introduced: output fell slightly, and there were complaints that this broke the work rhythm
f) Returned to 2 rest periods, but with hot meal provided free: output rose
g Operatives finished 1/2 hour earlier: output went up
h) They finished another 1/2 hour earlier: output steady
i) All improvements taken away: returned to original conditions. This phase ran for 12 weeks, and output was the highest ever recorded, at just over 3000 relays/week each. Again, the working conditions could not have been the sole determinant of improved performance, and Mayo concluded that this was further evidence of the influence of the group.

3 *The Bank Wiring Room experiment* – here Mayo was interested in the section producing telephone equipment. The group were on a production bonus, which gave increased earnings for higher output, but despite the fact that 7000 units was well within the capability of the group they produced no more and no less than 6000 units per day. The group appeared to have set this arbitrary standard, and dealt forcibly (both verbally and physically) with any individual who did not conform to the norm. By interview and observation it was discovered that the work group had developed spontaneously into a team with natural leaders (not necessarily coinciding with those put into positions of authority by management) who, within the group, had far more power than the official authorities. This experiment confirmed Mayo's conclusion that the work group was, and is, a major determinant of work behaviour (and of many of our industrial problems).

These three experiments emphasize the importance of the immediate social group in determining behaviour – in the drawing office and relay assembly experiments the subjects appeared to work harder as the result of some sort of group pressure, while in the bank wiring room the pressure was to limit the rate of work and thus output. So we can conclude that behaviour and attitudes can be influenced directly, and the strength of such pressure is very high – people were actually earning less money than they could have been due to the disciplines exercised by the two informal groups in the bank wiring room.

Additionally, these experiments gave us the concept of the 'Hawthorne Effect', where the behaviour of people taking part in an experiment ceases to be typical. This has been examined in some fascinating experiments in the USA – particularly the work of Milgram, who found that people would do extraordinary things (including apparently causing considerable pain to other human beings) so long as it was part of 'an experiment'. This is of considerable interest to us later when we consider the problems of investigating customers in Section 3.

The power of the group over individual members is considerable, with the need to conform and belong being so powerful. Evidence of this power came in another classic experiment.

Sherif – the Auto-kinetic Effect

In 1935 Sherif conducted an experiment in which students were placed in a darkened room. Each student was asked to judge in which direction and how far a spot of light moved. The spot, in fact, remained still and did not move at all – it only appeared to do so (the *auto-kinetic effect*). Sherif found that, under these conditions, each of the subjects develops a range within which he or she makes his or her estimates.

It also emerged that, if an individual made a judgement about the movement of the light in the presence of others, the judgement made was in the same direction and distance of the judgements around them – even if the original estimates, made when alone, were in the opposite direction!!

This highlights the great extent to which the individual subject is influenced by the group's judgement and the power of the group to ensure conformity of its members. This experiment, and others similar in design, have been repeated on many occasions and emphasize the influence that groups can have over an individual's perceptions and behaviour.

If groups are as powerful as these experiments suggest, they are of obvious interest to the marketing specialist. If they can change behaviour, it may be possible, through studying their processes, to understand and possibly influence buying behaviour.

People in groups – a review of concepts and theories

Think – What groups are you a member of? – Make a list of them. – Against each one indicate why you joined and your role within the group.

People join or find themselves in groups for a variety of reasons. Argyle (1989) has suggested that some of the reasons are conscious and deliberate, while others are situational or due to circumstances.

We may speculate on some of the reasons:

● To achieve a task which cannot be successfully completed alone. This may be an underlying reason for the human race developing tribal systems in the earliest stages of our evolution and continuing with them up to the present time. It could be argued that groups facilitate the satisfaction of Maslow's basic

physiological and security needs
- To obtain friendship, companionship and support. We will see in Chapter 6 that Maslow classified the companionship or love need as part of his hierarchy. This companionship need may be satisfied by informal groups, which can operate even within formal situations or organizations as we saw in the Hawthorne Experiments
- To obtain status (Maslow again) or to exercise power (as per McClelland's theory of motivation). By definition, status necessitates others as comparators for higher or lower status – and exercising power on one's own in a social vacuum is clearly an unsatisfying nonsense!
- To get what Handy calls 'a psychological home' – a source of warmth and psychological security.
- To get power, as in joining a trade union, and lastly,
- Because we have no choice – we are born male or female, the great majority of us cannot exercise choice over the families we are born into, we cannot affect the colour of our skin, etc.

Think – How does your list of reasons compare to those reasons given above?

As can be seen from this brief list, our membership of groups is both inevitable and complex, as it encompasses, and controls the satisfaction of, many aspects of human motivation.

So let us begin our discussion with a definition of what constitutes a group.

A *group* is a number of people (more than one) who have:

    a) a common purpose/goal/objective/task
and b) a sense of 'boundary' and, hence, an identity
and c) a minimum set of agreed/accepted values and norms governing behaviour within the group
and d) relatively exclusive interactions within a given context
and e) a self-perception, by the members, of themselves as a group.

Think – Using the definition above, does a bus queue constitute a group?
    – Does your CIM Understanding Customers class?
    – Does a group learning a foreign language in a language laboratory?
    – Does the crowd watching a football match?

Groups may be formal, informal, permanent or temporary.

Informal groups have the prime characteristic of being voluntary – both from the viewpoint of the existing group (do they wish to let the newcomer join?) and from the point of view of the 'applicants' (do they want to join, and how much?).

They are dominated by personal rather than role relationships and appear to exist to satisfy the personal and emotional needs of their members.

Think – Can you recognize any informal groups of which you are a member?
– Any of which you are not a member?

In addition to informal or friendship groups, much of our life is spent in more formal groupings, not least at work. Indeed, we spend a great deal of our waking hours in work situations, most of which constitute operating within formal groups.

Formal groups include departments/sections/classes and the like and are dominated by task activity and prescribed relationships. It is rare for formal groups to exercise control over membership, particularly at the lower end of the organizational hierarchy. Role relationships predominate (e.g. teacher/student, manager/subordinate). In some cases formal groups may adopt informal characteristics in order to maximize satisfaction for their members, but their very nature means that they remain formal.

Think – What examples can you identify of formal groups which choose to behave in an informal manner so that people feel more comfortable?

If you become a member of a group in order to satisfy your social affiliation needs, the price of membership is conformity.

Element (c) in the definition of groups highlights the point that they develop norms governing behaviour within the group. These may concern:

- the task or activities of the group
- the non-formal goals, such as relaxation or engaging in hobbies
- internal regulation, such as discipline, language or roles
- opinions, attitudes, beliefs about politics, unions, management outsiders, or anything else that the group is interested in
- physical appearance and dress.

Think – What are the behavioural norms governing the different groups of which you are a member?
– What does that mean in terms of your different behaviour when you are with different groups?

The idea of group norms governing the behaviour of a number of individuals suggests that individuals modify their behaviour according to the groups they are with. Thus we face the fact that human behaviour may be even less consistent and predictable than may be apparent from our studies so far. This idea of the human being as some sort of social chameleon, changing behaviour in order to match the group situation in which he finds himself, clearly only operates within limits which are likely to be a function of an individual's personality. Quiet individuals are unlikely to become raging extroverts, they just become more outgoing when in the company of other shy people.

Individuals who find their behaviour, values or attitudes deviating significantly from the norms of the group are placed in a difficult and uncomfortable position. Robertson and Cooper (1983) suggest that an individual in such a position has four options:

1 To leave the group.
2 To conform to the norms.
3 To try to change the norms of the remainder of the group.
4 To remain a deviant.

They believe that the option chosen will be a function of the individual's personality, the support of others in the group and the strength of feelings about the issue on which deviation occurs.

The idea of modifying behaviour in this way also means that some difficult adjustments may have to be made. Generally, conformity means compromise on the part of group members. However, we commonly deny that such compromise was either demanded or conceded – but it may well be the underlying reason why people as individuals sometimes behave differently from the same people when in a group.

The degree to which we will conform (and compromise) depends on:

- the strength of our desire for agreement on membership
- the strength of our wish to avoid 'aggro' or isolation
- the strength of our belief that the norm reflects our own view (*congruence*)
- the degree to which we doubt our ability to stand alone
- our belief in the group's goals.

These factors seem to define and measure our likely dependence on the group – but our need for Handy's 'psychological home' means that they are both universal and influential.

In the previous chapter we introduced the concept of the role. Roles also occur in groups, and tend to be fixed by two (sometimes conflicting) forces:

a) how we see ourselves, and
b) what others expect of us.

Some academics have described roles – such as spokesperson, peacekeeper, ideas person, comedian, commentator, deviant, specialist, etc.

Inevitably, most of us play the role of 'follower' most of the time!

> **Think** – Consider groups of which you are a member and
>   identify who plays which roles.
> – How were these roles allocated (or did it 'just
>   happen')?
> – What roles do you play?

Doing this exercise may highlight some interesting insights. Roles are often identifiable even within informal groups – even in something as informal as the Friday night drinking group one can often pick out the joker, the peacekeeper, the spokesperson and so forth. Some members may play more than one role, and those roles are allocated not by absolute characteristics but by a 'best available' process (i.e. the spokesperson role may well be allocated to the least introvert member of the group – even if they are all highly introspective relative to the population at large). Also, the allocation of roles in informal groups is commonly carried out at a subconscious and intuitive level.

Such an analysis can help to explain the problems which sometimes arise when dealing with the group spokesperson. The obvious and common assumption is that such a person is the leader of the group. Role theory could explain the problems that can emerge when this assumption is false and the spokesperson is merely the message carrier – not the one who can make a decision on behalf of the group.

Many textbooks have been written and many courses run on the subject of 'leadership'. Basically, the debate can be simplified and summarized by saying that some people believe that leaders are 'born, not made' and that leadership is a function of possessing the appropriate personality traits (sometimes rather rudely referred to as the 'boy scout syndrome'), while others believe that leadership is a function of the situation in which the group finds itself.

> **Think** – Which do you think is correct?
> – Why?

While there is some attraction in the notion of the born leader, it does seem a rather limited concept for wide application to groups. A major limitation seems to be the question of whether there are enough born leaders to go round, considering the vast number of groups which exist. Additionally, in formal groups the leader is sometimes appointed as manager or section leader by the organization, but he or she does not always command the respect of the subordinate group. Overall, the contingency or situational approach seems to be the most plausible, with leadership roles devolving to those individuals within the group who are perceived to have either the required personality characteristics or the relevant skills and knowledge. This approach implies that groups (particularly informal groups) will not have a single, permanent leader, but that different members will take on leadership as and when the remainder of the group sees them as leaders.

Types of group

It is useful for the marketer to distinguish between different categories of group in order to use them more effectively in the communication process. Behavioural scientists commonly identify a number of different types of group. These include:

- *Ascribed groups* are groups to which a person automatically belongs (e.g. the family, male/female, etc.)
- *Acquired groups* are those of which a person has sought membership (e.g. The Chartered Institute of Marketing)
- *Primary groups* are usually small, with close emotional contact and face-to-face communication (e.g. family, friendship groups)
- *Secondary groups* are more impersonal in terms of communication and are commonly larger (e.g. Societies, colleges, organizations)
- *Formal groups* have a clearly defined purpose or goal with defined roles (e.g. Behavioural Aspects of Marketing class with teacher/student roles)
- *Informal groups* usually exist to satisfy the social needs of the members. Roles still exist, but are rarely allocated formally. Examples would include groups of friends (which may exist quite comfortably within a more formal grouping)
- *Membership groups* are those groups to which an individual belongs, whether they are formal or informal, i.e. he/she is a member of that group
- *Aspirational groups* are those groups to which the individual does not belong but to which he or she wishes to belong
- *Dissociative groups* are those that the individual wishes not to be associated with (usually because of values and behaviour).

One final term which is used is that of *Reference groups*. These are defined as those which influence behaviour – thus all of the above categories are reference groups. Even dissociative groups fall into this category, as people may go to extremes of behaviour to ensure that they are not perceived as 'one of those'!!

One aspect which may need to be clarified is the idea that specific groups can fall into more than one category – for instance, your family group may well be both ascribed and primary as well as being a membership group.

Think – How would you classify your current work group? – Your drinking companions? – Your classmates studying marketing? – Heavy metal rockers? – The Chartered Institute of Marketing?

Once again, the issue of perception is critical. Some of you may have classified heavy metal fans as a dissociative group, while others may see them as an aspirational group. This is a similar problem to that faced by motor cycle manufacturers, who discovered that motorbikes were linked in many people's minds to Hell's Angels. For many, this was a turn-off, as they saw Hell's Angels as undesirable and hence they were a dissociative group. For others (only a minority), they were seen as a desirable aspirational group. In order to expand their potential market, many firms advertised in an attempt to change the general perception – 'You meet the nicest people on a Honda' being one of the more memorable and successful slogans.

> **Think** – What are your reference groups?
> – How do they affect your behaviour?
> – What impact does this have on your buying behaviour?
> – How do advertisements 'get at' you in these terms?

> **Exercise** – Discuss the relative importance of these different types of group to the practice of marketing.

The influence of different groups is also a situational variable.

> **Think** – What groups would affect your behaviour and your purchasing if you were:
> – arranging your wedding?
> – organizing the end-of-course celebration?
> – about to buy a new suit?
> – organizing a party for your parents' wedding anniversary?
> – deciding on the purchase of a mountain bike?

So, in summary, our behaviour is significantly affected by social groupings. Groups come in a variety of types and forms. The most important groups so far as marketers are concerned are reference groups, as these are the ones which affect behaviour and hence purchasing. The basic assumptions which underlie the marketing interest may best be shown in Figure 5.1.

The family

The family may be the single most important type of social grouping so far as marketing is concerned. Its importance stems from two separate, but crucial, processes in which it is a key factor. The first of these, consumer socialization – by which purchasing behaviours are learned and passed on from one generation to another we met in the previous chapter. The second process is that of the family operating as a consumer decision-making and purchasing unit.

However, before we look at these two processes it is worth spending a little time on consideration of the family as a social phenomenon.

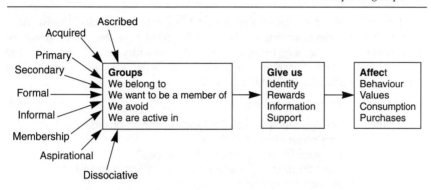

Figure 5.1 Reference groups – a pictorial representation

The family is defined by the Jarrys (1991) as:

a group of people, related by kinship or similar close ties, in which the adults assume responsibility for the care and upbringing of their natural or adopted children.

In terms of our earlier analysis the family is a primary group. Human infants undergo an extended period of maturation before they are capable of existing and surviving as independent adults. During this period they require extensive protection and support, and this very dependency helps us to explain the dominant role that the family plays in shaping our behaviour, attitudes, values and perceptions of expected roles – the socialization process, described in more detail in the next chapter.

Other key terms surrounding the concept of the family are the notions of the *family of orientation* – the family into which one is born – and the *family of procreation* – the family which one establishes by marriage.

Sociologists also commonly differentiate between the *nuclear family* (biological parents in a stable marital relationship, with their dependent children) and the *extended family* (the nuclear family plus parents, grandparents, in-laws, uncles, aunts and other relatives).

In either case the importance of the family is emphasized by the multiplicity of its functions – it is

a consumption unit
a purchasing unit
a financial resource
a source of information
a source of physical satisfaction
a source of emotional satisfaction.

The idea of the classic nuclear family demands that only two adults are involved in the activities of parenting – that is, they exist as sexual partners, biological parents, social parents – and the mechanism used to knit these different activities together is marriage. However, this is only one form of family grouping, and is very much a function of a particular European culture. Sociologists have argued that the development of this family format is the direct result of industrialization. The suggestion is that the mobility associated with the emergence of industrial development has led to the separation and isolation of the nuclear family from the wider kin networks.

Think – Do you still live close to your parents, grandparents and other close relatives?
  – Do your friends and acquaintances?
  – How does this closeness/distance affect family relationships and behaviour?

The nuclear family seems to be important in most cultures, and is often presented as being both the most common (descriptive) and the most culturally desirable (prescriptive) social formation. However, direct evidence shows that the nuclear family of mother and father plus 2.4 children is becoming much less common as divorce rates rise and the stigma of unmarried motherhood diminishes in the eyes of many people.

Additional complications arise from demographic patterns which are emerging. In the UK the birth rate declined in the 1970s and 1980s leading to smaller family units. Another factor which distorts the 'traditional' view of the family is the growth of the 'two-career family', with a wife who expects to continue her career and take full advantage of legislation enabling a speedy return to work after the birth of children. Such a two-income situation implies a possible doubling of income – but, as ever, the marketer is often more interested in disposable or discretionary spending power. For instance, the high earners may be mortgaged to the hilt, the second income may be swallowed up in child-minding costs or the demands of private education – so the amount which is 'free' for purchasing other products may be less than appears at first sight.

Thus we may conclude that the family, or at least the 'ideal' nuclear family, is undergoing some significant developments. The emergence of the 'single-parent family' calls many of the assumptions of the traditional family life cycle into question – so we may need to look at it again and question its 'normality'.

The situation can become even more complex when we consider the evidence which tells us that the majority of divorced persons remarry. This pattern of divorce followed by remarriage increases the options dramatically. The possibility of 'inheriting' a partner's older/younger children from an earlier marriage now needs to be considered. The pattern can become even more confused when this couple produce children of their own. The mixed extended families can become very large and difficult to explain.

Think – What examples can you find of 'non-nuclear' family images in current advertisements?

Reviewing the literature on the family sometimes suggests that the institution is in imminent danger of collapse. Looking at newspapers from past ages may lead us to the conclusion that this is nothing new – people have worried about changes in family roles and relationships for many years. The truth of the matter may be that the family, as a social construct, is continually changing and adapting to meet the perceived needs of the society. Thus there may be no such thing as the 'perfect' family set-up, and the idealized notion of the universal nuclear family may be only a dream of politicians and sociologists.

Authors such as Talcott Parsons have lent credence to such a view by charting the evolution of the family from a 'production unit' in early agricultural societies to the more fragmented, and apparently casual and less permanent, arrangements which we might recognize in our current society.

Those who decry the current divorce rate, and see this as evidence of moral degeneracy and the beginning of a breakdown of society, may be ignoring the fact that the low levels of divorce in, say, the Victorian era may well have disguised high levels of domestic friction and unhappiness. They may also be underestimating the degree to which the majority of people do, in fact, follow relatively traditional patterns.

In recent years, marketers have found it useful to consider the household as another, less limited, way of examining social groupings, as the rapid changes in the social norms surrounding marriage and the family have rendered some of the traditional views of the family less valuable as a tool for examining purchasing behaviour. Such a redefinition allows the identification and inclusion of persons sharing a flat or house who may not be married but who, nevertheless, indulge in group purchasing decisions for items such as washing machines and similar household items. As Lawson (1988) says – 'in all these instances the household is likely to be a better unit of analysis for much of consumer behaviour than the family'.

Consumer socialisation

Families are a major and significant source of the knowledge, attitudes and skills relevant to their functioning effectively as consumers in the marketplace. Being such an important source of emotional and physical satisfaction, the family exercised considerable influence on the values and behaviours of its members. However, despite the continuing interactive influencing that goes on within any tight-knit group, one of the key areas of interest for marketers is the way in which children pick up the attitudes, skills and knowledge which may stay with them for life and which influence their behaviour as consumers.

> **Think** – How has family socialization affected your views on such things as:
> - buying on credit?
> - the importance of a 'good' breakfast?
> - mail order shopping?
> - supermarket shopping?

- doing the football pools and gambling?
- looking smart?
- who does the shopping?
- who does the cooking?
- who does the cleaning?
- who does the ironing?
- who cleans the lavatory?

– What other consumer behaviours can you recognize as being 'learned' from your family?

Among the variety of social learning that occurs within the family setting, the part which interests marketers is the learning about what, when, where, why and how to purchase.

Hawkins, Best and Coney (1989) draw a distinction between *directly relevant learning*, which is concerned with activities such as how to shop, how to compare and evaluate brands and how to budget (which includes the development of attitudes about such aspects of marketing as the qualities and desirability of different retail outlets, products, brands, sales staff, clearance sales, mail order and advertising) and *indirectly relevant learning*, which is concerned with the knowledge, attitudes and values which cause people to want specific goods or services. In other words, this is the process of learning about differential evaluations of brands and products. Most of us learn that Rolls Royce produce excellent motor cars without necessarily purchasing one.

Think – How did you learn 'the value of money'?

In terms of directly relevant learning, there seems to be a general acceptance that, for some staple products, offspring may well purchase the brands that were used when they were growing up. This is obviously of great importance to marketers as it raises the possibility of an inherited lifelong brand loyalty! Examples of product categories which are thought to fall into this category are things such as toothpaste, breakfast cereals, laundry detergent and ketchup.

Think – To what brands do you owe lifelong loyalty?

Another related aspect of consumer socialization is the effect that advertising has on children. Numerous studies have identified that children spend many hours each week watching television, and exposure to advertising messages is a significant part of that experience. While any parent can attest to the value of TV as a surrogate childminder, it is not without its drawbacks as it may:

- become a source of conflict within the family ('Mum, I want a new bike'. 'You can't have one!')
- become a safety threat, by glamourizing unhealthy eating habits (especially high-sugar/high-fat products) or by giving rise to 'copycat' behaviours, such as magic tricks or other stunts
- raise unrealistic expectations of both products and society
- influence those vulnerable children who have not learned to distinguish between 'adspeak' and reality. Believing that toys shown in adverts actually move of their own accord would be an example of this
- establish values which the parents feel are undesirable – particularly those of materialism and those which are determined by stereotypes of gender and ethnic minorities.

An interesting offshoot of this research is that the UK 'watershed' of 9.00 p.m. for 'adult' advertising seems inappropriate when many children watch TV way beyond that time.

However, all is not doom and gloom, as the family will often mediate the message – parents might point out that sweets or snacks can cause tooth decay and toothache. But this last comment can only refer to situations where the child watches television in the company of a parent or parent figure. It will be completely inappropriate in other situations, where children are left with the television as 'childminder'. Thus mediation may well be a phenomenon of both class and culture. Perhaps more importantly, parents provide powerful role models which are likely to be even more significant than the images portrayed on television. The child will observe, at first hand, activities such as shopping, choosing and evaluating. American studies have suggested that male children tend to take up their father's shaving habits with respect to a preference for electric or wet (soap, brush and razor) shaving.

Families as consumer and purchasing units

The family is a group which has relatively fixed resources. We will see in the family life cycle that the focus of expenditure will tend to change according to the stage of development. This insight tells only half of the story, however, as different members of the family group will have different aspirations which may prove very difficult to satisfy within the budget available.

Family holidays can be a prime source of conflict, when one parent wants an adventure holiday, the other fancies a relaxing poolside break – and the child wants to visit EuroDisney!

Another example could be the new mountain bike for the teenager which uses discretionary funds that could have bought a weekend break for the parents, new clothing for brothers and sisters, materials for redecorating the kitchen, or a thousand and one other items desired or needed by members of the family group. Thus we may assert, with some confidence, that a degree of decision conflict will be present in many family purchasing decisions.

> **Think** – What other examples of decision conflict within
> families can you identify?

It is likely that the more expensive the item the greater will be the trade-offs required within the family group. Other factors which may affect the degree of conflict or agreement include the extent to which the item is for individual or family use and the extent of agreement between those family group members who may be expected to share the product.

Advertising messages sometimes seek to minimize this conflict by sending slightly different messages to the different parties. Children may be interested in the taste, image or personality of a breakfast cereal, while parents may be concerned with health, nutrition and similar issues. Carefully constructed advertising messages can reduce conflict by reassuring the parent while attracting the child. Recently, Shredded Wheat mounted a campaign which 'pushed' sporting hero images at the children while satisfying the parents by emphasizing the product's purity and lack of additives.

> **Think** – What other examples can you find of this kind of
> conflict reduction?

Roles and processes

It is generally accepted that family consumption decisions encompass a number of different roles. In Chapter 1 we looked at decision-making units in organizations. In this context we are often influenced by those individuals in our family DMU. These are other members of the family, and it is common for individuals to carry out more than one role and, often, more than one person playing the same role. The debate about customers and users which we explored in Chapter 1 is relevant in the family context. The DMU roles are as we described earlier, but in the specific family situation they are worth revisiting:

- *Gatekeeper* – this is the person who controls access to information and ideas. This may be in the sense of:
  a) giving a summary of relevant information – 'I saw a programme on TV which said that X was the best value'
  b) controlling access to information – 'No, you're not watching that!'
  c) mediating advertising messages as described above.
  One offshoot of the control function which is often seen in the family setting is the removal of advertising matter before others can see it – or, alternatively, ensuring that the advertisements are placed in positions where they will be seen by others.
- *Influencer* – this person provides information, expertise and/or preferences which are fed to the other members of the group. Sometimes such

opinions are sought by other family members, sometimes they are offered by the individual.

- *Decider* – this is the person with the authority or power to determine how the family's resources should be allocated. So this is where the decision as to whether a purchase is to be made finally rests. The deciders may well also use their power to influence both the product/brand choice and the evaluative criteria used in the decision process.
- *Buyer* – this is the person who acts as purchasing agent. In many product groups this means the one who does the shopping, calls the supplier, brings the products home and stores them appropriately.
- *Preparer* – this is the individual who fits the plugs on electrical appliances, prepares food, and similar functions.
- *User* – this is the person or persons who consume or use a particular product.

Think – Identify which individuals play (or played) the different roles in your family for activities such as:

- producing packed lunches for schoolchildren
- buying a new car
- redecoration of a room
- updating father's wardrobe
- choosing and buying breakfast cereals.

One of the most interesting roles is that of influencer, as this is likely to be a function of the interests, expertise and knowledge of the individual, not just the role of father or mother. As relationships change and become more varied within marriages, it may be that the father is the 'expert' on food and cookery rather than the mother. It seems logical that influence will come with expertise – thus we may have a child who is a technical electronics fan becoming the influencer (and, in some senses, the leader) in discussions about the purchase of a CD player or hi-fi system.

The patterns of influence will vary from family to family and from product to product. The complexity of the situation becomes clear with the realization that one individual can be an influencer in one situation, a decider in another, a buyer often or rarely, and a user of many products.

This type of analysis is particularly useful in marketing terms as it may give us ideas as to the best point at which to direct our persuasive messages. For example, if the decider and buyer are one and the same person, then the marketing effort should logically be directed towards packaging and point-of-sale advertising. However, if they are different persons, more effort will need to be directed to getting the message to wherever the deciders (and their surrounding influencers) might be reached. In some cases the evidence suggests that the user is neither the decision maker nor the buyer. This applies in areas such as pet food, where advertisements are aimed at the person who does the purchasing, not the end user. Similarly, surveys have suggested that 70 per cent of fragrances used by men are purchased by women (wives or girlfriends) and given as presents.

> **Think** – What are the marketing implications of your previous
> analysis of your own family decision making?

Some media which are widely shared by all the family – television, newspapers and such – offer the chance for marketing messages to be sent to all of the family (and, hence, all of the roles) at the same time. This may give a useful structure for thoughts as to the objectives and content of such messages.

Spousal roles

It seems likely that the husband and wife in the traditional family set-up will be the dominant decision makers within the group due to their roles, seniority and earning power. Historically, considerable research has been conducted into which partner makes the decisions about which products.

See Figure 5.2.

Writers on marketing decision making have classified the decisions into four categories:

1 Wife dominant
2 Husband dominant
3 Autonomic – equal number of decisions is made by each partner, but each decision is made independently by one or the other
4 Syncratic – where the decisions are made jointly and equally by the two partners.

This is often displayed in a triangular diagram such as Figure 5.3.

It is quite possible to plot your responses to the earlier 'who makes what decisions' exercise on such a diagram, and it would be of interest to compare your profile with that of others, as there is no right answer. It could be of even more interest to make comparisons with the responses of your partner and others in your family group, who may have different perceptions of the decision-making processes!

Another aspect of decision making within families is that the responses to the 'who makes what decisions' questions may vary with the decision stage. An example could be in the purchase of a car. The initiator/gatekeeper could well be one parent, with perhaps an older child contributing as influencer due to a special interest in motor cars which means that the offspring is more up-to-date and technically minded than the parent. This works quite well for the exploratory, information-gathering stages of defining the problem and identifying alternative solutions (possible purchases). But, as time goes on, it is likely that the decision becomes more joint, until the final decision involves an almost equal participation by the two parents.

Once more, we may have to draw a distinction between high-involvement, high-risk purchases and the more mundane buying activities centred on low-

Think – In your family, where on the scale does the decision usually lie for the following product groups? Mark an X at the spot.

Food

solely wife	mainly wife	joint	mainly husband	solely husband	could be either

Holidays

solely wife	mainly wife	joint	mainly husband	solely husband	could be either

Television sets

solely wife	mainly wife	joint	mainly husband	solely husband	could be either

Car

solely wife	mainly wife	joint	mainly husband	solely husband	could be either

Children's clothing

solely wife	mainly wife	joint	mainly husband	solely husband	could be either

Husband's leisure clothing

solely wife	mainly wife	joint	mainly husband	solely husband	could be either

Wife's leisure clothing

solely wife	mainly wife	joint	mainly husband	solely husband	could be either

Lawn mower

solely wife	mainly wife	joint	mainly husband	solely husband	could be either

Figure 5.2

involvement goods. The shift towards joint participation and away from autonomic behaviour tends to be most marked for products and services such as cars, refrigerators, television sets, paint and wallpaper and financial planning and investments. There is evidence to suggest that the family holiday may be the most democratic of a family's purchasing decisions.

Historically, it was assumed that some decisions were taken by men while others were taken by women. However, this tends to assume fixed roles within the family group for men and women. The stereotypical assumptions allocate women to caring, nurturing and child-rearing activities while men are seen as macho breadwinners.

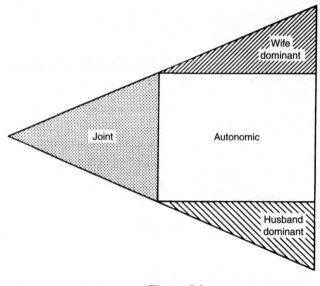

Figure 5.3

> **Think** – What examples can you identify of advertising
> material which portrays 'non-standard' sexual roles?

6 'That's all I need – a customer with attitude...'

Attitudes and social behaviour

Introduction

> A mental and neural state of readiness, organised through experience, exerting a directive or dynamic influence on the individual's response to all objects and situations with which it is related (Allport)

> An enduring organisation of motivational, emotional, perceptual, and cognitive processes with respect to some aspect of the individual's world (Krech and Crutchfield)

> ...certain regularities of an individual's feelings, thoughts and predispositions to act toward some aspect of his environment (Secord and Backman)

> An overall evaluation that enables one to respond in a consistently favourable or unfavourable manner with respect to a given object or alternative (Engel, Blackwell and Miniard)

All the definitions highlight the fact that attitudes relate to persons, objects or behaviours that are part of the individual's perceptual world. They represent our basic orientation towards the given stimulus and, as such, form an important part of the way in which people perceive and react to their environments. We have seen earlier (in Chapter 2) that individuals may select what they perceive from the environment. Thus attitudes influence, and are influenced by, our goals, perceptions and motivation.

At an intuitive level, the importance of attitudes in marketing seems obvious – if we believe that a product has certain desirable characteristics, it seems probable that we will like the product, and, should the appropriate situation arise, we would purchase the product.

All things being equal, people generally behave in a manner consistent with their attitudes and intentions. Certainly in everyday life we assume that there is a positive relationship between attitudes and behaviour – we attempt to 'change people's minds' about issues we care about in the assumption that this will result in the behaviour we desire. Gellerman has described attitudes as 'leading variables' to behaviour – i.e. attitude change predates and predicts behaviour – so we might suggest a relationship such as:

Attitude → Behaviour

On the other hand, we have all had the experience of indulging in a particular behaviour which has led to outcomes which have formed our attitudes. This suggests that we may also have a relationship:

Behaviour ← Attitude

The combination is usually represented by the symbol:

Attitude ⇌ Behaviour

This emphasizes that our attitudes may influence our behaviour, but our behaviour may also, in turn, affect our attitudes, either by changing them or by confirming them. In this sense it is very similar to connectionist learning theory (see Chapter 11), and generally it is agreed that attitudes are learned and are relatively enduring – they do change, but usually only slowly. They imply evaluation and feeling.

Attitudes have three components:

- *Affective* – emotional element may be positive or negative
- *Cognitive* – knowledge element concerning belief/disbelief
- *Conative* – predisposition or behaviour tendency element.

Earlier we used the phrase 'if we believe that a product has certain desirable characteristics' – this represents the cognitive element of our attitude. We continued: 'it seems probable that we will like the product' – this represents the affective part. 'Should the appropriate situation arise, we would purchase the product' represents the conative component.

See Figure 6.1.

> **Think** – Identify the cognitive, affective and conative elements of your attitude towards studying for the CIM Certificate.

So we could represent this as shown in Figure 6.2.

An attitude must have all three components, and it is this fact that distinguishes it from opinions and beliefs which have no affective or feeling component.

Others have highlighted the importance of the three components by defining an attitude by the expression:

Attitude = Belief × Value

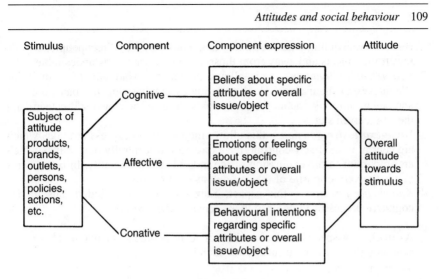

Figure 6.1

This approach (expanded later) bears a marked similarity to the expectancy theories of motivation discussed later in this chapter and also the rational model of decision making.

The functions of attitudes

Katz identified four functions underlying the motivational basis of attitudes:

1 *Instrumental or adjustive function* – this is the tendency of people to acquire attitudes which they perceive as being helpful in achieving desired goals or,

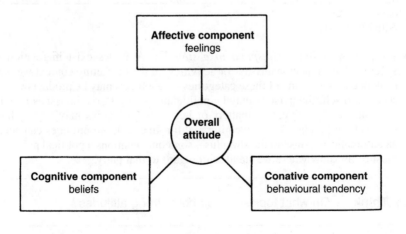

Figure 6.2

conversely, avoiding undesired outcomes. Thus they will direct people towards rewarding objects and away from those which are viewed as undesirable.

2 *Ego-defensive function* – this allows people to avoid admitting their in-adequacies to themselves. Holding attitudes emphasizing the bad points of another group may enable the individuals to raise their own self-esteem and their perceived status.

3 *Value-expressive function* – this allows individuals to express attitudes which are central to their self-concept, the expression of centrally held values which are important to the expression of the individual's personality. In many ways this is the very opposite of the ego-defensive function.

4 *Knowledge function* – this aspect, Katz claims, allows individuals to use cognitive processes in order to make sense of their world.

As marketing specialists we are interested in people's behaviour. This is the reason why the study of attitudes is of such importance.

Some key ideas about attitudes

Generally, attitudes are considered to be a characteristic of an individual personality, less enduring than temperament, but more enduring than a motive or a mood. It is another conceptual invention or hypothetical construct (like intelligence, personality, motivation) in that attitudes cannot be directly observed – so their study is fraught with many problems.

Think – Can attitudes be inferred from behaviour?
        – Can we believe what respondents tell us when we ask attitudinal questions?
        – Are attitudes actually predictors of behaviour, etc.?

Attitudes:

- *Are predispositions to respond to a stimulus.* Attitudes exist in relation to specific objects, persons, issues or activities. In the marketing context we may be concerned with any of these categories – the objects may be products we are seeking to sell; the persons may be politicians or pop stars; the issues may be environmental, political or matters of belief; the activities may be anything from selling holidays to not wearing real fur. In effect, our attitudes can act as an automatic response to the stimulus – someone mentions a political party and most of us know where we stand with regard to that party.

Think – On what topics do you hold strong attitudes?

- *May be positive or negative.* One of the major ways in which we recognize attitudes is in the way in which different people are polarized by the attitudes they hold. Drinkers commonly hold a positive attitude towards alcohol, while many religions hold that the consumption of alcohol is wrong.

> **Think** – Which of the attitudes you listed for (a) above were positive and which were expressed as negatives?

- *May be strong, weak, simple or complex.* Another important dimension of attitudes is their strength. A person may have a negative attitude towards a particular brand of coffee – but it may not be strong enough to prevent that person from accepting a cup of the brew when visiting a neighbour. We may have attitudes about many things, but only some will be held with strong conviction – others will be held with less confidence. The evidence is that those attitudes we hold with high confidence are the ones which can be most relied on to guide our behaviour and are the ones which are most difficult to change. Some attitudes are simple 'I like...' reactions, whereas others are much more complex. This must be borne in mind when attempting to measure attitudes.

> **Think** – Which of the attitudes you listed do you hold with most confidence? Which do you hold as less significant?

- *Are learned.* We have developed our attitudes as a result of prior experience. Many attitudes can be traced back to our childhood experiences, and so we accept that the family is a major shaper of attitudes which may last a lifetime. However, as marketers we commonly wish to change the attitudes of our consumers, so we will concentrate on environmental factors such as the volume and quality of the information and experience available or required to influence the consumers.

> **Think** – How did you learn these attitudes? How did they arise?

- *Persist over time.* Many attitudes that we hold are part of our make-up for long periods of time. They are both persistent and difficult to change.

> **Think** – Which of your attitudes have remained unaltered when you look back at yourself five years ago?

● *Are dynamic*. Despite the comment above, another characteristic of attitudes is that they can and do change over time. Perhaps the biggest problem for the marketer is controlling the timing, nature and direction of any change.

Think – Which of your attitudes have changed when you look back at yourself five years ago?

Theories of attitudes

Consistency approaches

Balance theory (Heider)
This considers the situation where person A receives positive or negative information from person B about an object. This results in either *balanced* or *imbalanced* attitude systems, as illustrated in Figure 6.3.

Faced with imbalance, the theory suggests that the individual will seek to reduce the tension by:

a) changing attitude to the person
b) changing attitude to the object

and thus establishing a balanced situation.

Congruity theory (Osgood and Tannenbaum)
Again, this considers positive and negative attitudes, but this time it attempts to measure the strength and resultant outcome of the attitudinal forces. Normally ratings are made on a scale running from +3 (highly favourable) to –3 (highly unfavourable). *Congruity* refers to the consistency of attitudes and suggests that we may be able to predict the outcome when a known person gives information about a known object. If we have a discrepancy (as described above in balance theory), then this will result in both attitudes shifting, but the outcome will be dependent on their relative strengths (Figure 6.4).

In this example, a negative attitude, X_1, towards, say, milk is countered by endorsement of milk by Linford Christie, an Olympic sprint champion, who is valued positively by the respondent (X_2). The outcome, O, according to this theory, lies midway between the two – the attitude to milk improving to neutral, while the resultant attitude towards Linford Christie has declined by the same amount to neutral. Thus equal strengths of attitude lead to equal shift (Figure 6.5).

In this next example, however, the positive attitude towards the endorser is stronger than the dislike of the object. In this case the theory predicts the outcome (O) as shown. Thus unequal strengths of attitude lead to a greater shift towards the more strongly held attitude.

It clearly matters how much the person believes the individual and the information given. It also suggests that changing attitudes has a cost in terms of

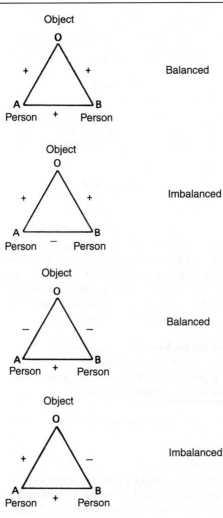

Figure 6.3

the attitude to the teller. This assumption may not hold up, however, if the change in attitude results in a change in behaviour which then gives satisfaction (i.e. following on from our earlier example, if I try milk as a result of the endorsement and find it an unexpectedly pleasant experience, I do not necessarily hold Linford Christie in less esteem, indeed, if I really enjoyed the milk I might even think more of him).

Cognitive dissonance (Festinger)
This is based on the assumption that attitudes held by an individual tend to be

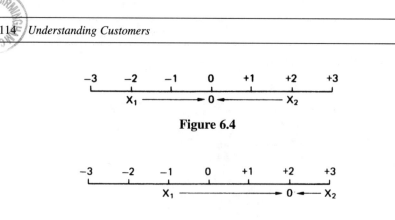

Figure 6.4

Figure 6.5

consistent, and they are consistent with his/her behaviour. Festinger's approach deals with post-decision (purchase) inconsistencies which arise when positive and negative attitudes to different elements have had to be weighed as part of the decision. Following a decision, information about the positive features of a rejected alternative will generate dissonance – similarly, information about negative features of the chosen alternative will also cause dissonance. The magnitude of this dissonance will depend on:

- the significance of the decision
- the attractiveness of the rejected alternative
- the number of negative characteristics of the choice made
- the greater the number of options considered.

The theory argues that we are uncomfortable with this dissonance and will seek to minimize it by:

- changing our mind/decision
- concentrating on positive features of the chosen option
- ignoring/devaluing information about negative features
- focusing on negative information about the rejected alternatives
- changing attitude
- consciously avoiding exposure to potentially dissonant information, e.g. by reading only newspapers which reflect our pre-existing attitudes (see also the discussion of selective exposure in Chapter 4)
- denigrating and devaluing the source of the dissonant information, e.g. we may ascribe characteristics of prejudice, ignorance or evil intent to those who hold differing views. Examples abound in the field of politics, and we have similar reactions from smokers to the evidence about the dangers of smoking when produced by anti-smoking organizations such as ASH.

As our attitudes are very much part of our self-concept, it is not surprising that the reactions to cognitive dissonance bear a strong similarity to defence mechanisms.

Compensation approaches

Fishbein Model
This is summarized by the formula

$$A_o = \sum_1^n B_1 a_1$$

where A_o = the attitude towards object o
B_1 = the strength of belief i about o
a_1 = the evaluation aspects of B
n = the number of beliefs.

Here evaluations of different aspects can cancel one another out. It is called a *compensating model* and has a marked similarity to expectancy theories and models of behaviour. Williams (1981) uses the following example (Figure 6.6):

Car attribute	Importance B_1	Evaluation a_1	Product B_1, a_1
Speed	1	4	4
Style	2	5	10
Price	3	3	9
Prestige	1	1	1

Total = Σ = 24

Figure 6.6

The success of this approach depends on choosing the relevant attributes to measure – but it can identify the important ones in the eye of the respondent.

The same author put forward what is known as the Extended Fishbein Model:

$$A_{act} = \sum_1^n b_1 e_1$$

where A_{act} = individual's attitude towards performing a specific act
b_1 = individual's belief that performing the act will lead to consequence i
e_1 = individual's evaluation of consequence i
n = the number of salient consequences involved.

However, the link between attitude and behaviour is not as clear as some theorists would have us believe. Many of us have had experience of people who have very poor attitudes to, say, bosses or teachers, but whose behaviour does not live up to their words!

Why don't attitudes always predict behaviour?

Peter and Olson (1990), in reviewing the relationship between measured behavioural intentions and observed behaviour, identify seven factors which reduce or weaken the predictive power:

1 *Intervening time.* The longer the time that elapses between the measure and the actual behaviour, the greater the opportunity for other factors to occur. These may modify or change the original intention so that the observed behaviour no longer matches the stated intention.
2 *Different levels of specificity.* When measuring intention the questions need to be specific and at the same level as the observed behaviour, otherwise the relationship may be damaged. I may hold strong views on the discomfort of wearing ties – but you may observe me on a day when I am going for a job interview and consciously decided that a T-shirt was inappropriate dress for the occasion!
3 *Unforseen environmental events.* You intend to purchase a particular brand, but your car breaks down and you are unable to go shopping – or, alternatively, when you do get there the shop is sold out and so you make do with a substitute brand.
4 *Unforseen situational context.* It is possible that the situation that the respondents envisaged when expressing their behavioural intention was not the same as the situation at the time of the behaviour. I may express the intention not to purchase X brand of beer because I view it as rather cheap and less enjoyable than my favourite German lager. However, faced with providing the drinks for a party to which many of my students are coming, the attraction of cheapness may overcome my preference – so I do purchase Brand X (in bulk!).
5 *Degree of voluntary control.* Some factors may be outside our control – I intend to take my family out for a picnic this weekend, but in the event, it may be pouring with rain, I may feel ill, etc.
6 *Stability of intentions.* Some intentions are founded on beliefs and attitudes that are both strongly held and stable over long periods of time (e.g. I do not smoke, I do not eat meat, etc.). These give rise to stable intentions and, generally, more predictable behaviour. Other behaviour may stem from much less strongly held attitudes and less important beliefs (e.g. I like these trousers) and these are much less dependable.
7 *New information.* I may receive information about important consequences of behaviour which leads to changes in my beliefs and attitudes towards the behaviour, and hence my intention. So my original intention no longer accurately predicts my eventual behaviour. Examples could include AIDS education regarding safe sex, or changing my intention to buy a particular second-hand car when I heard that it had been stolen.

To this list we can add a number of other possible reasons for attitudes and behaviour not coinciding:

- Lack of need for the object
- Joint decision making – taking a partner's wishes into account may give rise to compromise purchases which reflect neither party's attitudes!
- Inaccurate/incomplete measures of cognition or affect.

This implies that, while attitudes are significant, they may not hold the whole story of behaviour – this leads us on to another important and linked area of study: that of motivation – the attempt to answer the 'why?' of behaviour.

Motivation

Exercise – What is your purpose in undertaking this course of study?
Jot down your answer as fully as possible and keep it for later.

Many people see the study of motivation as being of prime importance to understanding behaviour. Certainly it has become a key and central plank of many management courses. The ideas and assumptions stemming from this chapter will influence many of the practical marketing applications we will look at later.

In order to understand the emphasis which is placed on the subject it is worthwhile trying to define some of the terms that are in use and the way in which the basic ideas interact.

Motivation is the mixture of wants, needs and drives within the individual which seek gratification through the acquisition of some experience or object. In many cases the goal or outcome sought will be less important in absolute terms, but will be valued for the reward or satisfaction with which it is associated or, alternatively, for the release from the tension of being in a wanting state (our ultimate aim could be to be unmotivated!). In fact, the prime objective of the marketer might be said to persuade or convince consumers that the use of their product will satisfy a specific need or group of needs.

This seems fairly straightforward until we realize that motives may be unconscious and multiple. Life would be much easier if our wants, needs and drives came one at a time – and easier still if we were fully aware of each. The word 'fully' is used here because often our motives are more complex than we realize. A person may state with all honesty: 'I am buying this car because it is economical and its carrying capacity suits my needs', but without doubt there will have been other motives that will have influenced the choice, some of which the person might partially recognize, while others might be completely unconscious. Here we have another example of the difficulties in the behavioural sciences (mentioned earlier in Chapter 1) where respondents may be unaware of their true motivations and reasons for their behaviour. On the other hand, few of us are willing to admit that we do not know why we do things, so we must treat with some caution the accounts that people give us of their motivation.

At a very crude level, Figure 6.7 proposes a simple cycle governing behaviour.

An example could be where Need = thirst; Action = get glass of water; Satisfaction = no thirst.

This may hold the key to the popularity of motivation as an area of study for marketing specialists:

IF we can determine the needs that people have, and

IF we can set up a situation where the only way in which they can satisfy that need is controlled by us,

THEN we may well be able to control their behaviour!!

In some circumstances this cycle bears remarkable similarities to what is called extortion!!

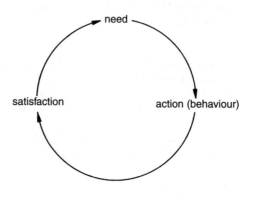

Figure 6.7

In a less extreme setting we can see the importance to marketing specialists – if we can identify (or create) the need, then we can offer our product as the satisfaction of that need.

But every individual is unique, and this raises a major problem: if we accept the uniqueness proposition at face value, the process of marketing becomes totally individualistic. Thus it will be of value to examine areas of similarity and attempt to develop ideas about some of the ways in which individuals' motivations are alike.

There is a consensus forming among psychologists that there are a number of ideas which are implicitly common to the many current theories of motivation:

1 *Causality* – the idea that human behaviour is caused, just as the behaviour of physical objects is caused by forces which act on them. Causality is implicit in the beliefs that environment and heredity affect behaviour and that what is outside influences what is inside.
2 *Directedness* – the idea that human behaviour is not only caused but also directed towards something – i.e. behaviour is goal-directed, people want things.
3 *Motivation* – the idea that underlying behaviour one finds a push, a want, a need or a drive.

These three ideas can provide the beginning of a system for conceptualizing behaviour in a slightly enlarged version of our earlier diagram, as shown in Figure 6.8.

The closed-circuit conception perhaps needs a little explanation. Arrival at a goal eliminates the cause, which eliminates the motive, which eliminates the behaviour. A typical example might be feeling hungry. However, not all of our goals will be physical. Many 'psychological' goals will not be finite and specific, e.g. can you consume a given amount of 'affection' and know that you will be sated? Love, affection, prestige and other psychological goals seem to be ephemeral and boundless. Some individuals may never obtain enough of these emotional satisfactions to inactivate the causes, and hence the motivation and the behaviour.

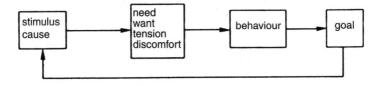

Figure 6.8

The notion of controlling behaviour through some sort of 'extortion' is generally not simple in the marketing context because:

- all customers and clients will be unique, as mentioned above
- marketers have to work with 'used', not new, humans
- marketers are themselves 'used' humans.

By the word 'used' we acknowledge that other outside, and perhaps historical, influences have 'got at' people – forming their attitudes, beliefs, perceptions, personalities and expectations. Also, these variables become facts in the real-life situation. While such thinking has only become explicit in the relatively recent past, assumptions about motivation (or 'what makes people tick') have been implicit in the major schools of thought about management during the last century.

All of this may appear fairly daunting – posh words (causality, drive, etc.) and complicated ideas – but have faith; I believe that thinking about motivation is something that we all do regularly. We say, for instance: Why is he buying rat poison? – Perhaps he's thinking of doing away with his wife, but probably he needs it to get rid of rats. Why did the chicken cross the road? – To get to the food on the other side. Why is she so grumpy this morning? – I don't know, but something must have gone wrong at home, and so on. We seem to spend most of our time ascribing purpose or motives to people in order to explain their actions.

Needs or motives can be either *unlearned* (primary) or *learned* (secondary). They can also be *positive* or *negative*.

Unlearned or *primary* motivation comprises the basic physiological drives for survival of the organism (hunger, thirst, sleep, etc.). It seems that the body has an inbuilt capacity for recognizing imbalance and for automatic response to restore the required balance. One example might be temperature control – if we overheat, the body sweats, the evaporation cools the surface of the skin and balance is restored. Similarly, if we are cold, our body hair stands erect, goosepimples form, the flow of air across the surface of the skin is reduced and with it heat loss, so we warm up. This self-balancing process is sometimes called *homeostasis*.

The sex drive appears to be an unlearned motivation throughout the animal kingdom (humans included) and is a very powerful and potent motivator.

There are also primary drives which involve a curiosity about the environment – a need to explore and be active, and a need for physical contact.

The exploration drive can be seen in both rodents and small babies – a hamster, on being released, will immediately explore the limits of the space by running around the walls, while babies are interested in their environment and respond to it from an early age. Babies also need physical contact with either other persons or with tactile substances (comforters). These basic needs coincide with what we will later call *lower-level needs* when we look at formal theories of motivation such as the Maslow Hierarchy of Needs.

Learned motives are many and various – in many ways this whole book is about the wide variety of learned drives. We learn how to gain approval of others; we are taught acceptable behaviour by family, school and friends; we learn to value certain rewards that society prizes; and we learn to avoid behaviour that will cause people close to us to withdraw affection. We learn to obey the laws of the land and to sublimate or redirect antisocial tendencies (often associated with the unlearned, primary motives) into behaviours that our society accepts.

Motivation may also be viewed as being positive or negative (similar in concept to the notions of positive and negative reinforcement). Positive motives are those we seek to satisfy while negative ones are those we seek to avoid. Much of motivation theory is expressed in positive terms, but I suspect that much of our behaviour will, at root, be negatively motivated – i.e. our behaviour will be directed towards avoidance of something that we perceive as unpleasant.

The idea of behaviour being goal-directed identifies further facets of motivation. Our goals may be general or specific – we may have a general need to keep healthy and extend our life expectancy, or we may have a specific need for a drink of water.

We may also reflect on the fact that our goals may be a function of the way we see ourselves and the way we would like to be. This idea of aspiration is of great significance in the marketing field as it is likely to form the basis of many of our advertising messages. This emphasizes the importance of perception in our study of motivation, and the fact that many of our motivations may be both learned and dependent on our culture, class and upbringing.

So, in terms of our earlier discussion, we need frameworks to describe, explain, predict and control behaviour – and motivation is a key element in that process. The whole area of human motivation is so complex that we do not have a single, unified, theoretical framework to work with. The ideas are fragmented and incomplete. They are also better at describing and explaining than they are at predicting or controlling. So it is important to review theories sceptically – think about the extent to which they fit your experience, the extent to which they adequately explain the phenomenon they claim and whether they can be used to predict human behaviour.

Theories of motivation

Hierarchy of needs – the work of Maslow

Maslow, starting from our initial assumption that a person's behaviour is directed to satisfying needs, groups these needs into broad categories, arranges them into a hierarchy of prepotency and theorizes on their relationships. The notion of prepotency implies 'overriding force' and proposes that some groups of needs will take precedence over others when the individual is faced with choices as to which needs to satisfy. The hierarchy is commonly displayed as a pyramid or triangle, but an alternative is a 'stepped' model, as shown in Figure 6.9.

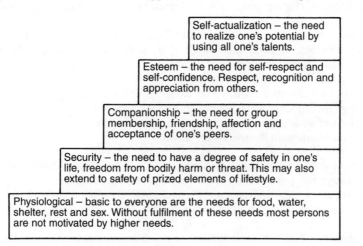

Figure 6.9

Maslow's hypothesis is that a satisfied need is no longer a motivator and that the hierarchy operates such that a person's behaviour will tend to be dominated by trying to satisfy the lowest unsatisfied need – i.e. physiological needs will tend to take precedence over security, companionship or esteem needs; companionship will tend to take precedence over esteem or self-actualization needs and so forth.

The notion is one of a needs ascending process, sequential in nature, whereby one particular class of needs must reach a sufficient level of satisfaction before the next needs level becomes operational. The emphasis is on sufficiency – each successive level must be relatively satisfied before the next level of need becomes more important in motivating behaviour. Thus the steps might be better represented by a more rounded, wavy line.

It has also been speculated that additional levels of need might be applicable. The freedom of inquiry and expression is sometimes quoted, referring to a need for social conditions which permit free speech and which encourage values such as honesty, justice and fairness.

Another high-level need that is sometimes proposed is that of knowledge and understanding. This suggests a need to explore and experiment in order to learn about, and understand, our environment.

Another view of the prepotency approach is that an individual is continually responding to the 'lowest' unsatisfied need. In reality, the different categories of needs may operate on very different timescales. Food needs could be defined in terms of calories/day, while self-actualization may be a lifetime target measured in years. This has given rise to the observation that, for many people, life is a struggle to achieve higher-level satisfactions against the 'obstacles' of lower-level needs. This has become known to some of my students as 'Rice's yo-yo', as they picture life whizzing up and down the hierarchy trying to satisfy very different needs!

Maslow's theory is perhaps the most all-embracing and influential theory in common currency. In a way this is both its strength and its weakness. We have a useful device for the description and explanation phase – but it is significantly weaker at prediction. Many discussions of its application rapidly become arguments on semantics, with more energy spent on defining words than on validating the model. This seems to reflect the importance of individual perceptions of what constitutes the needs in each broad category.

Other problems with the theory centre on:

- a lack of empirical evidence to support it. Physiological and safety needs are not always the predominant factor in determining behaviour – examples of heroism are sometimes recognizable and notable for apparently emphasizing the precedence of 'higher' needs over the individual's physiological and safety needs
- the absence of money from the list of needs worries some people. Here the answer would seem to lie in the argument that money is the means to an end. In motivational terms, we may be more concerned with what a person chooses to expend money on – it could be to buy food, security, status or to satisfy any number of needs
- self-actualization and esteem needs are likely to be a function of each individual's self-perception. This, in turn, may be socially conditioned. Thus we may question whether we are describing an innate need or something which may be defined by family, gender, culture and class.

It does, however, give us an interesting notion that 'behavioural efficiency' can be obtained by actions which satisfy more than one need at the same time.

Think – Which category of needs is your prime motivator?
– To what extent does this theory reflect white, male, middle-class Western values?

Marketing implications

Given its all-embracing scope, it is not surprising that marketers have found Maslow's ideas useful. Clearly we can associate certain products with appropriate levels of the hierarchy and so segment the market into large target populations – low-fat margarine with physiological, insurance with security, etc. It also offers the marketer the opportunity to offer the product as a solution to a problem or the satisfier of a need. The notion of 'behavioural efficiency' mentioned above can also be utilized – one TV advertisement for fitting a particular brand of security lock did it spectacularly well. Doing-It-Yourself clearly saves money and satisfies an economic need; locks satisfy the security need; the male doing the fixing was depicted as enjoying the companionship of his family; the looks given him by his children boosted his esteem while the glance from the wife figure would seem to confirm his high status in the eyes of his partner. One could hypothesize that self-actualization could stem from the achievement and use of his talents to solve a significant problem.

ERG – the work of Clayton Alderfer

A similar approach to Maslow's has more recently been suggested by Alderfer. He has developed a hierarchical, three-factor theory of needs known as ERG: Existence, Relatedness and Growth.

Existence is similar to Maslow's physiological and security needs, relatedness is similar to his companionship need and growth is similar to his esteem and self-actualization needs. He suggests that:

- the less a need is satisfied, the more important it becomes
- the more a lower-level need is satisfied, the greater the importance of the next higher-level need
- the less the higher-level need is satisfied, the greater the importance the lower-level need assumes. This suggests that if individuals cannot get what they want they will demand more of what they can get. This corresponds closely to what is called 'displacement behaviour' in other contexts.

> **Think** – What examples from your own experience can you find to support Alderfer's ideas?

Marketing implications

Given the similarities between the theories, it is not surprising that much of the comment on Maslow's approach will apply in this case. Alderfer does raise the notion of the possibility of 'displacing' frustration into the purchase of your product. If you cannot afford a Ferrari you may be persuaded to 'personalize' your Ford to satisfy 'status' needs.

Achievement – the work of David McClelland

McClelland argues that many needs are not as universal as Maslow proposes. He believes that some needs are socially acquired and picks out specifically the need for achievement, the need for affiliation and the need for power. The need for achievement reflects the desire to meet task goals; the need for affiliation reflects the desire to develop good interpersonal relationships; the need for power reflects the desire to influence and control other people.

He proposes a profile of needs – some people being high on achievement needs (high and visible performance targets), some high on power needs (in charge of a department or section), others high on affiliation needs (project or team work).

Think – Which is your principal need?
– What other examples can you think of?

Marketing implications

It is suggested that people with high power needs will be attracted to products which imply superiority – fast cars, 'power' clothing fashions and so forth. In contrast, those high in affiliation needs are likely to conform to group norms and select products that will be approved of by their friends and social contacts. They are also more likely to respond well to friendly and non-pressure sales techniques. Achievers will seek products which enhance their esteem and self-actualization needs, particularly those which indicate personal attainment.

Using such a framework we can both segment a market and shape appropriate marketing messages. The product could be portrayed as helping people achieve their objectives (computers, filofax, etc.) or suggest power (pinstripe business suits, large cars). It would also be possible to use similar ideas to reinforce a belief that the product will make the purchaser more socially desirable.

Expectancy – the work of Vroom

Vroom is the main name associated with Expectancy Theory. Under this approach individuals are assumed to make rational decisions based on the importance of the outcome to them and their perception of the likelihood of that outcome arising from an action. Vroom puts forward four premises:

1 People have preferences (valences) for various outcomes or incentives that are available to them.
2 People hold expectations about the probability that an action or effort on their part will lead to the intended outcome or objective.
3 People understand that certain behaviours will be followed by desirable outcomes or incentive rewards (e.g. a pay rise or increased status).
4 The action a person chooses to take is determined by the expectancies and preferences (valences) that the person has at the time. The relationship is

commonly presented as:

$$F = E \times V$$

where F = motivation to behave
E = expectation that the behaviour will be followed by a particular outcome (subjective probability)
V = valence of the outcome.

Normally a number of different outcomes will be associated with a particular behaviour. The expectancy equation has to be summed across all of these outcomes, so the formula becomes:

$$F = \Sigma(E \times V)$$

The hypothesis is that we will behave in the way which we believe will give the most desired outcomes overall.

Exercise – Buchanan and Huczynski (1985), in their book *Organisational Behaviour*, present the following activity:

First: List the outcomes that you expect will result from working hard for your 'Understanding Customers' course, such as:

1 High exam marks
2 Bare pass
3 Sleepless nights
4 No social life
5 ?
6 ? etc etc

Second: Rate the value that you place on each of these outcomes, giving those you like +1, those you dislike –1, and those for which you are neutral O. These are your 'V' values.

Third: Estimate the probability of attaining each of these outcomes, giving those that are certain the value 1, those that are most unlikely the value 0 and those for which there is an even chance the value 0.5. Estimate other probabilities as you perceive them at other values between 0 and 1. These are your 'E' values.

Fourth: Now put your E and V values into the expectancy equation

$$F = \Sigma(E \times V)$$

and add up the result.

Fifth: Compare your '*F*' score with the scores of your colleagues.

They predict that:

- those with higher scores are the course 'swots'
- those with the higher scores will get higher exam marks.

Think – Do we actually do this (without pencil and paper) for all behaviours?
– Are we really as rational as this theory supposes?

Marketing implications

Here there seems to be a clear parallel with the work of Fishbein on attitudes. If we accept the expectancy equation, it follows that we can attack the marketing problem in three ways:

- we aim to increase the perceived value of our product
- we aim to raise the expectancy of satisfaction
- we do both of the above.

This might account for some otherwise 'irrational' behaviour such as doing the football pools. As a relatively numerate person I am aware that my chances of winning the 'Treble Chance' are infinitessimal – but the value I place on winning a very large sum of money makes it worth trying!! Marketers must, of course, take great care not to raise consumers' expectations of a product beyond the level that it can satisfy. A very quick way to achieve a poor reputation is to promise things you cannot deliver.

These ideas underpin the PV/PPS model of consumer behaviour put forward in Chapter 10.

Social – the work of Mayo

Mayo conducted the famous Hawthorne Experiments in the late 1920s (see Chapter 5 for a more detailed account). This approach to motivation (often referred to as the 'Social' theory) reaffirms the ideas put forward in the previous chapter that an individual's behaviour is largely determined by the social groups he or she belongs to.

Think again – Which groups affect your behaviour?
– How?

The influence of groups on our behaviour and our needs for social contact and approval seem to be well established, and are discussed in much more detail in the chapter devoted to people in groups. The ideas underlying social theories of motivation are interesting in as much as they suggest that we may each be made up of a number of 'different' people who exist in different social settings. The problems associated with this multi-role experience, and the resolution of the inevitable conflicts that arise, are of great interest to the social scientist.

Marketing implications
Here we may decide to emphasize social acceptance as a benefit of using our product. Some may even offer fear of isolation as a threat for not using it! Positive images of consumers in group situations will become common. As we will see in later chapters, the media and advertising exert considerable influence on the way in which we define roles in society – so the marketing process itself may also help determine what is expected of certain roles.

Equity – the work of Adams

Another approach which centres on the individual's perceptions is commonly called 'Equity Theory'. Here it is assumed that the individual assesses his or her internal 'balance sheet' and will choose behaviours for which a fair exchange exists. The inputs are the costs incurred (effort, fatigue, anxiety, etc.). The outcomes are any events which contribute to need gratification. Comparison level is any standard used to assess the 'fairness' of a particular exchange.

Marketing implications
Here we may be looking at attaining a balance between what a consumer pays and what he or she gets in return – the idea of enhancing perceived value is not new in marketing terms and has resonances with other parts of the CIM course of study. Both expectancy and equity approaches stress the consumers' perceptions, and there is a possible application of both theories in reassuring consumers who have bought the product that they have made a sound choice while, at the same time, boosting expectations. 'Aren't you glad you bought...' style advertising falls into this category, and is an example of Festinger's Cognitive Dissonance theory.

Exercise – Look back at your statement from the beginning of this chapter.
– Which theory looks a 'best fit' for you as a consumer?
– Which theory do you think provides the best model for other people's behaviour overall?

There is one final contribution to our review of motivation theories.

Complex – the work of Edgar Schein

Schein, having reviewed the evolution of behavioural assumptions in our organizational systems, concludes that managers are far too susceptible to 'the bandwagon'. He points out that all of the theories are, in part, 'right', but none of them are adequate to explain organizational behaviour on their own. He goes on to propose the idea of 'Complex Man' – subsuming all the above theories, but believing none to the exclusion of others. He suggests a diagnostic approach to management (and, by implication, marketing), identifying probable problem variables and applying appropriate remedies. This should be followed by analysis of outcomes and reappraisal of the underlying assumptions if necessary.

This approach is compatible with that of my colleague, Professor Tony Watson, who has suggested that the best analogy for the motivation theories is that of waves breaking against the shore – one dominates temporarily, but rapidly mixes with the waves that have preceded it.

Marketing implications

As the essence of Schein's contribution is the denial of a single, universal theory, the implications are that we should reject a single assumption, analyse the situation, apply the most probable solution, monitor, measure and assess. If we are not successful, we can only assume an inaccurate diagnosis – so back to the drawing board!

The acceptance of Schein's view also implies that new ideas, hypotheses and theories of behaviour may emerge in the future and will join the existing canon of motivation theory for consideration in the same way. The obligation on us all as marketers will be to keep abreast of developments in the field.

Motivation theory – a summary

Theory	Name/ Originator	Assumption	Marketing implications
Self-Actualization	Maslow	Hierarchy of needs	Aim product at the appropriate need satisfaction
ERG	Alderfer	Existence, relatedness and growth needs	As Maslow Use 'displacement'
Achievement	McClelland	Achievement, affiliation and power needs	Identify product with satisfaction of these needs
Expectancy	Vroom	Motivation = Valence × Expectation	Raise perceived value and expectation of product satisfaction

Theory	Name/ Originator	Assumption	Marketing implications
Social	Mayo	Behaviour affected by social group (including informal groups)	Emphasis on social acceptance Fear of isolation
Equity	Adams	Effort/reward balance	Influence perceptions
Complex	Schein	None/all	Diagnose

Key learning points from Part Two

- Consumers make choices because their resources are limited
- Opportunity cost is the cost of going without the next best alternative
- Utility is the satisfaction or benefit derived by the consumer from the purchase of goods or services
- Consumers will seek to maximize the utility they get from their disposable income
- Price elasticity measures the extent to which a change in price will cause a change in demand
- The trade cycle (boom, recession, depression, recovery) influences employment, income levels, demand and confidence
- Perception is selective and depends on external and internal factors
- Products can be placed in the appropriate awareness set
- Consumers' self-concepts will influence the choice of products and will tend to enhance the consumers' desired self-image
- Subliminal perception is the perception of stimuli subconsciously
- Brand image is what distinguishes a product from its competitors
- Segmentation is a grouping of customers who have identifiable characteristics relevant to purchasing
- To be useful a segment must be measurable, accessible, substantial and relatively stable
- Demographics refers to population characteristics such as age, gender, occupation, etc.
- Geo-demographics links these factors with geography
- Status involves power and authority, and allows segmentation of markets by aspirational elements to low-status consumers or congratulatory elements to high-status consumers
- Class is another method of segmenting markets based on the traditional class systems in operation. However, as society becomes more open, and social mobility becomes more common, class declines in importance as a segmentation method
- Family Life Cycle (FLC) is a useful segmentation, using life stage as the basis

of identifying the focus of purchasing interest and level of disposable income
- Psychographics/lifestyle analysis is popular as a way of segmenting the market based on the attitudes, interests and opinions of consumers
- Industrial markets can also be segmented. In this case it is sometimes possible to identify and classify all potential customers
- Culture reflects the way of life of a society or group
- Cultures can vary widely and dramatically
- Micro-cultures are often based on class, race, religion, age, geography, gender
- Cross-cultural marketing offers opportunities and potential pitfalls
- There is a choice to be made between marketing a global product and modifying the product to the local environment
- Socialization is a key concept covering the learning and cultural values of the society
- Socialization takes place via family, school, peer group and mass media
- Families are important also as consuming and decision-making units
- Groups influence behaviour
- Groups can be ascribed, acquired, primary, secondary, formal, informal, membership, aspirational or dissociative
- Reference groups are those which influence our behaviour
- Attitudes have three components: cognitive (knowledge), affective (emotions) and conative (behavioural)
- Attitudes are thought to be leading variables to behaviour – but the relationship is both complex and difficult to predict
- Attitudes are thought to fulfil functions which are utilitarian, ego-defensive, expressive and knowledge-based
- Consistency theories (balance, congruity and cognitive dissonance theories) emphasize the importance of cognitive consistency for the individual's peace of mind
- Fishbein's theory is the principal one which suggests that attitudes may have a variety of different components
- Motivation is a key element in understanding behaviour
- Key motivation theorists are: Maslow, Alderfer, McClelland, Vroom.

Part Three   Investigating Customers

Introduction

Investigating customers involves the research methods associated with the behavioural sciences. So this section seeks to introduce key concepts from the behavioural sciences associated with the problems of investigating and measuring relevant aspects of attitudes and behaviour via an introductory look at marketing research and descriptive statistics. It introduces ideas such as:

- The scientific method – Hypotheses, theories, laws
- Experimental design and control groups
- Types of data
- Methods of data collection
- Problems of measurement
- Uses of behavioural sciences – description, explanation, prediction, control
- Ethical issues surrounding behavioural research
- Marketing research techniques
- Problem diagnosis, clarification of options, research design, data collection, data analysis, report presentation
- Data – qualitative and quantitative
- Secondary research – environmental scanning, sources of secondary data
- Validity – internal, external
- Question types and forms
- Questionnaire design
- Depth interviews and focus groups
- Sampling – random, quasi-random (systematic, stratified and multi-stage) or non-random (quota and cluster sampling)
- Data analysis – mean, median and mode
                – range, quartiles, deciles and standard deviation
- Data presentation – tables, graphs, pictograms, pie charts, bar charts, histograms
- Research reports – clear purpose, well organized material, well structured, well presented.

7 'There's nowt so strange as folk...'

The behavioural sciences – problems and methods

Introduction

Customers are people. The behavioural sciences are about people. This makes an understanding of some of the basic concepts of the behavioural sciences particularly relevant to this course of study. The concern for people and behaviour makes this field both the easiest and most interesting that you will tackle and also, in other ways, the most difficult.

The subject is 'easy' in as much as it is about life and our experience. At one level it should pose few problems, as it could be argued that we are all expert practical psychologists – we live in a complex world and cope with it successfully – so the main problem may be in understanding the ideas, language and mystique that surround the subject.

On the other hand, 'there's nowt so strange as folk'. People come in an infinite variety and are continually surprising. So the subject is very difficult in as much as it is very hard to know whether you are right in the same way that you can have confidence in having done a calculation correctly.

So far in this book we have already dealt with many ideas taken from the behavioural sciences – we have looked at ideas from economics, sociology and psychology. The alert reader will already have realized that degree courses could be followed in each of these disciplines – so, as we have already stated, this text is, in effect, edited highlights from those areas which will help to illuminate our understanding of the marketing process.

In order to explore some of the difficulties and issues involved, try the following exercise:

> **Think** – Imagine that you are asked to evaluate the effectiveness of the course of study you are currently undertaking.
> – How would you set about such a task?

> – Define the procedures, measures and timescales
> necessary to fulfil the request.
>
> Write down your thoughts on how you would tackle the
> assignment and keep the document handy as we will refer to it
> later.

We will start by looking at the problem of how we 'know' something.

Acquiring knowledge

There are a variety of ways in which we, as human beings, acquire knowledge: 'Experts' pontificate; preachers preach; teachers teach! We read newspapers, listen to gossip and generally learn by our own experience of life. Helmstadter (1970) formalized and described a number of processes which may be relevant to our course of study:

1 *Tenacity* – or the persistence of a belief. Here we are concerned with the beliefs which we hold on to and react to as if they were facts.

> **Think** – What beliefs do you hold?
> – How do they affect your behaviour?

2 *Intuition* – the process of coming to knowledge without reasoning or inferring. There is currently a lot of speculation about intuition stemming from the right hemisphere of the brain while logical thinking occurs in the left. There is interesting work going on regarding relaxation, releasing the power of intuition and of increased learning power.

> **Think** – What experience have you had of intuition?
> – How reliable has it been?

3 *Authority* – the acquisition of knowledge by accepting information because it comes from a respected source. This is rather different from taking expert advice – here the essence is the required acceptance. In this sense it can encompass religious absolutes (and also superstitions if the receiver believes them).

> **Think** – What strong beliefs (authorities) do you accept?
> – How do these affect the way you see the world?

4 *Rationalism* – the development of knowledge through reasoning. It assumes that 'good' knowledge is acquired if the correct process of reasoning has been followed. This can have unfortunate consequences if the initial assumptions are not valid. The computer expression GIGO (garbage in, garbage out) might be an example of the inadequacy of logically processing inadequate data. This is not to belittle the use of reasoning – indeed, it is a crucial part of the scientific method. Reasoning is used to arrive at hypotheses.

Think – What experiences have you had where reasoning has 'come unstuck'?

---

5 *Empiricism* – this approach focuses on our experiences. In, effect, it says, 'if I have experienced something, then it is valid and true'. So 'facts' that agree with our experience are true and those that do not are rejected. When we come to examine perception and the phenomena in that area we may well come to doubt the reliability of our own experiences. Once again, this is not to denigrate empiricism – it is a vital part of our intellectual armoury – but to counsel caution in unquestioning belief in our experiences.

Think – What experiences have you had which look different with hindsight?

Each of these approaches is 'real', but each has its difficulties as the basis for systematically acquiring knowledge about our world. The notion of belief or superstition is a reality for many people – 'lucky' mascots and rituals are common for many of us. As one acquaintance says, "I'm not superstitious – I just don't take chances walking under ladders". Clearly an awareness of superstition is relevant to our studies, but it is unacceptable as the basis for professional study in this area.

Similarly, intuition, authority, rationalism and empiricism all have limitations of greater or lesser importance when we are seeking to learn about people and their behaviour. Intuition is important, but we would be unwise to base our preparation for the examinations purely on 'I've got a feeling...' without any other back-up. Authority, in the form of deeply held religious beliefs, exists, but we may need to be aware that there are different (sometimes contradictory) beliefs which co-exist within our society. If we are to progress our studies, rational thought might be a requirement – but in our incomplete state of knowledge it might be unwise to deny other people's intuitions and apparent oddities. Lastly, our own experiences are a valuable source of input for our learning processes, but we have to face up to the question of how typical are we, and how typical was our experience?

In our society, and in this particular programme of study, the preferred method of acquiring knowledge is:

6 *The Scientific Method* – this represents a logic or method of enquiry, and is
  concerned with establishing general principles. Natural sciences (chemistry,
  physics, etc.) are based on direct observation, consistent relationships, experiments to test hypotheses and mathematical reasoning. Generally the following
  pattern is followed:

Idea – about things or relationships→
Hypothesis – a researchable statement, to be supported or refuted by facts→
Facts – to test hypothesis→
Theory – tested again to determine when true/when not→
Law – 'a statement of invariable sequence between specified conditions and
phenomena'.

This is shown diagrammatically in Figure 7.1.

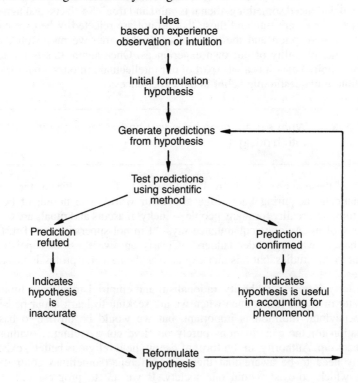

Figure 7.1   The scientific method

Clearly this could also be represented as a circular diagram, but we then realize
that we do not return to exactly the same point as the one from which we started.
Our investigation allows us to hold our prediction with greater or lesser

confidence – so we have moved on slightly with regard to our acquisition of knowledge. Thus it might be more realistic to think of this process as a 'spiral of knowledge'.

The behavioural sciences and the scientific method

The physical sciences utilize this method of investigation. Most of us remember physics experiments at school and are familiar with following the laid-down procedures and (hopefully) getting the 'right' results (some of us can remember not getting the right results and deciding that it was less hassle to copy someone else's results knowing that there was a 'right' answer).

There are significant problems, however, when we come to look at the behavioural sciences. Human beings are not identical. Indeed, it is a truism that every individual is unique. We also cannot subject humans to processes and experiences in the same way as we can deal with inert chemicals or materials. We have difficulty in 'repeating' experiments on people as they are clearly not the same the second time around, having already experienced the experiment – i.e. they can easily become 'contaminated'. Additionally, people are seldom subject to just one single influence at a time.

So if we are to understand behaviour we will need to conduct research in order to find and test relationships between a stimulus and a response, a given set of circumstances and an outcome, etc. We therefore need to spend a little time examining the problems associated with experimental design.

Experimental design

This stage requires a great deal of preparation, thought and planning. We need to ensure that the hypotheses stated are those that we actually test. We must control extraneous variables. We need to separate the experimental variable as well as the response variable.

Two important concepts need clarifying at this point:

1 *Internal validity*. This is concerned with answering the question as to whether the stimulus had any effect on the response.
2 *External validity*, which refers to the confidence with which we can generalize the outcome, or to what extent a result is peculiar to the subjects used, or the circumstances surrounding the experiment.

In order to protect internal validity we may need to guard against time as a variable (we could get different results from a survey today than we would have got six months ago – e.g. opinion polls are carried out regularly as we expect political feelings and intentions to change). If we are aiming to measure change we will have to use the same measure before and after, but the act of measuring before may give participants an idea of what it is you are interested in – so they may change their attitudes or behaviour in order to 'help' the experimenter. We have problems of who we choose to take part in the experiment – volunteers might well be untypical! What do we do about those who drop out? – their stories/views might be more significant than those who do not.

External validity is also prone to difficulties. Here we are concerned with whether our results can be applied more widely to people in general – so a significant problem may centre on whether our sample is representative. The time factor is another issue – by the time you have come to some conclusions, the situation in the world at large might have changed, so your results become irrelevant. The process of measuring may make subjects untypical in itself.

Most of these difficulties will be known to marketers because the market research activities are subject to these very same problems and constraints.

Experimental format

There are a number of different experimental forms that have differing strengths and limitations. We can set these out diagrammatically (Figures 7.2–7.6) where:

X = event in which we are interested, Tn = test or measurement

$$X \quad T$$

Figure 7.2

1 Case study or survey

> **Think** – The 'Walkman' personal stereo is an example of a
> successful innovation.
> – Why was it successful?
> – What can we learn which will ensure that our product
> innovation is also a success?

Here a situation/company/product is analysed retrospectively. This may provide useful suggestions for future actions (or hypotheses for testing), but care must be taken to ensure that future situations are comparable to the original case. Problems of '20/20 hindsight' abound, as we have no measure of the situation before the event.

2 One-group pre-test/post-test design

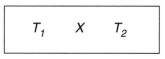

$$T_1 \quad X \quad T_2$$

Figure 7.3

> **Think** – Imagine that you have a steady level of sales of
> product X. You change your advertising agency,
> develop new advertisements, and sales rise.
> – Is this because of the new advertising campaign?

Here we start to deal with the problem of whether it was the stimulus that led to a change by measuring before and after. In the above example, we might discover that the increase in sales was due to some other factor. If, for instance, we were selling Do-It-Yourself products, the upturn in sales could be due to the economic recession and unemployment leading more people, literally, to do it themselves. We still have enormous problems of external validity (i.e. how typical was it?) and whether any lessons learned can be transferred to other situations.

3 Time-series design or survey

$$T_1 \quad T_2 \quad T_3 \quad T_4 \quad X \quad T_5 \quad T_6 \quad T_7 \quad T_8$$

Figure 7.4

This occurs where measures or tests are applied to the respondents over a period of time. Examples of this approach are *opinion polls,* when the effect on attitudes of a particular event are assessed, or *product panels,* which monitor responses by checking reactions to a product change over a period of time. Here the issues of sample size and of picking respondents who are typical of the group you are seeking to study become important.

4 Non-equivalent control group design

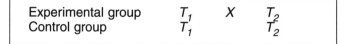

| Experimental group | T_1 | X | T_2 |
| Control group | T_1 | | T_2 |

Figure 7.5

Think – Imagine that you have a sales force of twenty representatives who are all on a fixed salary. A consultant has suggested that you consider a bonus scheme whereby their pay will be related to the level of sales that each rep attains. You decide to try this, but before adopting it for the whole department you decide to conduct an experiment. You pick the ten best salespersons and put them on the new bonus scheme. The remainder stay on their original salaries. The sales figures of the 'bonus group' increase over the previous level. The ten who stay on the old pay scheme show no change in their sales performance.
  – Does this prove that the bonus scheme improves sales performance?

This is a major step forward, as we have the idea of a control group emerging. This is a group who are subject to the same measures or tests, but who are not exposed to the stimulus. Thus they can act as a check as to whether it was the stimulus that gave rise to the response – if the change is due to an extraneous factor then both groups would show the same change and we would not be able to support our hypothesis that it was the stimulus that caused the change. Despite this being an improvement on earlier efforts, there are still significant potential problems surrounding the choice and representativeness of the two groups (i.e. are they actually the same or are they different – in the latter case, as in the example, it could be these differences that are being measured by any comparison, i.e. the fact of choosing the best ten for the bonus scheme may mean that it only works for good salespersons).

5 Classic experiment design

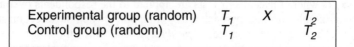

Experimental group (random) T_1 X T_2
Control group (random) T_1 T_2

Figure 7.6

Here the subjects are randomly allocated to the experimental and control groups and the measures are applied to both. This is the format which overcomes the majority of problems in terms of the scientific method.

> **Think** – In the previous 'Think' exercise, would offering the bonus to ten salespersons chosen at random and observing the improvement when compared with the performance of the ten control group (also chosen randomly) have improved the confidence with which you assess the effectiveness of the bonus scheme?

None of these designs is without its limitations, however. Even with the classic experimental design we commonly have the practical difficulty of access to suitable numbers of random subjects willing to take part in the study. We may also see 'unnatural' behaviour exhibited due to people knowing that they are part of an experiment.

The use of logic and reasoning

Earlier we referred to the use of reasoning as a method in acquiring knowledge, and much of the foregoing section involves the use of reasoning or logic. A central problem that is faced in the behavioural sciences lies in deciding what we can accept as 'evidence'.

> **Old joke** – A behavioural scientist was travelling with a friend, and on the journey they see a flock of sheep in a field.
> 'They've been sheared', said the friend.
> 'They seem to be, on this side', replied the scientist.

As we have seen, a second problem is the interpretation of the evidence, and the confidence we can place on the interpretation (which encompasses the internal/external validity issues discussed above).

Basically, the chain of reasoning can go one of two ways:

- *Inductive thinking* – the inferring of a general law from particular instances
- *Deductive thinking* – the inferring of particular instances from general laws.

Generally, as we have seen, the behavioural sciences are not strong on general laws, so deductive thinking is somewhat less common than in the physical sciences – the danger being that deductions are made from theories, hypotheses or hunches rather than true laws.

In contrast, inductive thinking is relatively common. The temptation is often to infer a general law from a single case study. The section on experimental method emphasizes the need for careful design to increase the confidence we might have in any conclusions. The case study approach is very common:

XYZ plc 'did it by the book' and succeeded,

but before we believe what is basically an anecdote we might like to examine:

Firms who did likewise, but who did not succeed,
Firms who 'did it all wrong' and succeeded
Firms who 'did it wrong' and failed.

Only then may we have the basis of a sound conclusion.

In dealing with the 'real world' it is sometimes difficult to set up rigorous experimental designs, so research is sometimes conducted 'after the event'. Data is collected and different aspects compared in order to develop hypotheses. It sometimes happens that high positive correlations are obtained between separate sets of information, but great care must be taken to test whether:

- A has led to B
- B has led to A
- a separate factor entirely has caused both, or
- it is just a statistical oddity.

This is the point at which sound experiments need to be conducted in order to test the various hypotheses and identify the proven from the disproven.

Description, explanation, prediction and control in the behavioural sciences

The scientific method has a number of aims which we can imagine as being at different levels.

First, it seeks to describe the event
Secondly, it seeks to explain what has happened
Next it moves on to predict the happening in advance, and
Ultimately it seeks to control the phenomenon.

The physical sciences give us good examples of this process. Returning to our memories of science classes at school or college, many of us will remember doing experiments which illustrate this method quite well – investigations of gravity, evaporation and expansion all spring to the author's mind. Each followed the process closely and resulted in describing, explaining, predicting and controlling – and all had to be written up in the standard form.

The predictability of these natural phenomena allows us to exercise control over processes which enable us to develop many of the machines which are so much part of our lives.

But we need to face up to the problem that these activities may be different in the behavioural sciences. We will examine each level in turn.

Description

The first objective/level of scientific enquiry is that of description – the accurate portrayal of a situation or phenomenon. This stage also seeks to identify the variables that exist and the extent to which they exist.

In the behavioural sciences we do face specific problems in attempting to describe things. Some behaviour is ambiguous, some of the variables are invisible. Some behaviours are difficult/impossible to observe and describe – an example might be learning. We cannot find physiological changes, but we can measure your knowledge at the end of a course (a problem then arises, as the knowledge might have been there before you started the course...). The process becomes even more difficult, however, when we have to rely on individuals' accounts of what they are doing – they may lie, they may tell us what they think we want to hear, or they may not know!

This focuses on the problem of the reliability of the data. There are three broad approaches we can follow in collecting data:

1 Observation

Non-participant observation
Here we have the researcher watching the subjects. This looks quite good until we realize that the act of observing people may cause them to behave 'abnormally' (as we saw in the 'Hawthorne Effect' mentioned in Chapter 5). We might therefore decide to go for 'hidden' observation, but even this has its problems. Observing pedestrian flow in a city centre from a hidden position does not appear too controversial, but other observations could seem a serious violation of privacy (e.g. Christensen (1988) reports a study which used hidden periscopes in a public lavatory!).

Participant observation
In this case the researchers 'disguise' themselves as ordinary group members/punters and observe what goes on 'from the inside'. Here we have problems regarding the influence of the investigator on what occurs – he or she could be the cause of the effect described, thus invalidating many of the conclusions. There are also some interesting and difficult ethical issues. The UK legal system rejects 'agents provocateurs' – why should marketing investigations be subject to less stringent controls?

Both approaches to observation are also subject to difficulties as to whether the observer is describing or interpreting. The element of subjectivity has to be guarded against when recording events.

Unobtrusive measures
This is where we look at outputs rather than ask opinions – a classic example is recording which books are taken out of libraries or sold rather than asking people what they read (few people 'admit' to reading Mills & Boon – but the evidence

that they do is overwhelming!). Similarly, carpet wear suggested that the reality of which exhibits were most popular in an art exhibition produced different results from those of the exit survey!

2 Analysing documents

Diaries, letters, minutes, accounts, policy statements, customer records, productivity measures, etc. may provide apparently 'neutral' data and facts. However, we must always be wary of the circumstances under which they were produced and the reasons for them.

3 Asking questions

One-to-one interview
These may be either structured or unstructured – the very straightforward meeting of the researcher and the subject where questions are asked and answers recorded. The structured interview gives manageable data, with the ability to follow up interesting or unexpected avenues that might arise from an answer. However, some people criticize the structure as defining an agenda which is the researcher's rather than the respondent's – e.g. if asked whether you are finding the course useful or not, you are likely to answer 'yes' or 'no'. Given a free choice, however, you might prefer to describe it in terms of interesting/boring, relevant/irrelevant, or any other construct which is relevant and meaningful to you.

Questionnaires
These are commonly used, but are really only highly structured interviews – so the key is asking the right questions first time! This needs careful development and pilot testing to avoid mistakes.

Explanation

At this level we are seeking the cause of a given phenomenon. We must, however, ensure that we get cause and effect in the right order, as we saw earlier when the processes of logic, inductive and deductive thinking were introduced in the section on rationality. An example of such a problem might be that race and criminality are claimed by some to be linked, but 'the facts' may not support the causal relationship – i.e. it may not be that black people are more criminally inclined, it could be that police officers are more likely to arrest members of the black community.

The laws of natural science are inviolate, but human laws are things that we can choose to disobey or amend. Many of our rules of behaviour will only apply in one society rather than be universal. Some of our behaviour will only be tolerated within certain social groups. On the other hand, the social sciences have the advantage that they can ask people why they do things – I can ask students how they feel about the course so far – whereas I tend to get no answer if I ask my bicycle why it is rusty!!

The difficulty of explanation is compounded by the fact that people appear to behave in accordance with their own theories of how the world works. The nature of our society is that we will tend to share these 'rules' with others in our groups (even anarchists share a belief in the absence of rules) – but we must also accept that we live with multiple realities (trade unionists and management may view industrial relations legislation very differently, as may marketers and consumers view the concept of 'profit'). We will see that many of these theories have been handed down through family links and standards, while others come from membership of certain groups or classes.

Another increasing problem is the use of 'technical', behavioural science language in everyday life. The colour supplements happily use words such as 'neurotic', 'intelligent', 'pathological' so that we get used to them. We may have to check that such technical jargon is being used with the correct technical meaning.

Prediction

In the behavioural sciences this is usually probabilistic rather than absolute – we can predict future labour turnover by cause, but we cannot determine exactly who will get an offer they can't refuse, have a heart attack, get pregnant, etc. There is also the danger of the self-fulfilling prophesy – you read something, believe it, act on it and it becomes true!! Predictions depend on the rules, but these are social phenomena and, as noted above, we can choose to disobey.

Control

Because of the choice element and cultural variations, social scientists can be critical of what they observe (unlike the natural scientist). Our judgements are based on the perceived evidence and our own values. Thus we become involved in the process – we cannot 'step outside' as the natural scientist can.

Most management activity may be viewed as being concerned with coping with, and controlling, an uncertain environment. This idea was explored in Chapter 1, and you were asked at that point to think about your reactions to assertions that our aim, in a course such as this, is to manipulate people more effectively.

> **Think** – What was your reaction to the 'Think' exercise in Chapter 1?
> – What is your reaction now that seven chapters have elapsed?
> – Why do you think you have changed (or not)?

This last exercise leads us on to discuss some more ethical considerations.

Ethical considerations

1 The relationship between society and science

This concerns the extent to which society and its cultural values should intervene in the process of experimentation and the acquisition of knowledge.

'He who pays the piper calls the tune' is a well-worn cliché, possibly because it is so often true – funding sources may define the focus of investigation and the development of knowledge.

> **Think** –   Your boss asks you to design and implement a study
> to show how effective a recent marketing initiative has
> been. As part of the briefing it is made clear to you
> that you will be expected to show that the initiative
> (which had been suggested by the boss) has been
> very successful.
> –   What will you do?

2 Professional issues

This is a linked issue and concerns the potential for faking in research. The scandal surrounding Sir Cyril Burt, the British psychologist who was knighted for his work on heredity and intelligence and who, it was alleged, faked some of his results, shocked the scientific world. The impact of the allegations was compounded by the claim that his work directly affected Government policy in the field of education and segregating children at 11+. The assertions discredited all his work (though it has never been shown that he faked results in all his studies) – so we lose what might have been valuable knowledge.

The pressure to give the client (paymasters as in (1) above) what they wish to hear can be very great.

THERE CAN BE NO JUSTIFICATION FOR ALTERING OR FAKING SCIENTIFIC DATA.

3 Treatment of subjects

This concerns the potential in the behavioural sciences for harming (either physically or psychologically) the subjects who take part in the studies.

Think – Imagine that you wish to find out more about the characteristics of people who buy your product. You watch outlets, spot purchasers, follow them to their homes and, at a later date, call on them, posing as health researchers conducting a random sample survey, and ask detailed personal questions about their lifestyle.

    a) Is this ethical?
    b) If not, which are the unethical bits:
- observing them
- following them
- questioning them on personal matters
- posing as a researcher with a different objective?

There are commonly ethical dilemmas for researchers when a judgement has to be made as to whether the potential benefits of a piece of research outweigh the possible difficulties for the participants.

The researchers concerned should not make this judgement, as they may not be impartial. They should involve other, independent, behavioural scientists in the decision to ensure the protection of the basic human rights of participants.

Deception poses problems for the dignity of subjects – yet often it is important to the very integrity of the investigation that the subjects remain unaware that they are taking part in 'an experiment'. TV shows such as 'Candid Camera' trade on the embarrassment of people being 'set up' in order to generate laughs at their expense. The problem centres on how we decide what is an acceptable joke/jape/trick and at what point the treatment becomes unacceptable.

Teachers may experiment with classes as a matter of course development – what rights have students in controlling the extent to which they are being 'experimented' upon? Teachers may be unwilling to admit that this is the first time they have tried a particular approach to teaching a subject. It can also be argued that if they announce, 'This is an experiment' the students may react unnaturally – thus invalidating any judgement as to the effectiveness of that particular approach.

Confidentiality of data is another issue that can become difficult in some situations.

Evaluation issues

Let us go back and consider the design you proposed at the beginning of this chapter for evaluating the course you are currently doing. In the light of the discussion about the behavioural sciences, how did you do?

Clearly, for a sound experiment or evaluation you should have included:

1 Measures of achievement, behaviour or knowledge both *before and after* the course.
2 A control group.

The reality is that evaluation, along with many investigations in the behavioural sciences, is very difficult to do well. Bloom (1956) observed that people are 'apparently so constituted that they cannot refrain from evaluating, judging, appraising or valuing almost everything that comes within their purview'.

There seems to be a paradox in that it is both difficult and we *do* do it all the time. Imagine two people settling down for an evening watching television. One chooses a documentary because she is interested in the topic, the other, seeking entertainment, chooses a comedy show. Assuming both shows lived up to expectations, both individuals would rate their decisions as 'right', thus highlighting the importance of *Criteria*. The obvious criterion for judgement is, 'did it achieve its objective?'

Think – In your evaluation of the course:
- What criteria did you use?
- Is it likely that students will all have the same objectives?
- Are they the same as those of others in your group?
- Are they the same as the tutor's objectives?
- Are they the same as the college's objectives?
- Are they the same as the CIM's objectives?

Some of you will have focused on outcomes (e.g. passing), others on process (e.g. enjoyment). Other issues that often arise from this exercise are:

1 *When* did you intend to evaluate? During the course, or after it has finished?
2 Do we look for unexpected outcomes or learning? Here we may have someone who came on the course to complete the CIM programme – but the prime learning might be that they discover that they are grossly underpaid relative to other course members doing similar jobs.
3 At what level do we evaluate:
- Reaction (like/dislike)
- Learning (it would need a pre-test to measure the start point)
- Behaviour (does it show?)
- Results (does it pay off? and for whom?)
4 Who will conduct the evaluation? and for whom?

There are many weak links in the chain – a major one being the issue of transferability of the learning from the classroom to the workplace. Other difficulties include inadequate analysis of the need, leading to unsuitable training design, using measures which show training success but which may not reflect job performance, using measures which show job success but which are unrelated to training, using measures because we have them rather than because of their relevance. Thus we may have a situation which could be described by means of Figure 7.7.

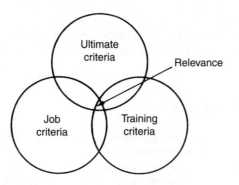

Figure 7.7 Evaluation criteria

As with any test, the criteria (measures) must be valid, reliable and relevant. The sources of unreliability are numerous – the sample size may be inadequate, the range of behaviours of the group may be too great, the instructions to the test may be ambiguous, conditions during measurement may not be consistent, or the instrument itself may 'help' the participant.

The problems increase still further if rating methods are used. Here the competence of the judges may be a problem, difficulties can arise with complex or simple behaviours, sometimes the behaviour is not overt, or observers may have difficulty in observing.

Reality poses even more problems – acceptability of the measures to both the organization and the participants, in terms of cost, time and inconvenience.

Generally evaluators seek to find a single measure that will pin down the behaviours required – but it is reasonable to assume that behaviour is affected by a number of factors, such as motivation, satisfaction, values and expectancy, so the logic is that we may well need a variety of criteria against which to judge the effectiveness of our training. The chances of positive outcomes against all of these criteria may be remote and perhaps unattainable.

Throughout there is a significant number of choices to be made regarding objectives, criteria, designs, etc. which will define the confidence with which you can conclude as to the value of the training.

While the exercise was chosen as being possibly the only common experience for all readers of this book, the parallels with marketing exercises that you might be asked to undertake are striking – in fact, if you were the publishers of the book you might make this request of your marketing staff.

On a lighter note:

An alternative view of the scientific method

In response to an examination question which concerned the explanation of 'theory/hypothesis, stimulus/response/intervening variables, experimental/control groups, illustrating each with examples from behaviour studies', one student came up with the following answer.

Theory/hypothesis

The critical difference between a theory and a hypothesis is one of evidence or experimentation.

One may have a hypothesis that, when poked in the eye, a person would say 'ouch'. However it cannot be said to be a theory until it has been tested and there is evidence to support it.

So, you go out and poke some people in the eye – let us take a sample of ten people. The first four people that you poke did, indeed, say 'ouch'; the other six, however, poked you back!

Having conducted this experiment you would then be able to say that, although your original hypothesis had been disproven, you have arrived at a new theory – that, generally, when poked in the eye, people will poke back.

In a marketing context this would come into play when planning a new product launch. Any statements regarding the product or its likely take-up would merely be hypotheses until some evidence had been gathered in the market.

You may well say 'What if an existing theory has been used, or a proven model of consumer behaviour?' The problem here is that such theories and models may only hold good for the precise circumstances in which they were created. They can be used to help arrive at a new hypothesis, but should never be taken as gospel.

Stimulus/response/intervening variables

Going back to our eye-poking example. In this experiment the original poke was the stimulus, and the victim's cry or counter-attack was the response.

However, the response was not simply caused by the original stimulus. It is affected by the intervening variables that are responsible for shaping the precise form of reaction.

So, if the victim of the original attack was a pacifist, their response might be different from that of a member of the SAS.

Similarly, if the original victim was a small and thoughtful person his (or her) response would be different from that of a six-foot, sixteen-stone professional wrestler.

In the real world and in a marketing context, intervening variables include social class, peer pressure, affluence, education, political opinion, etc.

These are all elements that people pick up (or are subjected to) throughout their lives. Their response to various stimuli depends largely on this sort of factor.

For instance, a marketer may use a politician to endorse a product in an advertisement (probably not a good idea in the real world). A consumer response to that advert will be determined by their attitude to politicians in general, their politics in particular and any preconceived ideas about the personality concerned.

Obviously, this is a very simplistic view of the subject. In reality the consumer's response would be affected by a great number of other factors as well – but it helps to understand the problem if one isolates the various components.

Experimental/control groups

When we were busy poking people in the eye and developing theories, we forgot to take into account one vital thing – what would be the response of the 'victims' had we not poked them in the eye?

In order to enhance the accuracy of any experimentation, but particularly in the case of behaviour, one must also set up a 'control' group. That is a group who are observed but who receive no stimulus.

If, in our control group, six people still poke us back unprovoked, and four say 'ouch' apparently without reason, we must abandon our old theory, develop new hypotheses and conduct new experiments since it is clearly not the poke in the eye that caused the response.

Such control groups are particularly helpful to those studying advertising and its effectiveness.

One group of people can be exposed to the campaign (the experimental group) while another group (the control group) are kept isolated from it. By observing the subsequent actions of the two groups (whether or not they buy the products concerned, etc.) a theory about the advertisement and its effectiveness can be built up.

This level of originality is very unusual under examination conditions – the candidate did get bonus points for making the examiner laugh while demonstrating a sound grasp of the issues involved!! I would happily acknowledge the authorship if I knew who the examinee was – in the event, I was marking 'blind', with only an examination number to go on – but thank you, 'anon from North London'!

8 'Excuse me, could I ask you a few questions...?'

An introductory look at marketing research

Introduction

If marketing is 'the management process responsible for identifying, anticipating and satisfying consumers' requirements profitably', there is a clear need for a continuing effort to match the capacities and efforts of the organization to the needs of customers. A key activity is researching the environment and the market so that these aims of marketing can be fulfilled.

This whole process of collecting the information on consumers in order to answer such questions is commonly called *marketing research*. It has been defined by the Market Research Society as:

> The collection and analysis of data from a sample of individuals or organizations related to their characteristics, behaviour, attitudes, opinions or possessions. It includes all forms of research such as consumer and industrial surveys, psychological investigations, observational and panel studies ...

What can market research do?

The process of marketing research is used by organizations for a number of purposes:

- To identify changes in the existing marketplace
- To improve market awareness so as to inform negotiations with suppliers
- To build up a bank of information
- To solve ad hoc problems
- To help in making plans for the future
- To monitor the success of current plans.

We could illustrate this by posing some of the questions which a marketing department may be asked to answer.

Some may centre on the *existing market*, e.g.:

- How big is a given market?
- Is it growing, contracting or stable?
- How profitable is it?
- What differing market segments are apparent?
- How are they different from one another?
- What other products/services are in the market?
- Who are the significant players/competitors?

Others focus on *potential markets*:

- How can we get ideas for new products/services?
- How do we choose which ideas to develop?
- How do we identify new market segments to target?

Strategic questions may be asked:

- Where do we stand in the market compared with our competitors?
- Should we get out of a given market?
- Should we go into others?
- What marketing strategies are being adopted by our competitors?

Product/service perceptions may need to be established:

- How do consumers see our product/service?
- What product attributes could be enhanced?
- What satisfactions do they provide?
- What is the consumer motivation for purchase?
- How can we choose a 'good' brand name?
- What constitutes a 'good' pack design?
- How can we make our product distinctive?

Pricing issues can be important:

- What are the competition charging?
- What are consumers prepared to pay?
- What do they expect to pay?
- What effect is price likely to have on sales?

Advertising demands answers to *pre-advertising* questions:

- What is the advertising message?
- Who is the advertisement's target?
- What is it going to cost?
- What media are likely to be most effective?

while *post-advertising* questions might include:

- What messages are being received?
- What level of consumer awareness have we achieved?
- Do the punters like the advert?
- What associations are consumers making?
- What impact on sales has the campaign achieved?

What can't it do?

Market research is very much a management tool, but:

- it cannot manage for us
- it cannot make decisions for us, although it can be crucial in terms of establishing evidence on which *marketing managers* can make decisions
- it is only strong at dealing with reactions to existing products, services or messages. It cannot reliably gain information about products which do not yet exist and of which respondents have had no experience or image
- in a dynamic marketplace it can only operate with the evidence that has been collected – it cannot predict future product life when it does not know what competitors will come out with and what the marketplace will look like in the future.

Market research is a key activity which must be integral to successful marketing. In one sense its very success has caused some problems. As techniques have developed and become a crucial source of competitive edge, so there has been a tendency to load more onto marketing research than can truly be justified. The fact that it usually has a quantitative element has led to a spurious belief in its accuracy. Similarly, it suffers from most of the weaknesses of the behavioural sciences in terms of prediction and control. It suffers from the potential hazards of the Hawthorne Effect when gathering data (people telling you what they think you want to hear) and it is always susceptible to claims of bias, self-fulfilling prophesies and 'getting the answer that the client/boss wants'.

Thus, in general terms, marketing research is a process of collecting, analysing, storing, retrieving and distributing all information relating to a market, brand or product. It involves direct contact with the sales force, accounts, purchasing, production, R & D and other members of the marketing department to assemble relevant internal information as well as dealing with outside agencies and the public to obtain external information.

However, there are some people who are less than complimentary about marketing research, pointing out that the results and predictions are sometimes wrong, that some successful organizations appear to do little research, while others who do invest heavily do not necessarily make profits. Others have suggested that our systems are better suited to developing existing products and markets. For example, some years ago the American academic and consultant Donald Schon, while giving the prestigious Reith Lectures on the BBC, argued that if he had a completely new and innovative product, he would go out with the marketing researchers to ensure that they got the 'right' answers that he wanted to hear!

The notion of 'right' and 'wrong' answers is interesting in the sense that it assumes two things:

- There is something that we may call 'right' or 'wrong'
- Marketing research is there to provide answers.

The first assumption is problematic in as much as it can be argued that we can only know whether something was right *after* the event. In this sense marketing research is like any other forecasting activity. It is easy to knock predictions after they have been overtaken by reality.

The second assumption is, to some extent, true – but only partially. If we take the view of marketing research which is outlined above, we could argue that it is not the place of marketing research to produce answers – only to provide data and information on which to base managerial decisions. While this might be counted as a defence in a debating society, it may not cut much ice in a busy organization seeking solutions to pressing problems, but the concerns hinted at in the previous chapter regarding pressures to satisfy the demands of our paymasters may be relevant.

In some ways it is silly to say that it produces the wrong answers, as this begs the question, 'What was the question asked?' (as the old saying goes, 'If you ask a silly question you get a silly answer'). So if we rephrase the question to, 'Does marketing research sometimes ask the wrong questions?', the answer would undoubtedly be, 'Yes – it sometimes does'.

The issue then becomes one of finding ways to minimize the chances of this happening. Here the answer seems likely to be found in the initial definition of the problem (or the MR brief) and in the design of the research project itself.

Lack of clarity as to the objectives of the research is likely to lead to wasted effort. This does not mean that all objectives need to be pre-defined – difficulties can arise if the formulation of the problem and the brief is based on unfounded assumptions. The project may need to do initial, exploratory, open-ended invest-igations to determine options, possibilities and probabilities before engaging in more detailed, positivist experimentation.

Even given this proviso, the scope for error due to ill-designed research is enormous. We may suffer from problems with the validity of the measures, the honesty of the respondents, the representativeness of the sample, and so on.

Nevertheless, it would be irresponsible on the part of the organization to risk capital, energy and effort on projects the utility of which had not been assessed. So the fact that marketing research may not always produce the 'right' answers is no reason to abandon it – it is a reason to devote more effort to getting it right.

There is a certain face validity in the assertion that marketing research is at its strongest when developing existing products and markets. We have real, tangible products (or at least experienced services) and real, live customers and users who have had direct experience of them.

In this situation it is realistic to ask for experiences, reactions, opinions and attitudes from those who have had experience of the product. It is quite realistic to ask them how they would like to see the product or service improved and developed. We can have a ready-made group of testers who can try out the new developments and give us first-hand feedback on the comparisons between the old and new products.

Thus in this area we have all the ingredients for a first-class, relevant and useful service. This can even be applied to innovations the benefits of which people may need 'convincing' of – who would have thought that a round teabag would have proved popular?

On the other hand, when dealing with new and innovative products, marketing research does run into some problems. It can be argued that in such circumstances the need for research is even more important. However, the main stumbling block is that respondents may be answering hypothetical questions without any first-hand experience.

If we ask people whether they would be interested in buying a cheap-to-buy, pollution-free, low-running-cost form of transport suitable for town use and commuting, the answer is likely to be a resounding 'YES' – it is the dream of a very large proportion of the population. If that is the question asked, we go ahead and produce something like the Sinclair C5 – one of the great marketing disasters of recent history!

The problem of hypothetical responses to hypothetical questions is almost insurmountable. It may be possible to produce examples or samples for a group of people to try out, but success will be a function of many things, including advertising and promotion. What may appear to be a duff idea may 'take off' and become fashionable – 'punk' style might be an example. The Sony Walkman is another example where the initial feedback was not encouraging – but the decision to press ahead and promote the innovative product has paid off many times over.

In general, we may conclude that marketing research is better suited to developing existing markets, products and services. But the cornerstone of success is innovation and there is still a place for the entrepreneur with vision, flair and an instinct for future public taste to be successful. Ask Richard Branson! Ask those who spot and promote pop groups! The risks are high, but the rewards for getting it right are huge.

Marketing intelligence

The information generated by marketing research is sometimes referred to as *marketing intelligence*.

One simple way of classifying different types of information is to draw the distinction between *internal* information, which is obtained from the organization's own records, results and forecasts, and *external* information.

External assessment

External intelligence is collected from a wide variety of sources and allows the organization to assess its competitive position. One commonly used format is known as *PEST analysis*:

● *Political*   – stability

- *Economic*
  - – constraints on investment
  - – GDP/GNP total and per head
  - – state of the national economy
  - – GDP/GNP gross and per head
  - – infrastructure
  - – costs, taxation, grants
- *Social*
  - – lifestyles
  - – religion/ethics
  - – demographics
  - – pressure groups
- *Technology*
  - – research and development
  - – energy resources
  - – labour force skills
  - – environmental impact.

Another commonly used approach identifies five forces acting on an organization:

- The power of competitors
- The power of buyers
- The power of suppliers
- The threat of potential entrants to the market
- The threat posed by substitute products.

This could be seen as another use of dependency theory, which we discussed in Chapter 1.

A more detailed categorization of different types of investigation have led Foster and Davis (1994) to classify ten types of marketing research which are defined by their focus of interest:

1 *Economic research* – the study of the economy of a country, region, industry or market – concerned with broad studies to establish the key economic aspects. The data obtained may be quite detailed, since this kind of research is intended to give insight into the current and future state of the economy under consideration.

2 *Market research* – a more detailed study of a market to identify total demand (usually for all products or services under consideration). It aims to establish how the market is changing, growing, contracting, the competitors in the market, market shares, prices and factors which may influence the market and its development.

3 *Demand studies* – a detailed in-depth study of the demand for specific products and services to get an up-to-date picture of what is happening to demand for the products/services in question. This sometimes stems from 2 above when the information gathered is found not to be detailed enough for detailed market planning.

4 *Consumer research* – detailed studies covering the attitudes, opinions and usage made of the products among an appropriate sample of people chosen from their personal, geographic or occupational characteristics. These studies

could provide information on the 'image' of the product, the profile of customers or users, attitudes to product characteristics, prices, reliability and quality. Information on preferences between brands might also be obtained – all by investigating a suitable representative sample of the population.

5 *Competitor research* – a detailed study of the competition – what they are doing, what products/services they are offering, how and why they are succeeding (or not). This can lead to a *competitor profile*, which may be used to predict likely competitor reaction to action, changes or innovations.

6 *Product research* – aims to establish what products/services are required, the types, specification, price and performance expected by customers and users. It may also attempt to establish the technical features required and may include information on the expected life of the product, after-sales service expected, etc. It may help clarify the product range for the organization.

7 *Sales research* – usually carried out on a continuous basis by sales administrators, the aim is to identify the flow of products/services, prices and distribution. It can provide a useful baseline against which to monitor and measure the effects of promotional activity, changes in systems, prices, etc.

8 *Distribution research* – this seeks to identify the physical distribution required to counter the competition effectively or to improve the service to customers. It may also be used to check on the efficiency and cost-effectiveness of current systems. Decisions about issues such as the location and size of depots, stock levels, transportation methods and the type of agents to be used may all be helped by the information gathered under this heading.

9 *Promotional research* – helps to determine the promotional activities required, the timing of them and the costs involved. It can cover all promotional activities or just advertising and sales promotion. The information gathered can be used to evaluate current promotions. It can also help with decisions regarding media selection and the nature, timing and costs of such activities.

10 *Market modelling* – these models aim to offer simplified views of complex situations. Some are based on statistical analysis, others on qualitative factors, but all have the aim of helping to decide whether current information is in line with expectations and plans – and ultimately to help predict the outcome of future action and plans.

The above categories of marketing research are only one way of classifying the activities. Other sources use different categories – one of the most common being to look at the source of the data we are collecting and subdivide the field into primary research (sometimes called desk research) and secondary research (sometimes referred to as field research).

Primary research involves the marketing researcher in collecting data for a specific problem which has to be solved or decision which has to be made. Primary data may come from surveys, questionnaires, experiments, etc. These approaches will be examined in more detail later. In contrast, *secondary research* is based on data which for the most part has been collected for some other purpose. Examples include environmental scanning, published statistics and bought-in reports.

Secondary research, although being somewhat less exciting and 'sexy' than primary research, is nevertheless a very important part of marketing research which is concerned with collecting, analysing and interpreting data which already exists and which is relevant to the organization and its environment. It is of use in helping to build up a database of information on the marketplace, to identify changes and increase awareness of opportunities. It is concerned with *secondary data* which is already in existence and which may have been collected for some other purpose, as distinct from *primary data*, which entails the collection of data specifically for the problem in hand and which usually involves interviews and questionnaires.

One specific area of secondary research, and thus examples of secondary data, is called *environmental scanning*. This is the professional's term for 'keeping one's ear to the ground'. It is about being aware of what is going on in the marketplace and may involve keeping an eye on competitors as well as a more wide-ranging sensitivity to what is going off in political, social, economic, technological and legal circles. In this case the secondary data sources will be:

- trade journals, such as *Campaign, Marketing*
- specialist magazines, such as *The Economist*
- the specialist press, such as the *Financial Times*
- academic journals, such as the *Harvard Business Review.*

Additional sources of data will include :

- conferences and exhibitions
- salesforce feedback (including customer reactions to competitors and their products)
- networking (including contacts with competitors, examining their products, financial statements, press releases, job advertisements, etc.).

Another important source of secondary data is *published statistics*, which are usually divided into *governmental* and *non-governmental*.

Examples of government statistics include publications such as:

- *Census* – numbers and location of the population
- *Household Survey* and *Family Expenditure Survey* – giving valuable data on spending patterns
- *Annual Abstract of Statistics* – data on housing, population, manufacturing output, etc.
- *Economic Trends* – gives economic analysis and indicators
- *Department of Employment Gazette* – concerned mainly with employment patterns, but contains useful data on (e.g.) earnings levels for areas and industries
- *Business Monitor* – gives information on specific industries.

Examples of non-governmental sources include:

- Chambers of Commerce
- Trade associations

- Banks
- Kelly's Directory
- CIM
- Financial Times Business Information Service
- Kompass
- News agencies
- Mintel

each of which provides reviews and data on various industries, sectors and localities.

Other significant sources of secondary data include bought-in information from *consumer panels* and *retail panels*, which we will look at in more detail later.

The difference between data and information

In describing information we need to make a distinction between information and data. The two terms are commonly used interchangeably, but from a technical viewpoint they are different:

- *Data* (the plural of 'datum') is defined as 'thing known or assumed as the basis for inference or reckoning'. It usually refers to groups of non-random symbols which represent qualities, events, actions and things. These are made up of characters which may be alphabetic or numeric or special symbols.
- *Information*, on the other hand, is 'knowledge or news'. Commonly it is used to refer to data which has been processed into a form which is meaningful to the recipient and which is of real or perceived value for the intended purpose. Data is therefore the raw material from which information (or 'news' in the dictionary sense) is produced. Information for one purpose in an organization can therefore be used as data to be further processed for a different purpose.

So, in summary, *information* is what marketing research is all about. It is what we seek in order to understand the marketing world in which we operate. *Data* is what we collect, analyse and interpret in order to get information.

Qualitative and quantitative research

Qualitative research is geared towards gathering qualitative information about things such as attitudes and motivation. As mentioned above under causal objectives, the researchers may utilize psychometric techniques such as word association tests or Thematic Apperception tests in order to explore respondents' deeper emotional values regarding the product.

Quantitative research is involved with numerical data, commonly generated by questionnaires and surveys.

Some research is done on a 'one-off' basis (sometimes called *ad hoc research*). This normally begins with an initial brief and ends with a report. It is not designed, for instance, to monitor change, but rather to find answers to specific problems, often using qualitative research methods. This should be contrasted with *continuous research* which has no identifiable beginning or end, but keeps the data constantly 'topped up' so that changes in the environment can be identified. Continuous research often requires a sophisticated management or marketing information system, and frequently involves panels.

Another useful way to distinguish between different types of marketing research is to classify it according to who the end-user of the product concerned will be. Hence *consumer research* concentrates on individuals and households, while *business research* looks at customers who are organizations.

There are various ways of categorizing marketing research, but in the writer's opinion classification by objectives is probably the most important. Indeed, the objective will often define the subsequent choices in research design, including who has the skills and capacity to conduct the research.

Information and data are the very lifeblood of marketing research. In order to achieve our aims we need to collect facts, figures, opinions and feelings. As a result, we are faced with the prospect of dealing with very different elements which need clarification.

Qualitative data in the marketing context usually involves the feelings, impressions, attitudes, likes, dislikes and prejudices of buying individuals who are quizzed by the marketing researcher, often during group discussion, but using quantitative research techniques such as questionnaires. The data itself can arise as narrative, commentary or statements, using words or pictures. Spoken words can be recorded; written words or drawn pictures can be captured on paper or computer. The data may take the form of isolated statements, often in response to open-ended questions, or of a description of a set of circumstances. Qualitative data is sometimes called 'soft' data because it is often about feelings and emotions and therefore is rather hard to measure. In marketing terms, the emotional values that the consumer attaches to a product or service are important determinants of buying behaviour.

In contrast, *quantitative data* is concerned with numbers, and so necessarily focuses on things that can be measured. As explained above, in order to be meaningful, a number must have some sort of context. It must also have some value in relation to the value of other numbers. For example, if asked my shoe size, I may respond by telling the market researcher that it is 11. This only has meaning and value if we are aware of the *comparitor* (i.e. the measuring system which is being used) – there could be confusion between UK, US and European scales. Many of us have had a nasty shock when we hear our waist measurement expressed in centimetres after years of hearing a much smaller number of inches! So quantitative data are the numbers that we collect and process. It may be that there is an interaction between the two systems, as even soft, qualitative research may need to be reviewed by allocating numbers to, say, interview interpretations, so that the results can be summarised.

We saw in the previous chapter that the behavioural sciences collect information via a number of different techniques and approaches – we listed observation, analysing documents and asking questions as the three main categories. In marketing research there are a number of methods which are relatively specific to the field, and it is perhaps worth looking at some of them in a little more detail as they are likely to be the 'tools of the trade' for marketing specialists.

(a) Consumer panels

These are made up of a representative sample of individuals and households whose buying activity is monitored either continuously (daily) or at regular intervals over a period of time. The panels are usually set up to examine a defined area – e.g. there are panels set up to monitor purchases of groceries, consumer durables, cars, baby products, etc.

For many years a well-known consumer panel was run which estimated the purchase of groceries and frozen foods for home consumption by using a sample of over 6000 households in the UK. More recently, it has been replaced by a high-tech superpanel. This allows the households to scan data directly from purchases into the database by means of barcodes after every shopping trip. Most consumer panels consist of a representative cross-section of consumers who have agreed to give information about their attitudes or buying habits (through personal visits or postal questionnaires) at regular intervals. Consumer panels with personal visits are called *home audit panels*.

Consumer panels generate a great deal of data which needs to be carefully analysed if it is to be useful to marketers. It is possible to purchase:

- *special analyses*, which may be relevant to a specific industry. Common ones include:
  - location of purchase analysis
  - frequency of purchase analysis
  - demographic analysis (in terms of household age, number of children, ACORN classification, etc.)
  - tracking of individuals, to show their degree of brand loyalty, how and when they change brands, etc.

in addition to the more general

- *standard trend analysis*, showing how the market and its major brands have fared since the last analysis, grossed up to reflect the entire UK population or a particular region.

(b) Retail panels

These are the equivalent process, but applied to the distribution system. 'Trade audits' are carried out among panels of wholesalers and retailers, and the term 'retail audits' usually refers to panels made up of retailers only. The research firm sends its 'auditors' to selected outlets at regular intervals to count stock and deliveries, thus enabling an estimate of throughput to be made. Sometimes it is possible to do a universal audit of all retail outlets. The adoption of EPOS (electronic point of sale) systems is making the process both easier and more universal.

These audits can provide details of:

- selling prices in retail outlets, including information about discounts
- retail sales for selected products and brands, sales by different types of retail outlet, market shares and brand shares
- retail stocks of products and brands (enabling a firm subscribing to the audit to compare stocks of its own goods with those of competitors).

Perhaps the best known example of a retail audit is the Nielsen Index, which has operated since 1939. This monitors sales and stock levels for three product groups: food, drugs and pharmaceuticals. The Nielsen Food Index audits about 800 grocers bi-monthly, and reports on each brand, size, flavour, etc. specified by the client, together with an 'all other' category, showing the following:

- Consumer sales in units and £
- Retailer purchases in units
- The source of delivery (co-operatives, multiple stores depot, independent wholesalers)
- Retailer's stocks and stock cover (in days/weeks, etc.)
- Prices
- Details of out-of-stock items
- Press, magazine and TV expenditure.

The report is subdivided into shop types (all grocers, co-operatives, multiples, major multiples and independents) and television regions.

Usefulness of the data
The information collected by this method is potentially extremely valuable, as it is about what is actually happening. The main advantage is that the information is 'hard' – it is not about intentions, attitudes or opinions, it is about what people actually did. As we are talking about purchasing actions, we are looking at what the customers actually parted with money for.

In the previous paragraph the word 'potentially' was used as the actual value will be greatly reduced if the panel is not representative or if the data is out-of-date.

In terms of usefulness, the two sources can be seen as complementary to each other – one acting as a check on the validity of the other's results.

Difficulties
As mentioned above, the main problems with panels centre on the extent to which they are representative of the population as a whole. It is difficult to select a suitable panel, as it must be typical of:

- all the customers in the target market
- the decision-making units who will make the purchase decision (e.g. male as well as female partners).

This is an issue of segmentation, and requires a great deal of attention when setting up a panel.

Secondary problems of consumer panels include the difficulty of access to researchers and the need for complete information and accuracy of data. The electronic approach using barcodes (mentioned earlier) is both quicker and more reliable. Other problems with consumer panels include:

- Panel members tend to become sophisticated in interviewing techniques and responses and so the panel becomes 'corrupt' (but the superpanel may overcome this to some extent by eliminating some of the 'social' element).
- It is difficult to maintain a stable personnel; the turnover of members may be high, and this will affect results as new members are enlisted.

The problems with retail panels are less marked, as there are fewer retailers and wholesalers, the linkage with the EPOS systems eliminates much of the drudgery of continual manual auditing and, once recruited, the organizations seem to be more stable than the household units of the consumer panels.

These panels are typical of secondary source material which may be relevant to a marketing specialist seeking 'off the shelf' information. Other sources stem from the 'asking questions' option for data collection, and are usually referred to under the generic title of 'Surveys'. This approach can be primary data – where the organization goes out to seek the answers to specific questions needed for its own research – or, alternatively, it can be secondary – here a research organization would undertake a survey and sell on the results to interested buyers. We will look at this approach in a little more detail.

Surveys

Most of us will have had some experience of being stopped and canvassed for our views. This usually happens when we are shopping, or in a hurry. It is typical of much UK market research as it takes place as face-to-face interviews. The interviewers are sometimes freelancers, sometimes employees of the organization seeking the information, sometimes employees of a market research organization and sometimes students trying out survey methods! Its prime characteristic lies in it being a face-to-face encounter.

Types of survey
- *Street surveys* take place typically in busy town centres, with the interviewer approaching individuals as they pass by. They need to be brief (5 minutes is too long for most people in their lunch break or going to or from work) and should not require too much concentration from the interviewees, so getting them to consider display material should be avoided. A survey taking place in a shopping centre requires the centre manager's permission, and a fee may be payable.
- *Shop surveys* take place inside or just outside a particular shop, obviously with the shop's permission.
- *Hall surveys* take place in a pre-booked location such as a hotel, where people are invited to attend to answer a few questions, usually being recruited from

the street and being enticed by a give-away or refreshments. More complex tasks can be performed by the interviewee – for instance, a display can be permanently set up and considered.

- *Home interviews* are held in the interviewee's home (or on the doorstep), with the interviewer recruiting simply by knocking on doors. They can be pre-arranged by phone or by dropping a note through the door. Larger, in-depth interviews often result, but these are time-consuming, expensive and prone to interruption. Many people are reluctant even to answer their doors, let alone let an interviewer in, so recruiting for home interviews is often frustrating for the interviewer.
- *Business surveys* take place on the interviewee's business premises and are always pre-arranged. Again, they are prone to interruption and/or last-minute cancellation.

Thus the main distinction between the different types of survey is that they take place in different locations. As has been hinted at, this may well influence the depth and detail into which it is possible to go in the encounter.

It should always be remembered that people taking part in interview surveys are doing the researcher a favour, so the least the interviewer can do is ensure that he or she is well prepared and efficient. It is vital that the questionnaire or interview schedule is clear, unambiguous and accurate.

The interviewer may have to carry out additional tasks, which can include locating respondents. It is essential that this is done properly if we are to avoid sample bias (e.g. stopping individuals in the street, calling house-to-house as instructed by the researcher), asking questions in a consistent manner and recording the responses accurately. It is essential that the selection and training of interviewers is thorough in order to minimize interviewer bias.

Alternatives to face-to-face

The two main alternatives to the above methods are *telephone* surveys and *postal* surveys.

(a) Telephone surveys

These are relatively cheap and quick to conduct. There is a standard sampling frame – the telephone directory – which can be systematically or randomly sampled. A wide geographical area can also be covered without incurring travel costs.

On the downside, we can get a biased sample as a significant proportion of the population do not have telephones. This may be more or less important depending on the range of socio-economic grouping we are seeking to sample. Other problems include:

- People may resent being called (a common reaction following pestering by telesales personnel)
- It is not possible to use 'showcards' or pictures

- It is not possible to see the interviewee's expressions and it may be harder to establish a rapport.

(b) Postal surveys

This usually includes all methods in which the questionnaire is given to the respondent and returned to the investigator without personal contact. Such questionnaires could be posted, but might also be left in pigeonholes or on desks.

Postal surveys are relatively cheap, so more people can be sampled. It is usually possible to ask more questions because the respondents can do so in their own time. As all respondents are presented with the questions in the same way there is less opportunity for bias.

On the other hand, the use of postal surveys is not without its disadvantages:

- Response rates may be low, causing significant bias
- Questionnaires may not be fully answered, causing similar problems. Low response rates can be avoided by supplying stamped addressed envelopes (raising costs), offering incentives to respondents, etc.

All of the survey methods discussed have both advantages and disadvantages, but overall the use of interview methods may have the edge on the grounds that:

- respondent suitability can be checked at the outset
- respondents can be encouraged to answer fully
- there is better control of data collection
- response rates are higher.

Survey and questionnaire design

When you are designing a questionnaire you should clarify the following points in advance:

- The target population
- The main items of information you want and what form it should be in for subsequent analysis
- Any subsidiary information which would be of interest (for example, so that you can compare the responses of men and women or old and young)
- Whether the questionnaire will be filled in by the respondent or by the interviewer. This determines how 'user-friendly' it needs to be.

Next you need to decide which type of questionnaire is appropriate:

- A *structured questionnaire* lists all questions to be asked in a logical sequence, specifying the precise wording to be used in the response and providing categories for recording the replies.
- An *unstructured questionnaire* may simply be a set of open-ended questions to which the respondent can write replies in his or her own words.

- A *self-completed questionnaire* is completed by the respondent rather than an interviewer.
- An *interviewer-completed questionnaire* or interview schedule is used in face-to-face interviews or telephone interviews.

The next step is to draft the key questions. They are never as easy to get right as you expect!

Questions

Both interviews and questionnaires operate on a question and answer format. While we all ask questions every day of our lives, it may be of use to identify some of the defining characteristics of questioning techniques.

First, the person asking the question usually controls the exchange – we are all socially conditioned to answer when someone asks a question.

Next we need to realize that the question asked – the actual words we use – may well define the type of response we get. For instance, if I ask, 'Do you smoke?' I am likely to get a much shorter response than if I ask, 'How do you come to be working in marketing?'

We can recognize three broad categories into which questions fall in terms of what they seek to find out. These are:

1 *Behavioural* questions find out what the respondent has done in the recent past, such as recent purchases of a product. In order to help recall, it is better to ask specific questions – 'have you bought X in the last fortnight?' is more likely to prompt recall than 'how often do you buy X?'
2 *Attitudinal* questions seek to measure relatively enduring likes or dislikes. We can set about this task by:
    - asking for ratings from positive to negative for a particular factor
    - instructing the respondent to pick a pre-defined statement which most nearly accords with his or her own attitude
    - asking the respondent to agree or disagree with certain statements, providing a scale to measure the degree of agreement or disagreement
    - asking the respondent to place items in order of preference.
3 *Classification* questions are a specific type of limiting question which market researchers may find particularly relevant as they seek to define the demographic characteristics of the respondent (age, gender, marital status, occupation, accommodation, etc.). This information is necessary to define the population of the survey and to analyse how far demographic characteristics 'explain' (or distort) the survey's findings.

Formulating questions

When designing a questionnaire it is useful to understand that different types of questions produce different types of information – and that there are some simple rules of thumb to help us. It is often helpful to draw a distinction between *closed, limiting* and *open* questions.

1 *Closed questions* – these are questions which demand a yes/no answer. Our example 'do you smoke?' falls into this category. We can often identify the closed question by the words we use. Look out for:

'Do you...'
'Have you...'
'Would you...'
'Can you...'
'Should you...'
'Could you...'
'Presumably you...'.

We can tick off the yes/no responses very easily while interviewing. Closed questions tend to focus on facts.

2 *Limiting questions* – these are questions which give us information, but which do not invite elaboration and expansion. We can hear ourselves using the words:

'Who...'
'Where...'
'When...'.

In such cases we get facts which can usually be recorded simply. For example, 'Who does the weekly shopping in your household?' may allow the ticking of boxes which identify the options.

3 *Open questions* – these are the ones which are likely to get us into attitudes and opinions, values and motivation. We use the words:

'What...'
'Why...'
'How...'.

Here we are likely to establish a situation where the respondent is doing most of the talking and, as a result, it can sometimes be difficult to record the responses as they can be both long and unpredictable. This type of question often gives relatively 'soft' data. They allow the respondents to 'tell it like it is' – but, unfortunately, your set of respondents may all see the world (and the product/service you are interested in) differently. So, while open-ended questions have an important part to play, they are difficult to classify, analyse and convert into useful data.

4 *Introductory questions* – these are questions which are an open invitation to the respondent to talk. You may hear yourself saying things such as:

'Tell me about...'
'What about...'.

Because of their very 'woolly' nature, such questions often yield responses which are very difficult to classify. They may well be of most use at the beginning of an encounter, when trying to establish a rapport before getting down to the real meat of the interview.

5 *Set choice questions* – in this case we have a list of possible answers from which the respondents choose. This can be a simple yes/no format, yes/don't know/no, through to rating scales, or even lists which can be checked off (e.g. 'Which of the following have you purchased in the last month?'...). The answers are pre-coded or numbered before the respondent (or interviewer) completes the questionnaire, so that the answers can be entered as numbers for analysis and summary.

Needless to say, the foregoing presents a rather simplified outline of the process, and I am sure that some readers will have spotted that question technique is a little more complex than described. For instance, 'how long have you worked here?' is actually a limiting question establishing a factual piece of information (it is really a 'when' question rather than an open 'how' question). Similarly, 'what car do you drive? is not an open 'what' question. However, thinking in terms of what you wish the question to attain will help in both questionnaire design and interview practice.

Next we need to consider each question in turn and think:

- Is it really necessary?
- Is it posed in a way that will provide the information and any subsequent analysis that you require?
- Will interviewers be able simply to read out the words, or will they need to 'ad lib', which might introduce bias?
- Is the question posed in a neutral, unbiased way, or is it a 'leading' question which inclines towards a particular answer?
- Are respondents likely to find the question too personal or offensive?
- Is it clear and unambiguous?
- Is it understandable?
- Is the question simple enough for the respondent to be able to answer fairly easily?

Try them out informally on people similar to, but not from, your target population. If respondents cannot understand or relate to the questions, it is your problem, not theirs. Rewrite the questions if necessary. After writing the questions, try to leave them for a day or two and then re-examine them.

Laying out the questionnaire
1 Explain the purpose of the survey at the beginning of the questionnaire and, where possible, guarantee confidentiality. Emphasize the date by which it must be returned.
2 If respondents have to complete the questionnaire themselves, it must be approachable and as short as possible. Consider the use of lines, boxes, different typefaces and print sizes and small pictures. Use plenty of space.
3 Start with quota control (classification) questions so that the interview can rapidly determine whether the interviewee is the right type of person.

4 Questions should be in a logical order as far as possible, but if difficult questions are necessary it may be more appropriate to put them at the end.
5 At the end of the questionnaire, thank the respondent and make it clear what he or she should do with the completed questionnaire.

ALWAYS PILOT TEST TO CHECK IT OUT BEFORE 'GOING LIVE'.

Attitude measurement

The assessment of the differences in attitude both within and between people is an important element of market research. It means that we need measurement that is both reliable and valid. As we saw in Chapter 7, reliability is to do with consistency or stability, and validity is concerned with whether we are measuring what we wish to measure (or, indeed, what we think we are measuring). There are a number of approaches to the measurement of attitudes – we will consider some of the more relevant ones.

Likert scales

One of the most popular measurement techniques is that credited to Professor Rensis Likert (1932). It is relatively straightforward to understand and is in common usage. A statement is made and the respondents indicate the degree to which they agree/disagree with it. For example, we might use the statement:

'*I enjoy studying Understanding Customers*' (see Figure 8.1).
   The subjects are asked which of the five ratings they agree with. The numerical value indicates the weight attached to the response. In this case the respondents choose their own degree of agreement with the statement.

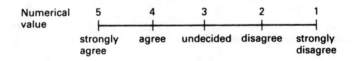

Figure 8.1

   The total score of the subject is the sum of the values given to all the statements on the issue under consideration.
   This is generally seen as being simple to construct and it also appears likely to be reliable. It has high face validity in that it deals directly with the individual's response to the statement made. One potential problem, however, is that this approach can provide an attitude score which can be arrived at by strikingly different patterns of response.

Semantic differential

This approach is associated with C. E. Osgood and was originally put forward in 1957 in a book jointly written with G. J. Suci and P. H. Tannenbaum. In its original form, the authors were investigating the nature of meaning, but it has become widely used in the measurement of attitudes.

Osgood argues that, as the basic function of ordinary language is the communication of meaning, ordinary language can be used to discriminate and differentiate between concepts and also to measure their meaning.

The respondent is given a number of bipolar adjectives, each with a seven-point scale inserted between the opposites, so that the given topics, objects or issues can be assessed on each scale. This allows the respondent to indicate both the direction and intensity of each judgement.

Osgood and his fellow workers, in a large number of studies involving both different scales and different concepts, used the technique of factor analysis and identified three basic dimensions underlying semantic differential ratings. The dimensions are:

- evaluation
- potency
- activity.

The evaluative dimension is characterized by scales such as:

good – bad,
clean – dirty,
beautiful – ugly

the potency element by scales such as:

large – small
strong – weak
thick – thin

and the activity factor by scales such as:

fast – slow
active – passive
hot – cold.

So a semantic differential questionnaire might look like Figure 8.2.

The emergence of three dimensions is convenient in that it allows us to imagine the attitude mapped into a three-dimensional space – so most people find the concept of attitude difference or shift relatively straightforward to visualize. This aids the description of difference or change, so a person's attitude regarding a product may have shifted to see the product as being, for example, more potent, less active, but much better.

This is an interesting approach which has some useful factors. The theory suggests that there are three main dimensions – evaluation, potency and activity. This may provide useful information for the marketer in determining the focus of marketing messages aiming to either reinforce or change attitudes. The notion of three dimensions is a happy one, as it allows us to imagine an attitude being defined in three-dimensional space, which also allows a visual representation for attitude change.

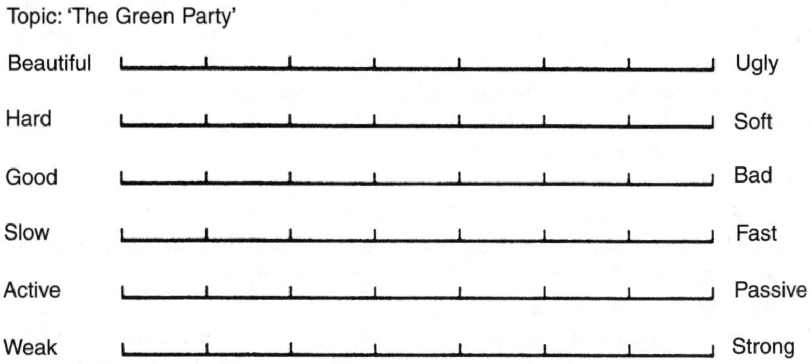

Topic: 'The Green Party'

Beautiful		Ugly
Hard		Soft
Good		Bad
Slow		Fast
Active		Passive
Weak		Strong

Figure 8.2

Repertory Grid

The Repertory grid technique can be used to compare attitudes towards products or brands. A representative sample of respondents are interviewed to establish the key dimensions (constructs) of the ways in which they perceive the brands or products. We can then take (say) the eight most popular constructs to emerge, and form a grid which is applied to the respondent group in which we are interested.

Analysis is then possible in terms of the 'distances' between constructs (useful for designing the marketing message) and the 'distances' between the elements (in this case, competing products), so it can be used to identify competitors.

Perhaps more importantly, we can begin to focus our marketing message on different groups or clusters which we may have identified, emphasizing the 'positive' points as elicited by the grid. Alternatively, we could attempt to design attitude change strategies in order to make our brand more attractive to the other groups of respondents who do not perceive our product positively.

Motivation research

As early as 1924, Copeland introduced a framework for marketing decisions that drew a distinction between rational and emotional motives. Notions of value for money, efficiency and utility would fall into the former category. However, it is now widely accepted that products have symbolic values that go way beyond these rational factors. Engel, Blackwell and Miniard use this format when discussing motivation to buy, but use the terminology of 'Utilitarian' (objective product attributes) and 'Hedonic' (subjective/emotional benefits).

Motivation research is the area of marketing research activity that seeks to find the underlying 'why?' of our behaviour and, in particular, 'why' we purchase one product in preference to another. It focuses very strongly on the hedonistic benefits encompassing emotional responses, sensory pleasures and other aesthetic considerations. If we can identify common perceptions and motivations associated with our product, we can use the information, emotions and symbols to promote it further.

Motivation research seeks to identify the attitudes, beliefs, motives and other pressures that affect our purchasing decisions. In marketing terms, it came of age in the 1950s, when researchers such as Ernest Dichter used Freudian psychoanalytical ideas to explain behaviour on the basis of unconscious motivation. Statements such as 'Women bake cakes because of an unconscious desire to give birth' gave rise to Pillsbury's slogan, 'Nothing says lovin' like something from the oven'. In other words, motivational research concentrates very much on the emotional and symbolic values of products.

Packard produced his classic and best-selling *The Hidden Persuaders* in 1957 and in that book reports the problems of the Ronson lighter company in determining its advertising strategy. Motivational research suggested that the key characteristic of the product was the flame, which was seen as having phallic symbolism. Eventually the company advertised without showing a lighter at all – only the flame and the logo 'Ronson'. Sales rocketed! Similarly, the Mary Baker cake mix had poor response in the marketplace despite being a product that seemed destined for success. Perfect cakes, and all you had to do was add water. Motivation research suggested that some women felt that it had made the process of cooking too easy! As a result, the company modified the mix so that the cook had to add an egg and beat the mixture. The claim was that this would enable the 'mothers' to fulfil their roles concerning a need to be actively involved in making a contribution to caring for their families. Again, sales rose dramatically.

Motivation research methods

There are a number of techniques associated with motivation research and, as mentioned above, they come primarily from the field of clinical psychology.

(a) Depth interview

This is normally a one-to-one interview which is relatively unstructured. The pattern is commonly to explore the 'why?' questions in depth. Attempts are made to get the subject to talk about the product rather than answer predetermined questions. The aim is to probe below the surface to uncover and expose the underlying motivational influences. Commonly the interview starts at a relatively broad and shallow level, but becomes more detailed and focused on the key topics as it progresses. This is sometimes done by coming back to 'why?' Those readers who have been questioned by small children using this technique will know how quickly it is possible to reach a position where you really have to think about the answer!

This approach offers a one-to-one framework to explore the issues. It is more flexible and unstructured than the questionnaire format, and involves sensitive prompting and probing by the interviewer/researcher.

As with any research, it is crucial that the subject (respondent) is representative of the population towards which the research is directed – he or she should be involved in the decision-making process, whether as an individual or as an organizational customer. Respondents should be given due warning and agree to be asked relevant (and sometimes personal) questions. They may need to give approval to the recording system being used – most people are happy for the interviewer to take notes, but may be less willing for tape or video recording to be used.

Depth interviews will vary in length according to the topic being investigated. If we are researching reactions to a new packaging design, we may be able to get all the information we require in 10–15 minutes. If, on the other hand, we are investigating the emotional meaning of food to an individual, we may need hours!

Being an interactive encounter, it is very flexible and can be as structured as the interviewer wishes. However, if we are to make the most of the meeting it is likely that the emphasis will be on unstructured, open-ended, probing questions.

(b) Group discussion or focus group

The aim of such a group (usually numbering no more than ten persons) is the same as the in-depth interview, but here the respondents are invited to discuss their motivations in a relaxed, informal setting. There is usually a skilled group leader to guide the discussion in such a way as to ensure that the relevant issues are aired, but without pre-empting or determining the outcomes. Most of the communication should be between the group members – the moderator should introduce the topic, get discussion going, keep the group focused if it wanders, and wrap up the discussion at the end.

The moderator's role should not involve too much questioning of individual group members. On the other hand, the moderator is the person who will recognizse if a significant point has been made in the discussion and who may choose to emphasize it and ask others' opinions. Another part of the role is that of summarizer. The belief is that such a setting provides an opportunity for people to interact and to allow the thoughts of one person to stimulate others. The theory is that people will talk more freely in such a setting and the process will yield much richer information than is possible from more structured and sterile questionnaire techniques.

Clearly there are some subjects that respondents may find too personal or embarrassing to discuss or admit among a group of strangers, so group methods are not universally applied. The role of the discussion leader (or interviewer) is also crucial, and one which requires a very high level of skill. Groups may have the additional weakness of being 'hijacked' by a strong personality or of the discovery of an 'opinion leader' within the group (see Chapter 13).

The development of tape and video techniques for recording group processes has given the researcher a useful tool to help overcome bias in the observer, allowing a group session to be replayed to a panel of specialists who can compare and agree ratings. Many practitioners feel that discussion groups can bring out more than one-to-one encounters, as participants may generate ideas better with other people to 'bounce things off' than if they are operating solo.

Both approaches have advantages and potential drawbacks. These may be summarized as follows:

Group discussions	*Depth interview*

Advantages

● Less intimidating	● Decision-making processes
● Easily observed	can be analysed
● Range of attitudes can	● Majority and minority
be measured	opinions can be captured
● Social aspect reflects	● Sensitive topics more
the real world	easily discussed
● Dynamic and creative	● 'Unusual' behaviour can
● Cheaper	be openly discussed

Disadvantages

● Participants may not	● Time-consuming
express what they really	● Less creative
think – they may be	● More expensive
inhibited or they may be	
showing off	
● Views may be unrealistic	
– meaningful in a group	
context but not for the	
individual	
● Undue influence of one	
'strong character'	

The final choice of method will depend not only on the relative importance of the various factors summarized above, but also on the nature of the product or topic being researched. For instance, group discussion of sensitive industrial products would be very difficult to arrange and potentially undesirable if it meant revealing the state of a development to the very people who could (and probably would) inform competitors.

(c) Projective techniques

There are a number of these methods which come primarily from clinical psychology, where they are used to examine aspects of personality and perception. In the marketing sphere it is possible to alter the focus of the process slightly to encompass the product we are considering.

- *Thematic Apperception Test (TAT)* – here the respondent is shown a picture, drawing or photograph which is suitably ambiguous and which could be interpreted in a number of ways. He or she is then asked questions such as, 'What story does the picture tell?', 'What led up to the events in the picture?', 'What is happening?', 'How are things going to work out?', etc. Many respondents identify with the characters in the pictures and reveal feelings, motives, emotions and desires associated with the situation shown. It is thought that, by putting things into the third person and telling stories about imaginary people, it may allow them to reveal things that they would be unwilling to admit to themselves (or of which they may be genuinely unaware).

  A similar technique involves respondents in filling in 'balloons' or captions on a cartoon. This again allows the subject to express perhaps deep feelings but in the third person, without having to 'own up' to them.

- *Word Association Tests* – this involves the researcher presenting a word to the subject, who has to respond with the first word which enters his or her head. Many of the stimulus words used are neutral 'dummies', but interspersed with these are a number of 'test' words – the reaction to which we are particularly interested in. The responses to these test words may give us insights into the perceptions and feelings that the respondent has towards the product concerned. However, there is a significant problem in such approaches that concerns the assumption that words have the same meanings (both in facts and emotions) to all respondents.

- *Rorschach Test* – this consists of a random inkblot which is presented to the subject, who is then asked what it represents to him or her. As the pattern is random, it is suggested that any perceptions must be from the respondent's subconscious, and hence analysis of responses may give insights into personality and perceptions. However, while this test is a staple of the psychiatrist, it does seem to have limited use in the field of marketing due to the difficulty of introducing specific products or product types into the process to analyse.

- *Psychodrama* – in this technique respondents are asked to improvize mini-plays about situations, products, etc. Again, the assumption is that, in getting people to act out (for example) a painkiller dealing with a headache, the researchers can gain valuable information about the way the process is seen. In our example the painkiller could be viewed as 'fighting off' the evil pain or, alternatively, comforting the sufferer.

Think – Can you identify analgesics using these different perceptions and marketing messages?

Some researchers are using a development of this approach by inviting subjects to relax and make clay models which represent the product, service or organization. They claim that analysis of the outcomes sheds light on the respondent's inner feelings.

Motivation research is big business. Advertisers seek the maximum return from their investment, so considerable effort is put into discovering the underlying motives of consumers. But it is not without its problems. If we go back to the previous chapter on the scientific method, we can see that the approaches described suffer from significant flaws.

First, we have difficulty with the process of interpretation of evidence. In all the techniques the researcher's interpretation is crucial – but, more importantly, the interpretation is rarely standardized. Thus we are open to researcher bias.

We also have difficulties with both internal and external validity. Internal validity is at risk due to the inadequacy of the experimental method and the subjectivity of the interpretation. To this day there is a lack of convincing proof of many psychiatric assumptions. That they work in many instances is not denied, but this may be as a result of the processes involved rather than the truth of the underlying assumptions. Similarly, external validity is suspect if the number of respondents is not large (and commonly it is not, due to the costs involved in one-to-one testing) as we are then faced with the problem of how typical respondents are of the population at large. We may have a difficulty in as much as it could be hypothesized that people who willingly subject themselves to this kind of exposure might not be 'normal'!!

Summary

Qualitative research is about understanding consumer behaviour. It is concerned with perceptions, feelings, attitudes, opinions, etc. In other words, it focuses on the emotional aspects of products, services and the decision-making process. Because of this emphasis, the majority of qualitative research tends to be carried out by talking to people, asking the open-ended 'why' questions to try to get to the real values underlying what may be a relatively superficial 'I do not like that!' reaction. Thus the form is primarily narrative and descriptive, and the main methods are depth interview and group discussion.

Sampling

In many situations in which we find ourselves we will need information, and the population that we need to get the information from will be too large for us to ask everybody. An example with which we are all familiar is the opinion poll. Newspapers and television companies regularly want to produce pieces which will tell us how we will vote in an election (either real or imaginary). This is a typical situation when the population is too large to carry out a complete survey and only a sample will be examined. It is not possible to ask everyone of voting age how they are going to vote: it would take too long and cost too much (the same as the General Election we are investigating!). So a sample of voters is taken, and the results from the sample are used to estimate the voting intentions of the whole population. Similarly, we will come across research which purports to tell us what the nation thinks of the Royal Family at a given point in time – but I have never met anybody who has been asked!

Some definitions

Census – Occasionally a population is small enough for *all* of it to be examined – for example, the attitudes of the class of students who are taking the 'Understanding Customers' course. When all of the population is examined, the survey is called a census.

Sampling – This is the selection of groups and individuals who will be used to represent the total population. It may appear that using a sample is something of a compromise, but you should consider the following points:

- It can be shown mathematically that, once a certain sample size has been reached, very little extra accuracy is gained by examining more items.
- A census may require the use of semi-skilled investigators, resulting in a loss of accuracy in the data collected.
- In practice, a 100 per cent survey (a census) never achieves the completeness required.
- It is possible to ask more questions with a sample.
- The cost of a census may be very high and may not be worth it in terms of the extra information generated.
- Things are always changing. Even if you go to the expense of a census, the information gathered could well be out-of-date by the time you have completed it.

One crucial requirement of sample data is that it should be *complete* – that is, the data should cover all areas of the population to be examined. If this requirement is not met, then the sample will be *biased*.

For example, suppose you wanted to survey the attendance of students at a college, so you went along every Monday and Tuesday for a few months to see who was there. Would this give us a complete set of data? The answer is no. We might have gathered very thorough data on what happens on Mondays and Tuesdays, but you would have missed out the rest of the week. It could be that the students, keen and fresh after the weekend, attend more at the start of the week than at the end. Alternatively, they may be in college much less, as many are recovering from weekends of excess! In either case, the data will give a misleading attendance figure. Careful attention must therefore be given to the sampling method employed to produce a sample.

Random sampling

To ensure that the sample selected is free from bias, random sampling must be used. Inferences about the population being sampled can then be made validly. A *simple* random sample is a sample selected in such a way that every item in the population has an equal chance of being included.

If we continue our earlier example, we might choose to interview a random selection of students present in the college, to investigate in more depth their attendance patterns. This would be flawed, as we would not be interviewing the absentees – the very people we are most interested in! The only way would be to select our respondents randomly from the whole student population.

If random sampling is used, then it is necessary to construct a *sampling frame*. A sampling frame is simply a numbered list of all the items in the population. Once such a list has been made, it is easy to select a random sample simply by generating a list of random numbers.

For instance, if you wanted to select a random sample of students, start with the enrolment list and number each person registered.

Using these numbers, we can select our sample using random number tables.

A sampling frame should have the following characteristics:

- *Completeness*. Are all members of the population included in the list?
- *Accuracy*. Is the information correct?
- *Adequacy*. Does it cover the entire population?
- *Up-to-date*. Is the list up-to-date?
- *Convenience*. Is the sampling frame readily accessible?
- *Non-duplication*. Does each member of the population appear on the list only once?

Two readily available sampling frames for the human population of Great Britain are the *community charge register* (list of dwellings) and the *electoral register* (list of individuals).

Examples of different sampling approaches

(a) To determine attitudes towards the canteen provision in a small organization employing 53 people
Here the population is small enough to contemplate a census. Conducting 53 interviews would probably be too expensive for the likely outcome, so it would seem sensible to go for a 100 per cent sample (if that is not a contradiction in terms) with a questionnaire.

(b) To determine attitudes towards the Royal Family in a town of 35 000 people
Here the need for a sample is clear. The electoral register would make a good, relevant sampling frame, and the required number of persons from that total population could be chosen by the use of random number tables. It would probably be sensible to back this up with interviews to ascertain attitudes.

Think – How would you go about determining
a) the level of support for a 'neighbourhood watch' scheme?
b) the attitudes of the population of the UK towards abortion?
c) the potential market for a small motor to assist cyclists?
d) the views of the population of a small town as to the desirability of a bypass?

In each case think of the sample you would utilize, the form of data collection and the types of question that might be employed.

Experiments as a form of marketing research

Think – You have been asked to evaluate the effectiveness of two alternative pilot advertising campaigns so that an enlightened choice can be made as to which is the most appropriate to be rolled out nationally.
– How would you tackle this assignment?

Projects such as this are not uncommon in the marketing field. Inevitably marketing departments are having to make choices between alternatives (packaging, prices, products, promotions, etc.).

To produce a professional and supportable answer to the question we will have to design an experiment.

Think back to the discussions in the previous chapter. We would need measures of consumer recognition, attitudes, purchasing patterns, market share, etc. before and after any trial. We would need to identify two comparable areas in which to run the two competing campaigns. We would then be in a position to compare the impact of the campaigns, both in their own area and in comparison with one another – thus enabling a sound judgement to be made.

9 'What do you mean – I'm about average...?'

The presentation and interpretation of data

One more time – the difference between data and information

We have already discussed the expressions 'data' and 'information'. The two terms are commonly used interchangeably, but from a technical viewpoint they are different.

Consider the numbers 4057, 4091, 4064, 3994, 4051. They are data. If these figures (data) are set in context, it may be revealed that they represent the closing values of the FTSE Index on five trading days of the week. Thus we can inform people that 'the stock market had a variable week – it fell sharply on Thursday and broke the psychologically important "4000 barrier". However it rallied strongly on Friday, to end the week down only six points'. This is information!

Information is what marketing research is all about. It is what we seek to understand the marketing world in which we operate. *Data* is what we collect, analyse and interpret in order to get information.

So we can define data as 'things known or assumed as the basis for inference or reckoning'. It is common in the marketing situation for this data to be expressed in numbers. In contrast, we define information as 'knowledge or news', and we observed that the expression information is commonly used to refer to data which has been processed into a form which is meaningful to the recipient and which is of real or perceived value for the intended purpose. To reiterate, we said that data is the raw material from which information is produced.

We have also referred to both qualitative and quantitative data, and we observed that we may express the 'soft' data of qualitative measures, such as attitude measures, using numbers.

So this chapter is about handling numbers, analysing data and creating information and presenting it so that it may be of use to us in our work as marketers.

We will start by looking at ways in which we present data.

Presentation of data

Tabulation

Data often makes more sense if we set it out in a table. This is a process which is called *tabulation*. To create a table we put the data into a matrix of columns and rows and, in order to make things clear to our readers, we will need to label the columns and rows clearly and also give the whole thing a title.

A table is two-dimensional, and so we need to be very clear about what the two variables we are showing represent.

A very simple table might be:

Year	Sales of product X
1995	56
1996	60

Table showing sales of product X in years 1995 and 1996

In this case the two variables displayed are the year and the sales figures for the specified product. We can, of course, create more complex tabulations which would give more detail, such as:

Year	Quarter 1	Quarter 2	Quarter 3	Quarter 4
1995	12	10	16	18
1996	12	11	17	20

Table of quarterly sales of product X in years 1995 and 1996

In turn, this could be broken down and summarized still further:

Year	Quarter 1 Sales	%	Quarter 2 Sales	%	Quarter 3 Sales	%	Quarter 4 Sales	%	Total
1995	12	21	10	18	16	29	18	32	56
1996	12	20	11	18	17	28	20	33	60

Table of quarterly sales of product X in years 1995 and 1996

In summary, tables are a useful way of displaying data. Tables should have: clear labels for both columns and rows

- a clear and helpful title
- sub-totals, where appropriate

- a total column, where appropriate (usually the right-hand column)
- totals may be included for each of the columns, where appropriate
- a clear uncluttered layout.

Many people are terrified of statistics. This is often because they do not have an understanding of mathematical processes. They often convert this fear into an attack on statistics via the well-known saying, 'There are lies, damned lies, and statistics'. One important way of making the process of data presentation simpler is to tackle it visually – by means of graphs, charts and diagrams.

Graphs

These are representations of two variables which interact. One example might be sales per quarter, such as we have in the previous example. You may remember that we got as far as a tabular representation, as follows:

	Quarter 1		Quarter 2		Quarter 3		Quarter 4		
Year	Sales	%	Sales	%	Sales	%	Sales	%	Total
1995	12	21	10	18	16	29	18	32	56
1996	12	20	11	18	17	28	20	33	60

Table of quarterly sales of product X in years 1995 and 1996

Here we have two variables: the quarters and the sales. These can be displayed in graphical form by making the time element the x-axis (horizontal) and the sales the y-axis (vertical). It is usual to call the measure expressed on the x-axis the *independent variable* and that which is shown on the y-axis the *dependent, variable*. Setting things up in this way we obtain our graph, as shown in Figure 9.1.

Graphs need to have the axes clearly marked and scales given so that the data can be recognized easily and quickly.

Charts

The purpose of a chart is to convey the data in a way that will demonstrate its meaning or significance more clearly than a table of data would. Charts are not always more appropriate than tables, and the most suitable way of presenting data will depend on:

- what the data is intended to show. Visual displays usually make one or two points quite forcefully, whereas tables usually give more detailed information
- who is going to use the data. Some individuals might understand visual displays more readily than tabulated data.

There are three types of chart that might be used to present data.

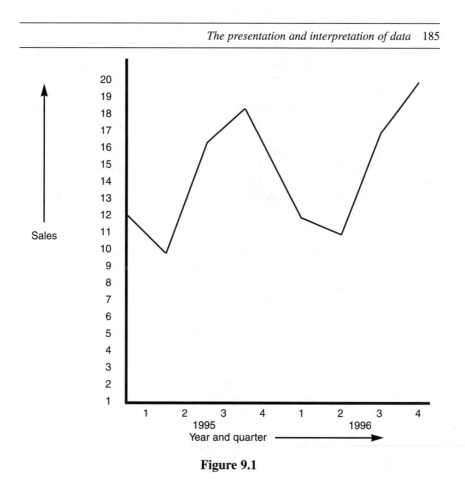

Figure 9.1

Pictograms
A pictogram is a statistical diagram in which quantities are represented by
pictures or symbols (Figure 9.2). Thus a pictogram showing the number of

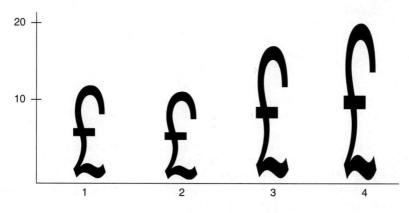

Figure 9.2   Quarterly sales 1996

customers visiting a supermarket might represent the quantities using pictures of people. Depending on the numbers involved, each figure might represent 10 (or 100) customers. To make a good pictogram, the symbols should be clear and simple; the quantity that each symbol represents should be clearly shown in a key to the pictogram; care should be taken to ensure that bigger quantities are shown by more symbols, not by bigger symbols.

The advantage of pictograms is that they present data in a simple, readily understood way. Pictograms convey their message to the reader at a glance, and are consequently often used on television and in advertisements. However, they can only convey a limited amount of information, and they lack precision.

Pie Charts

A pie chart is used to show pictorially the relative sizes of component elements of a total (Figure 9.3). It is called a pie chart because it is circular, and so has the shape of a pie in a round pie dish, and because the 'pie' is then cut into slices. Each slice represents a part of the total.

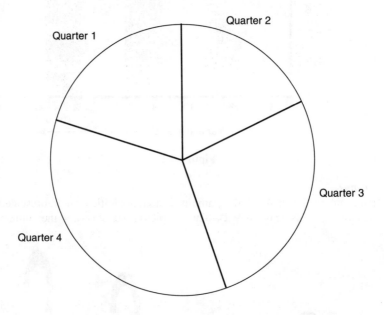

Figure 9.3   Quarterly sales 1996

The advantages of pie charts are that they give a simple pictorial display of the relative sizes of elements of a total and they show clearly when one element is much bigger than others. On the other hand, they show only the relative sizes of elements. Also, they involve calculating degrees of a circle and drawing sectors accurately, and this can be time-consuming.

Bar charts

This is a chart in which quantities are shown in the form of bars (Figure 9.4). They can be *simple, component* or *multiple* (or compound) bar charts. In a bar chart the length of each bar indicates the magnitude of the corresponding data item.

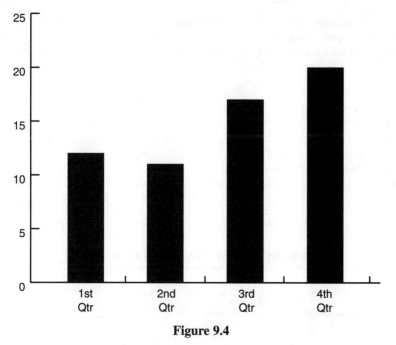

Figure 9.4

Bar charts give another simple pictorial display of the data – a compound bar chart can give additional information concerning the make-up of the overall figure – but changes in the make-up are not always so easy to compare.

Making sense of data

Note: There is no need for students of the CIM programme to be overly worried about statistics, as the Chief Examiner has assured us that there will be no calculations in any of the examinations. However, in order to explain some of the tricks of presenting data we will use a simple data set – *purely as an example – DON'T PANIC!*

Here is the data:

10, 8, 20, 8, 14

At first sight this data is relatively meaningless – until we know more, it is very hard to make any sense (create information) from it. The first thing we need to know is what this data represents – on their own the numbers are relatively meaningless. A crucial piece of information is to know what units are represented by the numbers and the context in which they exist. For instance, they could represent the ages of children in a family, the number of items bought by five people chosen at random at a supermarket checkout, the amount of coins in five people's pockets.

We will assume that they represent the number of calls on customers made by five sales reps last week.

We could set the data out in a column:

10
8
20
8
14

but that does not help us very much.

We could set it out linking the number of calls with each of the sales reps, as shown:

Table A

Sales rep	Number of calls last week
A	10
B	8
C	20
D	8
E	14

This has made the data a little more tidy, and it has increased our understanding a little – we now know who was making what number of calls.

A significant problem is that the data is not arranged in any coherent way – this is often the case when responses are recorded in some relatively arbitrary way such as alphabetical order. It might help us if we were to arrange the data in ascending or descending order of number of calls made, as in Table B:

Table B

Sales Rep	Number of calls last week
B	8
D	8
A	10
E	14
C	20

In this case we get easier confirmation of the range of the calls made – we do not need to search for the highest and lowest figures, as they are clearly identifiable at the top and bottom of the array.

Sometimes we find it useful to organize the data into groups. In this instance we might group the number of calls as follows:

No. calls	No. reps
0–9	2
10–19	2
20+	1

This could also be displayed as a simple bar chart if we thought it worthwhile. (Note that when we draw a bar chart for grouped data it is called a *histogram*.)

It is also possible that we might sometimes find it useful to express information in *percentage* terms. This can be particularly helpful if we wish to compare data. Establishing percentages is one way of taking care of the problems which arise when samples or sets of data are of unequal size.

Another way of looking at the data we have (called a *data set*) is to consider the *average* value of the data given. These are ways of finding the middle or typical value of the data set and are sometimes called *measures of location*. There are three main measures of location which are based on different ways of looking at the notion of 'the average'.

The first, and most commonly used, is called the *mean*. This is the one you most probably remember from school and the one that most people think of when they speak of the average of a set of data.

The *mean* is the sum of all the items in a data set divided by the number of items.

If we ascribe symbols to the items in the set – $x1, x2, x3,....xn$ we can express the mean by the equation:

$$mean = \frac{x1 + x2 + x3 + ... + xn}{n}$$

So if we go back to the data set we have been using – the sales reps call rate – we can calculate the mean by first of all adding up all the numbers of calls made:

$$10 + 8 + 20 + 8 + 14 = 60.$$

If we now divide that figure by the number of sales reps (5) we find that the mean number of calls made last week is 60/5 = 12.

So we can say that the mean number of calls made by our sales force last week was 12 calls per rep.

Another useful measure of location, and probably the second most used after the mean, is the *median*. If we arrange the data in an array of either ascending or descending order (as we did in Table B above), the median is the value which falls in the middle of the array. If we have an odd number of items in the array, then the median will be the middle number. However, if we have an even number of items, we calulate the median by taking the mean of the two middle numbers.

If we look back at Table B, we see that the middle value is 10.

So, the *median* value of the sales call rate is 10 calls.

The third, and final, measure of location to examine is called the *mode*. This, very simply, is the value which occurs most frequently in the data set. Thus it can be obtained fairly easily if we have constructed a frequency distribution.

If we look back at Table B, we can see that the most frequent call rate was 8. So this is the mode.

So, to recap, we have looked at some figures, established what they represent, identified the units that apply and looked at three different averages – the mean, the median and the mode.

In the example we worked through we obtained three different values:

The mean was 12 calls in the week
The median was 10 calls in the week
The mode was 8 calls in the week.

Think – Each of these measures can be called 'an average'. Which would you use if you were:

a) a sales manager wishing to tell the sales force that they are not working hard enough?
b) the sales reps trying to make the point that they are not idle?
c) a manager wanting the information to determine whether an extra member of staff can be justified?

So, in summary, the *mean* is the sum of the values of items divided by the number of items.

Advantages
- The most popular and best known
- Every value in the set contributes to its calculation
- It is useful for statistical analysis.

Disadvantages
- May not coincide with any value in the set
- Can be distorted by very high/low values.

The *median* is the value of the middle number of the set of figures when they are arranged in order of size.

Advantages
- Useful when we need to know what the middle item is
- Useful for identifying changes over time
- Unaffected by very high/low values.

Disadvantages
● Does not use all of the data
● Less useful for statistical analysis.

The *mode* is the most frequently occurring value.

Advantages
● Uses the most popular value, therefore very useful in some circumstances, e.g. when we want to know what is most popular
● Not influenced by 'untypical' values
● It can be used for non-numerical data.

Disadvantages
● It ignores dispersion entirely
● It does not take all values into account
● We can have more than one mode.

Hazards of presentation and interpretation

In addition to misleading by an inappropriate average there are some potential problems when displaying data – statistics can be misleading. Below are some things to look out for when looking at statistics (or presenting them). This may also be a useful checklist for 'mistakes to avoid' if you wish to communicate accurately and effectively.

Decimals and spurious accuracy

Imagine that you ask some of your friends how long they slept last night. You get the following answers:

Six hours
Eight hours
Seven and a half hours
About six and three-quarter hours
About seven hours
Seven hours
Seven and a quarter hours.

You wish to calculate the *mean sleeping time* so you do the sum:

$6 + 8 + 7.5 + 6.75 + 7 + 7 + 7.25 = 49.5/7 = 7.0714285$ hours!!

The decimal points make it look very precise and accurate, but all we were doing was averaging a series of guesses which at best were only accurate to a quarter of an hour. So giving the result to seven decimal points gives a totally spurious illusion of accuracy (the 'real' answer should have been 'about seven hours').

Gee whiz graphs

Here we present the graphs with one of three flaws. We can alter the length of the x-axis, which can give a false impression of the rate of increase or decrease (Figure 9.5). Alternatively, we can create the same effect by starting the y-axis at something other than zero (Figure 9.6). Or we can even present the graph without any scales (usually on the y-axis, but sometimes on both), as shown in Figure 9.7.

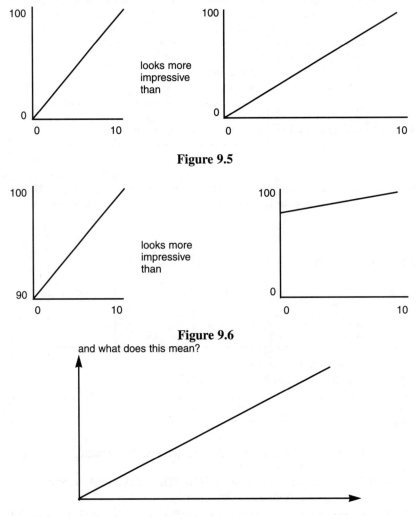

Figure 9.5

Figure 9.6

Figure 9.7

Example – You may think that no-one would really do this in the real world – but here is a recent example found on the packaging of a new yoghurt type product which made some interesting claims:

'Gaio can actively reduce cholesterol levels'

Clinical research in Denmark has proved this. For a six-week period a group of fifty-eight people aged 44 years old ate 200 ml of Gaio as part of their daily diet. During the research period, everything else they ate and the amount of exercise they took remained unchanged. Scientists from Aarhus University Hospital monitored their LDL cholesterol levels throughout the trial and found that these had been reduced by 10 per cent.

So far so good – but the real clincher comes with the accompanying graph (Figure 9.8):

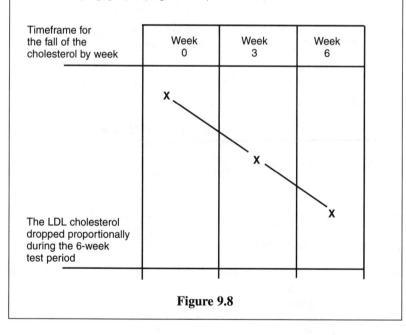

Timeframe for the fall of the cholesterol by week	Week 0	Week 3	Week 6

The LDL cholesterol dropped proportionally during the 6-week test period

Figure 9.8

Exercise – Look out for these kinds of presentational errors in advertisements, news programmes, political statements, etc.
Collect the examples, as they may prove useful examination fodder.

Misleading claims

This is the famous 'nine out of ten cats prefer Pussikins'. This looks powerful, until we ask what is the basis for this claim.

How many cats took part in the trial?
How was 'prefer' measured?
How many 'tens' were used before they found one with nine preferring Pussikins?
Were the cats chosen for their liking of Pussikins?
etc.

Similarly, you may be able to see the flaw in the research report which said that a questionnaire survey found that 93.42 per cent of respondents enjoyed filling in questionnaires!

Misleading averages

The average number of children in UK families is 2.4.
This looks fine until we realize that *no family in the land has that number of children*!!!

Not letting on which average you are using

Dwellings in a particular road vary, from large Victorian houses split into flats, through smaller Victorian villas (semi-detached), to modern bungalows. Valuation of the properties gives a lot of numbers at the low end (the flats), several in the middle range, and a few very expensive ones. Using the mean, median or mode may give significantly different answers – but if we just say, 'the average price of property in the road is £X', we can make whatever point we like!

Pictograms (especially three-dimensional images)

Using pictograms is a dramatic way of making your point. They can be very useful – but they can mislead.

If we wish to represent the doubling of sales of breakfast cereals, it is very naughty to represent this by drawing two cornflake boxes, the second one twice as big in all dimensions as the first – the image is of an eightfold growth. It is slightly less misleading if we use a two-dimensional image – because it only looks four times as much!

Over-confident claims

Surveys of 1000 individuals assessing their strength of will and size of chin came up with the following matrix (Figure 9.9).

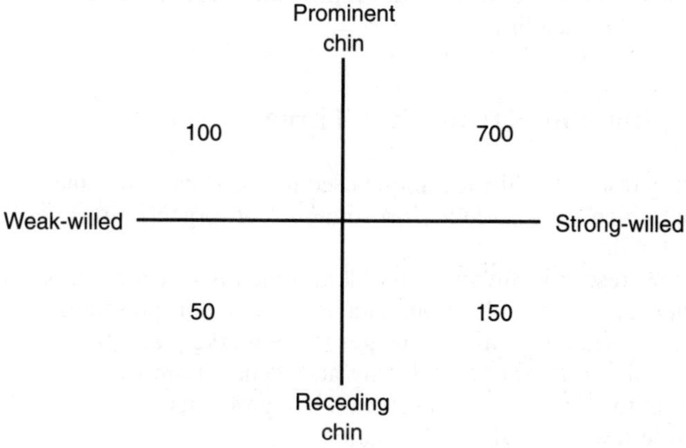

Figure 9.9

This could result in dodgy conclusions, mainly due to sloppy use of English, e.g. 'This shows that people with prominent chins are strong-willed' – the dubious word being 'are'.

Shaded maps

Take any figure you are interested in – unemployment, sales of Sudso.... Plot the figures on the map and shade in the areas where the phenomenon is high/low. This is commonly misleading because if (say) unemployment were low in (say) East Anglia and high in Birmingham, the map would show a large area identified as 'low' and a small area as 'high'. The reality could be that, due to the huge difference in density of population, the large area represented a very much smaller number of unemployed people than the small area representing Birmingham.

Presenting research findings

This is not the place to give detailed checklists for report writing, as most people studying *Understanding Customers* will also be taking a separate course on communications.

Suffice it to say that an effective report:

- gives a clear indication of its purpose and terms of reference
- summarizes the main findings in an executive summary
- has a clear structure, including an introduction, methodology, results, findings, conclusions, recommendations, action taken, appendices, acknowledgements, references, etc. as appropriate

- the presentation of the data should follow the rules set out in this chapter and should avoid misleading the reader.

Key learning points from Part Three

- Marketing research is the technique used to investigate customers. It is a broad concept which can include investigation of organizations, economies or psychographics
- Marketing research involves problem diagnosis, clarification of options, research design, data collection, data analysis, report presentation
- Marketing research identifies changes in the marketplace, builds up a database of information relevant to marketing and, hence, improves market awareness. It can help to make plans and solve ad hoc problems
- Data is the raw material of information
- Qualitative data comes from narrative and commentary
- Quantitative data is numbers
- Secondary research stems from desk research
- Environmental scanning is a process of establishing market intelligence
- There are numerous governmental and non-governmental sources of secondary data
- Data can be bought in from marketing research organizations
- Secondary data may be suspect due to factors such as different reasons for gathering the data, time lag, etc.
- Experiments investigate the effect on dependent variables of changes in the independent variables
- Experiments need to have internal validity (measuring what they purport to via control groups, pre- and post-measures, etc.) and also external validity (able to generalize the results)
- Experiments can be 'laboratory' (artificial) or 'field' (real world)
- Questions may be closed, limiting or open
- Questions can be attitudinal, behavioural or classificational
- Questionnaires can be structured, unstructured, self-completed, interviewer-completed
- Qualitative research involves depth interviews and focus groups
- Samples are regularly used for collecting data – they may be random, quasi-random (systematic, stratified and multi-stage) or non-random (quota and cluster sampling)
- Data can be analysed using averages – mean, median and mode
- Data can be presented in tables, graphs, pictograms, pie charts, bar charts, histograms
- Histograms are used to display grouped data
- Research reports should follow normal good report writing principles:

  clear purpose
  well organized material
  well structured
  well presented.

Part Four   Predicting and Influencing Customer Behaviour

Introduction

This section brings together many of the ideas explored earlier in the book. At this stage we are hoping to move beyond the description and explanation stages of the behavioural sciences and move into the predicting and controlling phases as described in the previous section. Inevitably life is rarely so simple, and a variety of approaches to predicting and forecasting will be looked at. At the end of this section the reader should be familiar with and able to use, in a marketing setting, ideas such as:

- The consumer modelling approach
- Types of models
- Evaluation of models
- Black box, personal variable, decision process, comprehensive or 'grand' models
- Innovation
- Diffusion process
- Adoption process
- Opinion leaders
- Adopter categories
- Product characteristics that affect adoption
- Influencing and learning – conditioning and cognitive approaches
- Demand forecasting
- Changing attitudes.

10 'Whatever made you buy that?'

Consumer decision making and modelling

Introduction

A model in this context is a representation of consumer behaviour. The aim is to provide a simplified portrayal of consumer processes to aid our description, explanation and control of buying behaviour.

One important fact to understand is that models are real, they are not solely the prerogative of the academic. For instance, if you are asked what your reaction would be to raising the price of vending machine drinks at your place of work, you might answer that it depended how large the increase was. If your investigator gives you a series of amounts you may be able to make some guesses as to your likely reaction. So you might respond that a 10 per cent increase would make little difference, a 50 per cent increase would make you drink less from the machine and think about alternative sources of refreshment, while a 100 per cent increase would mean that you definitely would not use the vending machine. This suggests that you have a model of your own behaviour which is inside your head. It is a model which links consumption (buying behaviour) with price. Such a model is extremely common, and we rarely pay a great deal of attention to them in that they are 'implicit' models. In this chapter we are looking at similar approaches which have been formalized and written down. They attempt to clarify the processes underlying consumer behaviour.

Models come in a variety of forms – we shall look at simple models and more complex versions. Some people find it hard to understand why there can be more than one model of consumer behaviour. They argue that if the models are correct, all the representations of a phenomenon should be the same. Perhaps the best explanation comes by analogy.

A map is a representation of a real-life phenomenon. But not all maps are the same. You will probably have seen a road map with towns, motorways and road links clearly marked. Also, you can probably remember your school atlas, which contained the same map but with the waterway systems highlighted. Other maps gave the average rainfall and the height above sea level. Some even displayed which parts of the country are made up of limestone, which are sandstone and which bits are granite and so forth.

Each of these maps is the same in one sense – it is a representation of the country – but has been modified and designed to give the reader different information.

Another important fact is that a map or model does not have to be 'accurate' or 'realistic' in order to be useful. One of the most famous visual images in the UK is the map of the London underground system – it appears in most diaries and even crops up on T-shirts. This colour-coded map fits neatly onto the paper, the lines are mostly straight and the whole thing is easy to follow and a spectacularly successful piece of design work. The map works excellently so long as you know where you are and which station you wish to get to. It does not work very well if you do not. Additionally, if you were to superimpose the underground map on an ordinary street map of London you would find that the stations and routes do not coincide. In some cases stations on different lines are shown as being quite a long way away from one another, when in 'real life' they are only yards apart. If you have travelled on the underground you will also realize that few of the journeys are straight lines.

Thus, in order to make a representation or model of the underground system which was understandable and 'user-friendly', it was necessary to distort and simplify the 'normal' map of London.

Models in the fields of consumer behaviour are somewhat similar to maps. They attempt to give simplified representations of behaviours and influences so that we may better understand them. We have used models throughout this book – but without drawing specific attention to them. This chapter looks at them as an approach to consumer behaviour that will hopefully act as a means of drawing many of the threads together into a more coherent whole.

Variables and relationships

Chapter 8 looked at the process of scientific enquiry. You will remember that the scientific method aims to establish the relationships that exist between variables via the idea–hypothesis–theory–law progression which reflects the confidence with which the relationships can be shown to have been established. Throughout the book we have examined ideas, hypotheses and theories regarding human behaviour and have used different variables according to the subject under discussion. Some of the categories have been defined earlier, but here we can attempt to review and summarize the different groups of variables.

These can be classified as:

- *Stimulus variables* – the inputs to a situation. Within the contexts we have examined which would come into this category would be perceived needs, social influences (family, class, culture and reference groups) and situational stimuli such as advertising messages.
- *Response variables* – the behavioural outputs from the situation. So within the marketing context we are looking at purchases, rejection, further search activity and similar manifestations of buyer behaviour.

- *Intervening variables* – the influences which can only be inferred from the exhibited behaviour and which are assumed to mediate the process between the input and output variables. Examples would be perception, attitudes, learning, beliefs and values.
- *Endogenous variables* – these are factors which have a clearly defined effect and which can therefore be built into a model with some confidence. They are similar to the predictable factors discussed in Chapter 1.
- *Exogenous variables* – in contrast, these are factors whose exact influence is hard to define. In this sense they are similar to the unpredictable factors in the control cycle discussion in Chapter 1.
- *Internal variables* – these are, as the name implies, factors which are internal to the individual, and so we would place motivation, perception, values, attitudes and learning in this category. There is a noticeable overlap with the 'intervening' category described above.
- *External variables* – these are the outside influences on behaviour which are sometimes sub-divided into:
  a) past experience
  b present environment
  c) future expectations.

Classifications of models

Following the boom in modelling approaches at the end of the 1960s, the British Market Research Society set up a Study Group on modelling. They developed a number of classifications for different types of model. Some of the categories defined by this group were as follows:

Micro or *Macro*
Such models focus on a single element of a situation, i.e. they have a relatively narrow focus and may centre on an individual or single action.

These deal with a wider picture of processes and action – often the whole population, environment or process.

Data-based or *Theory-based*
These models are based on the logical analysis of the available data and may also be a function of the methods of analysis used.

These models are developed by logical extension of existing theories – sometimes of marketing, but often from other disciplines.

Behavioural or *Statistical*
Based on assumptions about how people behave, e.g. stimulus response theories.

No built-in assumptions about relationships or motivation. Analysis identifies linkages.

Generalized	or	*Ad hoc*
Such models are designed to apply to a wide range of markets.		Such models are designed to apply to a single market.

Qualitative	or	*Quantitative*
These models do not measure any specific variables.		These measure specific variables and their relative weightings.

Static	or	*Dynamic*
These are a 'one-off snapshot' of a particular phenomenon at one specific moment in time.		These models attempt to take account of changes which might occur over a period of time.

The group also drew distinctions between the different ways in which the models might be displayed:

- *Verbally* – most of us will put our assumptions about consumer behaviour into words in order to explain them both to ourselves and other people.
- *Algebraically* – some of our ideas are best transmitted via an algebraic equation. Weber's Law (page 32) or the Fishbein model of attitudes (page 115) would fit into this category.
- *Pictorially* – almost every diagram in this book can be viewed as a model – a diagram illustrating some point about the topic under discussion.

In addition, they identified categories such as *descriptive, diagnostic* and *predictive* models (see also the comparable discussion in Chapter 7 where the aims of scientific investigation were outlined as being description, explanation, prediction and control) and a rather more subjective pair which were called *successful* and *unsuccessful*.

Perhaps the most used set of categories is that of *low, medium* or *high-level* models. In this case the level refers to the level of complexity – so a low-level model would be a relatively simple representation of the phenomenon, while a high-level model of the same event would be much more complex and detailed and include many more variables.

Think – Here are some 'models' we have used already in this book.
Classify them using the categories outlined above:

a) 'attitudes are leading variables to behaviour – i.e. attitude change predates and predicts behaviour...' (Chapter 6)

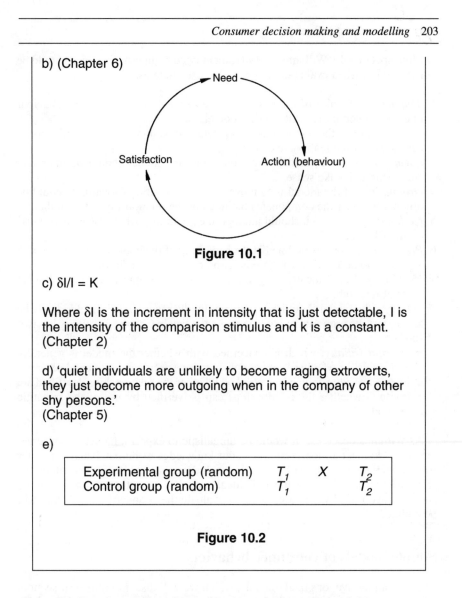

b) (Chapter 6)

Need

Satisfaction

Action (behaviour)

Figure 10.1

c) $\delta I/I = K$

Where δI is the increment in intensity that is just detectable, I is the intensity of the comparison stimulus and k is a constant. (Chapter 2)

d) 'quiet individuals are unlikely to become raging extroverts, they just become more outgoing when in the company of other shy persons.'
(Chapter 5)

e)

Experimental group (random)	T_1	X	T_2
Control group (random)	T_1		T_2

Figure 10.2

Criteria for the evaluation or construction of models

In the marketing context, the modelling approach has two key objectives:

1 Description, explanation, prediction (and ultimately control) of consumer behaviour.
2 Aiding researchers in their task of developing 'better' hypotheses and theories about the relationships and processes involved in consumer behaviour.

Thus models can be evaluated overall against their ability to satisfy either or both of these objectives.

More specifically, Williams, in 1981, mentioned eight criteria which should be borne in mind when evaluating a model. He lists them as:

1 *Simplicity* – the aim of models should be to break down complex behaviour into its simpler, more easily understood elements.
2 *Factual basis* – they should be consistent with known facts in order to be descriptive of the reality concerned.
3 *Logic* – to be understandable and plausible, the model should be internally consistent and make sense.
4 *Originality* – if the model is to move our understanding forward, it should be original in either the components included or the relationship between them.
5 *Explanatory power* – it should attempt to explain the 'what', 'why' and 'how' of the behaviour.
6 *Predictive power* – as outlined at the beginning of the book, one of the aims of a model should be to assist the prediction of consumer behaviour.
7 *Heuristic power* – ideally, a 'good' model should suggest new or additional areas of research.
8 *Validity* – the model should be verifiable. In other words, one should ideally be able to test the proposed relationships. As we saw in Chapter 7, validity has two sub-sets:
   ● *external validity*, which is concerned with whether the model is generally applicable, or whether it only applies in one specific experimental setting
   ● *internal validity*, which is centred on whether the relationships described are true and whether the relationships can be verified by use of the scientific method.

As Williams observes, 'it would be unrealistic to expect a model of consumer behaviour to meet all these criteria as our knowledge of human behaviour is far from complete and we still lack the techniques to evaluate adequately the relationships postulated in the individual models'. Nevertheless, these criteria should prove useful when attempting to evaluate the 'standard' models that will be outlined.

Simple models of consumer behaviour

The comprehensive, or grand, models, which we will discuss in the next section, attempt to define and relate all of the variables which affect consumer behaviour. Lower-level, or simple, models, in contrast, fall into three broad categories: *black box* models, *decision process* models and *personal variable* models.

Black box models

Black box models do not consider internal variables. They focus on inputs and outputs, without concerning themselves with the intervening mental processes which might determine the outcomes. So an example of a black box model would be a 'map' of the decision environment such as Figure 10.3.

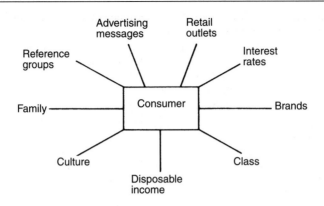

Figure 10.3

Similarly, we could produce a black box model of the buying process which was as simple as Figure 10.4.

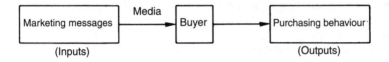

Figure 10.4

Despite their simplicity, black box models can be of value to the marketer, as they are based on identifiable, observable and measurable variables. It is possible that input variables can be adjusted and the outputs observed. In this way, the economist theories regarding supply and demand can be tested, or, alternatively, ideas about the effects of price reductions on sales can be tried out. It can be argued that if it is found that price reduction increases sales, then marketers can make informed decisions, without necessarily understanding exactly why such a reaction results. The emphasis on external stimulus variables is significant, as it can allow the marketing specialist insight into the actions that might be taken in order to achieve the desired objectives.

Another advantage is the relatively limited number of variables that are considered. This can be an aid to decision making, as it may prevent the process from becoming bogged down in complexity.

The limitations lie in the black box model's inability to explain or predict behaviour in a wide range of situations.

Decision process models

These are fairly common in the field of marketing. They attempt a simple description of the stages which consumers progress through in reaching purchasing decisions.

Most are variations on the classic problem-solving/decision-making process of:

Define problem
↓
Generate alternative solutions
↓
Evaluate alternatives
↓
Decide
↓
Implement
↓
Monitor

Marketing 'editions' of this include the innovation adoption model:

Awareness → Interest → Evaluation → Trial → Adoption

The core of the Engel, Blackwell and Miniard comprehensive model (see Figure 10.7) is:

Motivation and recognition of need
↓
Information search
↓
Evaluate alternatives
↓
Purchase
↓
Outcomes

and even the promotional 'AIDA' model shows a similar pattern:

Attention → Interest → Desire → Action

These approaches give a sound basis for marketers seeking to devise strategies which are appropriate for each stage. Inevitably they are not strong on explanation or prediction without considerable elaboration, which makes them fall into the comprehensive model category.

Personal variable models

In contrast to black box models, personal variable models omit external variables. So these models focus on the mental processes of decision making – internal elements and processes such as perception, motivation, beliefs and values.

One classic example of a personal variable model, which we have already met in Chapter 6, is the Fishbein model.

You may remember the model – it is summarized by the formula:

$$A_o = \sum_{1}^{n} B_1 a_1$$

Where A_o = the attitude towards object o;
B_1 = the strength of belief i about o;
a_1 = the evaluation aspects of B;
n = the number of beliefs.

The Rice Perceived Value/Perceived Probability of Satisfaction (PV/PPS) model

This is the author's own attempt to synthesize decision process and personal variable models introduced at the beginning of the book. To reiterate, it is based on the view of decision making as a process in which, when faced with a choice, behaviour is determined by two factors:

- The value attached to outcomes (perceived value {PV})
- The perception of the probability of each outcome occurring (perceived probability of satisfaction {PPS}).

The idea is that we may attach suitable values to each and produce a Subjective Utility (SU) score, using the formula:

$$SU = PV \times PPS$$

One example used by George Wright in his book *Behavioural Decision Theory* (1984) is that of deciding between revising for an examination and going out for a picnic. He points out that the Perceived Value of each option might depend on the weather, so one could allocate a score out of 10 for each of the options depending on the weather conditions which might apply. Thus we could produce a table of perceived value which might look like this:

Perceived value	Fine and sunny	Cloudy but dry	Wet and windy
Revising	2	4	8
Picnic	9	6	0

The next stage is to assess the probability of each type of weather. We may ring up the Weather Bureau to get a forecast for our area and we could allocate probabilities to the various types of weather in the light of that information. We could assess the probability of the weather in each category as:

Fine and sunny   0.3 (3 chances in 10)
Cloudy but dry   0.6 (3 chances in 5)
Wet and windy   0.1 (1 chance in 10)

(Remembering our statistics classes and the fact that a probability of 1.0 means complete certainty and that the probability of all the options must add up to 1.0.)

We can then multiply up the scores for each 'hole' in the matrix to give Subjective Utility scores of:

Subjective Utility	Fine and sunny	Cloudy but dry	Wet and windy
Revising	0.6	2.4	0.8
Picnic	2.7	3.6	0

So we decide on the option with the highest score – we go for a picnic!

> **Think** – What would you decide if the weather forecast had not been so good and you had assessed the probabilities as:
>
> Fine and sunny   0.1 (1 chance in 10)
> Cloudy but dry   0.5 (1 chance in 2)
> Wet and windy   0.4 (2 chances in 5)?

There are significant similarities between this approach and other topics that we have discussed earlier in the book, most notably Expectancy Theory and Fishbein's Compensatory Model of Attitudes, discussed above and in Chapter 6.

We can modify this approach to fit into the marketing situation. Consumers will purchase when they perceive the product and the associated outcome to have both high value and a high probability of satisfaction (or, at least, a $PV \times PPS$ score higher than that of competing products).

The influences could be displayed as shown in Figure 10.5.

Such an approach encompasses most of the material contained in this book and justifies the study of topics such as perceptions, attitudes, learning and social influences. Additionally, it is in line with one of the main themes of this book – the overriding importance of perception in the study of human behaviour.

It also allows us to analyse purchasing behaviours by setting the two dimensions as axes of a grid, as shown in Figure 10.6.

This diagram suggests that consumers are more likely to indulge in extended problem-solving behaviours when the perceived value of the product (or the outcome of its purchase) is high. Conversely, limited problem-solving behaviour is associated with low perceived value.

When the value is perceived to be low, and the probability of satisfaction is also perceived to be low, then the prediction is that purchase will not occur.

The lower right-hand quadrant is concerned with purchases which are of low

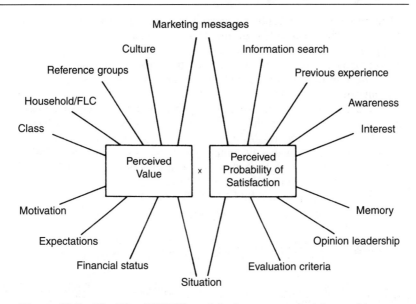

Figure 10.5 The Rice PV/PPS model of consumer decision making

perceived value in themselves, but which have a high probability of satisfaction. Here an example might be a situation of running low on petrol while travelling down a motorway. Government quality standards assure the driver that there is little to choose between brands of 4-star petrol, so the car is filled with whichever brand the next service station happens to sell. Many petrol companies attempt to increase the perceived value of their brand by offering Air Miles, Green Shield stamps or their equivalent.

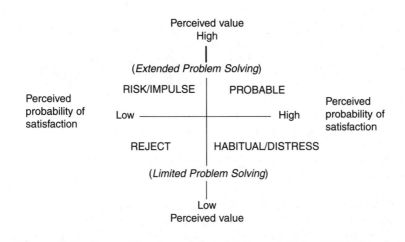

Figure 10.6 Type of purchase analysed in terms of Rice PV/PPS model

The above example could be classed as a *distress* purchase, but a similar process could be predicted in habitual buying at supermarkets. Low-involvement purchases are often made on the basis that there is little or nothing to choose between brands – so it becomes easier for the consumer to make all purchases in one single visit to a superstore, rather than shop separately for each item on the shopping list.

The top left-hand quadrant is interesting (high value, low probability) as it may go some way towards explaining otherwise apparently irrational behaviour. An example might be gambling. Millions of people in the UK gamble on the football pools – despite the chances of winning a fortune being infinitessimally small. Here the hypothesis would be that, for many people, the very high value of winning a very large sum of money (with its attendant outcomes of travel, giving up work and being able to afford luxuries) more than compensates for the very low probability of that outcome occurring. Thus this can be classed as a *risk* or *impulse* purchase.

The top right-hand quadrant is the marketers' dream: high value and high probability of satisfaction – the combination that is most likely to result in probable purchase.

The model clearly identifies two key objectives of marketing effort and communication as being:

- to raise the perceived value of the outcomes of purchase
- to raise the perceived probability of satisfaction following purchase.

Comprehensive (grand) models of consumer behaviour

In this section of the chapter we will examine three of the most famous of the high-level models. These grand models are the more complex formulations of consumer behaviour, and they commonly attempt to encompass all the factors and elements which the authors feel to be relevant to the behaviour.

Note: Many readers find that the complexity of the diagrams is overwhelming at first sight, but be reassured – the Chief Examiner has stated on many occasions that *candidates will never be expected to reproduce these complex diagrams*. So we will look at the models, control our panic and attempt to 'pick the bones' out of each.

The Engel, Blackwell and Miniard model

This is a development of the classic Engel, Kollat and Blackwell model first introduced in 1968 and updated and modified in the 1990 edition of their book *Consumer Behaviour* (see Figure 10.7).

This model takes the process of purchasing as a *problem-solving/decision-making* exercise. The assumption is that the consumer has a problem which is solved by the purchase of a suitable product. The most common everyday problem-solving sequence is:

Define problem → Generate alternative solutions → Evaluate alternatives → Decide → Implement → Monitor

(the simple model of the decision-making process referred to above).

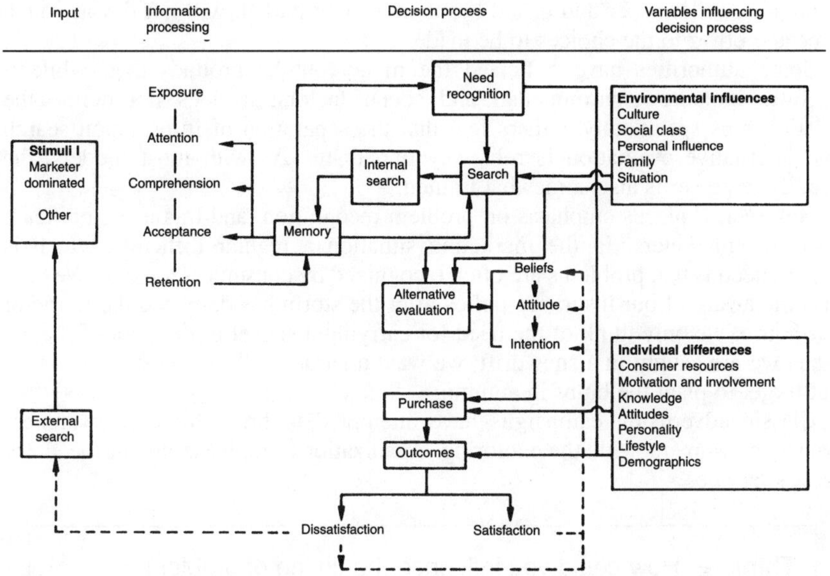

Figure 10.7 A complete model of consumer behaviour showing purchase and outcomes. *Source*: Engel *et al.* 1990

In the marketing context, Engel, Blackwell and Miniard suggest that this becomes:

Motivation and recognition of need
↓
Information search
↓
Evaluate alternatives
↓
Purchase
↓
Outcomes

(another simple model).

If we keep our nerve, we can find the part of the model which identifies each part of the process and, hence, how the model is built up. This forms the basis of the model which is developed.

The authors draw attention to the fact that a modified form of the model can be used to describe low-involvement, limited problem-solving behaviour. They suggest that the key difference between EPS (extended problem solving) and LPS (limited problem solving) is not that the process is different only in the extent to which time and effort are put into external information search and alternative evaluation. In other words, they predict that shoppers, faced with a shopping list containing toilet paper and baked beans in a supermarket, will not devote much time and effort to the choices to be made.

Some authorities have criticized the model on the grounds that, while it usefully includes environmental and social factors, it does not define the relationships specifically. Others feel that the separation of information search and alternative evaluation is relatively unrealistic. As with most models, the predictive power is also somewhat limited.

However, it places emphasis on problem recognition, and this is a significant issue for marketers. In the marketing situation a regular difficulty which is experienced is that problems are often recognized by consumers too late. We only become aware of our insurance policy after the storm has damaged the fabric of our house; we only think of the need for carrying a shovel in the boot of the car when we are caught in a snowdrift; we want a garden full of flowers in spring – but forget to plant the bulbs in autumn.

Classic advertising campaigns have attempted to bring forward awareness among consumers with the motoring organizations emphasizing the need for rescue services.

Think – How could you influence the timing of problem recognition for:

- Home insulation?
- Life insurance?
- Dental floss?
- Car engine tuning?

Exercise – Try using the complete Engel, Blackwell and Miniard model to analyse the behavioural implications of the purchase of:

- a new car
- a house/flat/apartment
- a personal computer
- a new cooker
- hi-fi equipment
- a new autumn outfit.

The Howard–Sheth model

The next grand model we will look at is that devised originally by Howard and then revised and published jointly with Sheth. It is another comprehensive model comparable to that of Engel, Blackwell and Miniard.

The full Howard–Sheth model is presented as Figure 10.8.

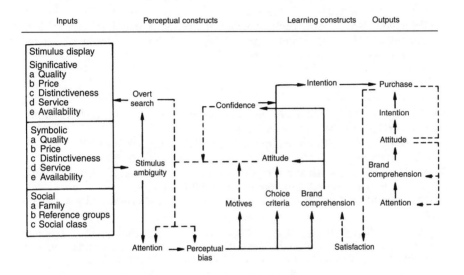

Figure 10.8   The Howard–Sheth model. *Source*: Howard and Sheth 1969

This model is characterized by four major elements – *inputs*, *perceptual constructs*, *learning constructs* and *outputs*. We can attempt to clarify their roles as follows:

Inputs
These cover the sources of information which provide the input, or stimuli, concerning the brand or product to the individual. As can be seen, they draw a distinction between stimuli which are:

- *Significative* – concerning the physical attributes of the product
- *Symbolic* – concerning verbal and visual elements of advertising messages
- *Social* – concerning inputs from the individual's social environment.

Perceptual constructs
This part of the model shows four elements:

- *Stimulus ambiguity* – this suggests that the consumer may be unclear about the messages being received and may attempt to resolve uncertainty through
- *Overt search* – similar to the Engel, Blackwell and Miniard section on external search, this may involve interrogation of opinion leaders, purchasing relevant literature or visiting appropriate outlets to obtain more information. Implicit in such activity is
- *Attention* – in the sense of concentration on the material to hand, and the whole process is admitted to be subject to
- *Perceptual bias* – as a result of many of the issues that were discussed in Chapter 2. Thus expectations and situational factors (not included in the model) may have a significant impact.

Learning constructs

In this model Howard and Sheth attempt to identify the learning processes which are concerned directly with the product.

The perceptual constructs outlined above will, in turn, influence:

- *Motivation* – the satisfaction of the consumer's perceived need. In a similar fashion to our earlier discussion, this will influence the
- *Criteria for choice* – here the authors suggest that if criteria do not already exist, a process of extensive problem solving will be required; if criteria are already established, but brands have not been evaluated, limited problem solving will be required; and if the criteria are known and the brand evaluation has already been conducted, then routinized buying will suffice
- *Brand comprehension* – this is concerned with the overall perception of the product which, the marketer hopes, will have been influenced positively by the marketing messages sent. This, in turn, will influence
- *Attitude* – here the consumer forms attitudes towards product and brand, and the influences will be all of the elements discussed in Chapter 6
- *Confidence* – this is another important element of the decision process. The attitudes held and the evaluations carried out will determine the level of confidence the individual may have about the capacity of the product to satisfy the perceived need. The combination of attitude and confidence lead to
- *Intention* – to purchase the product, so the final stage becomes the act of
- *Purchase*.

The final stages concern post-purchase

- *Satisfaction* – this is very much as described in the section on Engel, Blackwell and Miniard, and will feed back into the consumer's perception of the brand.

Outputs

Here Howard and Sheth look on the actual decision-making process as the output, which becomes a relatively straightforward sequence of:

Attention → Brand comprehension → Attitude → Intention → Purchase

The dotted lines in the model represent feedback, which influences attitudes.

This, in turn, may affect attention and brand comprehension.

Overall, the Howard–Sheth model provides an interesting comparison with the Engel, Blackwell and Miniard model described earlier. Here greater emphasis is placed on perception, attitudes and learning processes. The two models are similar in as much as they both propose a rational consumer, but one who is prepared to 'satisfice' where appropriate.

As ever, there have been some criticisms. As with the previous model, the relationship between variables is relatively ill-defined and is the cause of most of the reservations.

It has also been pointed out that another limitation is its relative weakness in modelling choices which are made between different families of product – i.e. it is better at describing the choices made between brands than the choices made between unrelated alternatives, such as between spending money on a new house or on private education for the children.

Exercise – Try using the complete Howard–Sheth model to analyse the behavioural implications of the purchase of:

- a new car
- a house/flat/apartment
- a personal computer
- a new cooker
- hi-fi equipment
- a new autumn outfit.

The Nicosia model

This model differs from the previous two in that it specifically includes the perceived attributes of the selling organization. Thus a key feature of the model is the relationship between the firm and the customer. The firm influences the consumer through its promotional and advertising activities and is affected, in its turn, by the customer. It shares with the earlier models the insight that the consumer's buying experience influences future buying behaviour.

As can be seen from Figure 10.9, the model is based on four fields:

Field One

This is divided into two sub-fields, the first of which concerns the characteristics of the firm and the second the characteristics of the consumer. The two interact via marketing communication processes and this communication is subject to all the potential distortions of perception and memory. This field would also include social and environmental influences which might affect awareness, motivation and attention, and thus perception. The aim of the communication (so far as the firm is concerned) is to link with the consumer's existing value system in such a way as to result in a positive attitude towards both the firm and the product.

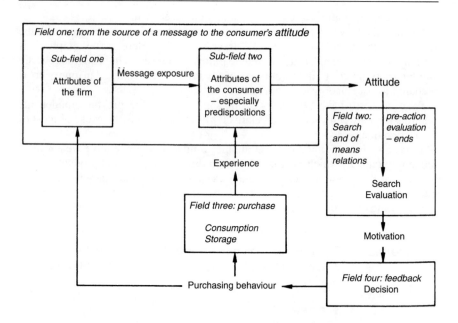

Figure 10.9   The Nicosia model – a summary flow chart.
Source: Nicosia F. M. 1966

Field Two
This centres on information search and evaluation, very much as outlined in the previous two models we have examined. The importance of the positive attitude is the belief that it will encourage problem-solving behaviour. In the diagram there is an implication that such problem-solving behaviour will result in a positive outcome for the firm, but it is clear that the result of such behaviour could be a decision to reject the product.

Field Three
This follows the assumed motivation stemming from Field Two will lead to the act of purchase – so the output from this stage is shown as purchasing behaviour.

Field Four
This is the post-purchase feedback which will affect both the consumer's predispositions and attitudes. The feedback for the consumer is in the form of experience, while that for the firm is in the form of sales information that can be used to modify the marketing strategy. So this field implies potential behaviour change for both parties.

The model emphasizes that interactions between the four fields may occur either simultaneously or in sequence – that the process can be initiated at various stages, i.e. by the firm via marketing messages or by the consumer.

It has the relative advantage of showing the process as interactive; of not considering the consumer in isolation from the firm and its advertising; and, additionally, it does not assume that attitude leads directly to purchase, but that it triggers a decision-making process.

Criticisms have included the assertions that it is descriptive rather than explanatory or predictive, and that areas such as Field One need expansion to do full justice to the rich complexity of the interaction between firm and consumer.

Exercise – Use the complete Nicosia model to analyse the behavioural implications of the purchase of:

- a new car
- a house/flat/apartment
- a personal computer
- a new cooker
- hi-fi equipment
- a new autumn outfit.

11 'Teach me tonight...'

Learning

Introduction

One way of looking at the problem of predicting and controlling behaviour is to consider that our aim is to 'teach' the consumer about our product. Consumers learn from their experiences – our ultimate aim is for them to 'learn' brand loyalty.

If we take this view, it would be helpful to clarify some of the ideas about how people learn and to consider the application of these theories to marketing situations.

Unfortunately, defining learning is somewhat difficult, as we have at least two contrasting views of what learning is.

Behaviourist approaches are solely concerned with observable behaviours. Behaviourists argue that mental processes are unobservable and must therefore be inferred. They believe that learning is shown by changes in behaviour which have their roots in the associations developed between stimuli and the resulting responses. They focus on learning resulting in behaviour change, i.e. behaviourists view learning as the process of acquiring, through experience, knowledge which leads to changed behaviour.

Cognitive approaches, in contrast, emphasize the changes in knowledge and focus on the processes by which people learn information. Here, 'learn' is used to imply that the changed knowledge has been stored in long-term memory. An example of this approach is given by Hawkins, Best and Coney (1989), who define learning as 'any change in the content or organisation of long-term memory'.

However, not all learning is 'used' immediately. Knowledge may lie dormant for long periods before a situation arises in which it is useful; so an even more all-encompassing definition might be that learning is:

a relatively permanent change in potential response which occurs as the result of reinforced practice.

Behaviourist approaches

Trial-and-error learning
This is the trying out of different responses in a problem-solving situation until a response which is effective in solving the problem is hit upon. This approach implies that learning comes from direct experience and is not mediated by any processes of thinking or reasoning.

Think – To what extent do you think that consumer behaviour
is a series of trial-and-error experiments?

Classical conditioning
This approach is typified by the well-known experiments with dogs conducted by Pavlov. He noticed that after the dogs had been in his laboratory for a period of time the mere sight of food, or even the sound of footsteps of the attendant bringing the food, caused the dogs to salivate. He proceeded to set up a series of classic experiments which investigated the phenomenon we now know as the *conditioned reflex*. He arranged for the amount of saliva produced by the dogs to be measured. Then he sounded a bell slightly before food was placed in the animals' mouths. After a number of repetitions it was found that the bell by itself would produce salivation and therefore the dogs had been conditioned (or had learned) to respond to the bell rather than the food.

Operant conditioning
Skinner was the researcher most closely associated with this approach. Whereas Pavlov's dogs had been passive recipients of the stimulus and the reward (bell and food), Skinner's experiments had the subjects as active participants. The emphasis in this approach is very much on what the subject does to elicit the response. By giving reinforcement, usually in the form of food, immediately following particular actions, the animals became more likely to repeat those actions. They could also be 'taught' to exhibit a wide range of behaviours – for example, there are accounts of pigeons being taught to 'play' table tennis.

   Thus operant conditioning is different from classical conditioning primarily in that operant is essentially voluntary on the part of the subject whereas classical deals with involuntary behaviour – i.e. in operant conditioning the subject is active as opposed to the passive role of the subject in classical conditioning.

   On the other hand, the two approaches are similar in that they both accept and agree that motivation, association and reinforcement are key concepts.

Cognitive approaches

Iconic rote learning
Cognition is a word which means mental activity. There is a form of learning

which is purely mental and which is called rote learning. Technically this is a process whereby two concepts are associated in the absence of conditioning – an example might be the way in which many of us learned our multiplication tables. Eventually we learn to associate the statement 'four fours are...' with the appropriate end to the statement, which is 'sixteen'. However, there are other approaches to learning which also imply cognition, and which are rather more complex.

Insight learning
Kohler was a leading proponent of this approach, which sees learning as a problem-solving activity. His experiments suggestd a lengthy pre-solution period in which the subjects appeared to run through a number of 'hypotheses' as to the effective ways of solving the problem. The discovery of the 'right' solution is called *insight*. The magic of insight is usually accompanied by some sort of release of tension in which we make sounds of satisfaction and show signs of excitement when 'the penny drops'. This phenomenon is also called the *'aha' or 'ooh-aah' reaction*.

The characteristics of insight learning are that the transition from pre-solution to solution is sudden and complete – what we sometimes refer to as 'a flash of insight', and that a principle obtained by insight can be easily applied to other problems.

Latent learning
Tolman was an American psychologist whose view was that learning was essentially a process of discovering what leads to what in the environment. Tolman thought that, in everyday language, what was learned was what we often call 'the lie of the land'. He believed that the subject gradually develops a picture of its environment which it then uses to get around in it. He called this picture a *cognitive map*. His idea was that the organism, having developed its cognitive map, can reach a goal from any number of directions. If one commonly used route is blocked, then an alternative one is taken. He suggested that the subject will always choose the shortest route or the one requiring the least expenditure of energy. This he called the *principle of least effort*. For Tolman, the idea of reinforcement as defined by other investigators was less important. He argued that the confirmation of a hypothesis was the real reinforcement – and only confirmed hypotheses were retained in the cognitive map.

This leads on to the important concept of *latent learning* – learning which occurs but is not necessarily used immediately. This gives rise to the idea of a brain containing many solutions to problems and selecting the 'best' one for the current problem being faced.

The foregoing sections have attempted to summarize some of the important ideas that have influenced our view of the learning process. In following the accounts the reader may have noticed that the experiments described have largely been conducted with animals – cats, dogs, rats, pigeons and so forth.

The question may need to be posed:

> **Think** – How useful do you think findings based on animal
> behaviour are for predicting human behaviour?
> – If you feel that animals are not suitable models for
> human behaviour, what do you think are the
> characteristics that make human learning different?

There are no simple answers to these questions. Humans possess advanced cognitive processing skills which seem not to have been developed by most animals. Language development is further advanced. Human beings have also generated views on philosophical issues such as 'right and wrong' and have whole belief systems which are built on the notion of individual responsibility and the ability to control our own destiny and affect our own world.

On the other hand, few of us will be unable to recognize conditioned responses – answering a ringing telephone, lighting a cigarette before beginning to write a letter, the ritual behaviours we indulge in which precede a good night's sleep, and so forth.

> **Think** – What conditioned responses will you admit to?

Cognitive theories appear to be more attractive in the sense that they propose a rational, planned, purposeful approach to life – something to which I am sure most people would aspire. Many of our life experiences reflect insight learning and much of education is inevitably likely to depend on latent principles.

> **Think** – What cognitive learning can you identify in your life?

The likelihood is that we learn in both of these dominant fashions. It may be fruitful to consider what sort of things you learn on a conditioning basis and what on cognitive principles.

> **Think** – What sort of learning has governed your study so far
> on this course?

Some other approaches to learning are described below.

Observational learning

Bandura, working more recently (in the 1970s and 1980s), introduced this approach. This is the process, widely accepted for many years within our society, whereby people are believed to learn from observing other people and to imitate many of the observed behaviours. Bandura suggested that observational learning may be a human rather than an animal characteristic, dependent on cognitive processes such as language, morality, thinking and the notion of self-regulation of behaviour. Observational learning or imitation falls into three categories:

1 *Same behaviour.* Two or more individuals respond to the same situation in exactly the same way – for instance, we applaud at the end of a play in the theatre or stop at red lights.
2 *Copying behaviour.* An example might be learning to swim. One person's behaviour is guided by another and rewards are given when things are done 'right', therefore reinforcing the behaviour. Much teaching in schools falls into this category.
3 *Matched-dependent behaviour.* This is where the learner receives reinforcement for blindly repeating the actions of a model. One way of coping in unfamiliar situations is to look round and observe what others are doing – and then copy it! Examples could include being in a foreign country for the first time or eating in company with unfamiliar cutlery.

Think – What experiences have you had where you have learned by imitation?

It does seem likely, however, that there is more to vicarious learning than pure imitation.

Think – Imagine you are walking down a freezing road in winter. You observe the behaviour of the person walking ahead of you and see them slip and fall on a patch of ice.
 – Do you then imitate their behaviour?
 – Or are you more likely to take extra care?

This approach gives rise to the notion of the role model, and is one which is important to marketing.

Experiential learning

Kolb's view of the learning process is that human beings learn by experience. In the first stage we experience something. The second stage is the observation of what happens and the reflection on the experience. Thirdly comes the conceptualization and generalization of the event. The final stage is when we test out our ideas and theories. This, in turn, gives us another experience to reflect upon, theorize about and test (see Figure 11.1).

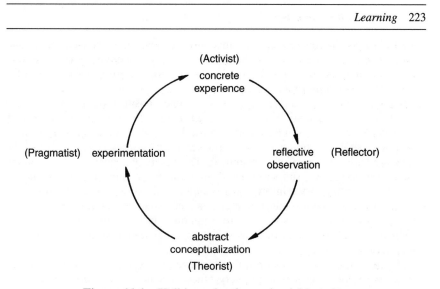

Figure 11.1   Kolb's cycle of experiential learning

More significantly at this stage, the ideas of Kolb have been developed by the work of Peter Honey and Alan Mumford, who believe that each of us, as individuals, will have developed a *preferred learning style*. Thus they suggest that some people prefer the concrete experience (Activists), others are happier observing and thinking (Reflectors), some enjoy the process of conceptualizing (Theorists), while others are concerned primarily with trying out the ideas and making things work (Pragmatists).

Activists tend to be doers – they are likely to get bored just sitting and reading a text book, so they may need to think more about ideas that are being put forward (reflection); reviewing the evidence and ideas in the light of their own experience and developing their own modifications and reservations regarding the theories being discussed. Finally, they may need to consciously think about the application of these ideas in 'real life'.

Reflectors, in contrast, are relatively happy reading and thinking about the material being presented. Their main task is likely to be questioning theories, testing practicalities and getting involved in activities.

Theorists are likely to need to reflect more, and also to go beyond the theory to the application to marketing situations.

Pragmatists, being concerned with whether things work, will need to put effort into understanding and learning the theories and reflecting on their experience of the marketing world.

If Kolb is to be believed, then it is necessary to go through all four stages of the learning cycle.

So, to recapitulate some of the key issues in the field of learning, and their application to human behaviour:

1 *Association*. Fundamental to all behaviourist theories is the notion that we must

make an association between a stimulus or cue and the response. The author, after many years of being called 'Chris', suffers a momentary onset of fear when he is referred to as 'Christopher' – this appears to be associated in his mind with being in trouble as a child!

2 *Reinforcement.* The notion of a payoff, either positive or negative, which confirms the association that has been made. Positive reinforcement is something which is perceived as a reward and seeks to confirm a positive linkage between stimulus and response. Negative reinforcement may be regarded as some sort of punishment. The result of negative reinforcement should be to lead the subject to avoid situations where such a response may be forthcoming. Primary reinforcement is aimed at satisfying a basic need such as food or water. We no longer live in a society where withholding such basic elements is acceptable, so it is more common to use secondary reinforcement, which depends on such things as social approval which we generally assume are desired by people.

It must be stressed, however, that the idea of positive and negative used in the context of reinforcement is very much a matter of the perception of the individual. Offering meat to a vegetarian will be a negative reinforcement, while the same offer would be a reward to a meat-eater.

3 *Motivation.* The reader will have noticed that the primary motivation throughout most of the experiments described in this chapter has been hunger. As mentioned above, such crude methods are rarely appropriate or acceptable when we are dealing with people. Much of the thinking on the place of motivation in the learning process seems to tie in closely with our earlier examination of the internal factors affecting attention and perception. Tolman's argument that the need to explore the environment is enough to 'cause' learning may just be another statement of motivation – i.e. he assumes that individuals are motivated to explore and understand their environment.

Marketing implications of different approaches to learning

We will consider applications of learning theory and its associated ideas to marketing situations.

Trial and error learning. This was one of the earliest theories to have been put forward and, while we can see it applying to certain situations, its application to marketing is relatively limited. Few consumers find themselves in situations where their behaviour is completely undirected and unprogrammed. The basic principles, however, apply to most conditioned learning, and the notion of trial and error is developed much more by Skinner's ideas, which are discussed above under the heading of operant conditioning.

Classical conditioning is of more direct interest. Many advertisements create associations between the product and desirable outcomes – Bounty chocolate bars seem an obvious example of this concept of linking the product to an image of paradise. Another example may be of shoppers in a supermarket following a standard route around the store and filling their baskets with a standard range of goods while 'shopping on autopilot'. One reason for changing store layout from time to time is to ensure that shoppers get to see ranges that they may miss due to habituation.

The notion of familiarity has already been discussed when we looked at habituation in the chapter on perception. It is also of interest in this context, as there is evidence that prior experience of a stimulus can, in some cases, undermine the conditioning process. Some have suggested, for instance, that a tune created specifically for a product is more effective than a well-known song. However, many products are now linked with classic pop music of yesteryear, most notably jeans. Here there may well be more potent and significant associations with happier times past when the consumers were both younger and more carefree.

Think – What associations do these songs have for you?

Operant conditioning has fairly obvious and strong links with consumer behaviour. The assumption of an active subject who is rewarded according to behaviour fits well with the marketer–consumer relationship. The aim is to get the consumer to purchase your product and to ensure that the purchase results in positive reinforcement or reward. The reinforcement should lie in satisfaction with the product, so the implications for marketers are first, that quality is a key determinant of satisfaction and so should be high on the organization's agenda: secondly, the concept of the perceived value of the product is important; and thirdly, it does not pay in the long run to claim in advertisements benefits that the product cannot deliver.

Shaping is an expression used by some psychologists to describe the reinforcement of successive behaviours which ultimately lead to the desired response. In many of the animal experiments the researcher would have had to wait a very long time before the animal produced the desired complex behaviour unaided. So animals are often taught by rewarding increments of behaviour. Similarly, it is possible to break down the desired consumer behaviour into a number of stages – and reward each successively. So we may realize that people are unlikely to purchase if they do not visit our store – we could therefore decide to reward attendance through devices such as door prizes or loss leaders. Another example is the practice of some motor manufacturers and garages of offering a prize for undertaking a test drive in a car. Thus shaping encourages the marketer to examine the behaviours which must precede purchase and to consider ways in which those prerequisite behaviours can be encouraged via appropriate reinforcement.

Generalization. The phenomenon of Pavlov's dogs responding to stimuli that were similar to the original has significant echoes in the field of marketing. Some organizations make use of generalization through using *family branding* – the labelling of all company products with the same name or logo so that the positive associations with one product will spill over on to others. BMW uses the tag 'the ultimate driving machine' to cover their entire range of cars, from the largest to the most compact. Many companies will introduce a new product as a product line extension rather than developing separate brand identities – Crest Tartar Control was presumably so named to build on the existing positive ratings of Crest toothpaste; the advertising for SAAB cars emphasizes the organization's links with high technology by using the SAAB fighter plane as a counterpoint image to the car; the name Rolls Royce covers both cars and aero engines and has become a generalized synonym for excellence.

However, there are some potential limitations to family branding, especially where a company wishes to market products at different ends of the quality range. Additional problems can occur when competitors have company or brand names which are similar to those of market leaders. It is for this reason that legal action is often taken to prevent the use of confusing titles.

Another aspect of generalization that can also result in litigation is what is sometimes called the 'me too product'. Here some manufacturers seek to encourage sales by using packaging which is very similar to that used by a leading competitor. The producers of such goods are seeking to evoke the same positive response that the competitor has spent a great deal of time and effort in generating.

Generalization is therefore something of a two-edged sword for the marketer – highly desirable in some circumstances, and highly undesirable in others. An example of this was the famous series of advertisements for vermouth which were made by Joan Collins and the late Leonard Rossiter. They became a cult, watched by millions and loved by all. Unfortunately, few of the consumers were clear as to whether the advertisements were for Cinzano or Martini. The net result was that sales for both brands went up. Whether or not you think generalization is a good thing or not may well depend on whether you are paying the bill!

Discrimination is the converse of generalization – the process where a subject learns to exhibit a response to one stimulus, but avoids making the same response to similar stimuli. It is important because, in many circumstances, marketers want consumers to differentiate clearly their products from those of their competitors. Discrimination is usually achieved by emphasizing the unique qualities, benefits or features of a product. In blind taste tests it has commonly been found that consumers cannot distinguish between different beers, cigarettes and spirits – so marketers often have to create distinctive 'personalities' for such products to make them distinctive.

Another approach to making your product 'different' is the use of what is sometimes called 'knocking copy' – criticizing competitors' products. This occurs fairly often with motor car advertising, but one of the classic examples is Qualcast's advertising of their lawnmowers as being 'much less bovver than a hover'. 'Knocking' is also commonly used in political election campaigns, where the parties devote most of their advertising effort to discrediting the others. So, in the UK, Conservative party political broadcasts and posters often talk about Labour and vice versa.

Repetition is a key concept in conditioning theory, and is significant to advertisers. Experiments measuring recall of advertising messages show that the average recall rises when commercials are repeated – the exact improvement varies from study to study, but figures in the range of 60 per cent increase in recall by repeating the message four times as opposed to a single showing. Our earlier consideration of awareness in Chapter 2 suggests that repetition could backfire if receivers either get annoyed by the repetition or get bored. Too much repetition could cause receivers to actively shut out the message, pay no attention, or evaluate it negatively. Thus advertisers need to get the balance of repetition right in order to maximize the impact of their messages.

Another aspect of repetition of interest to the marketer is the *frequency* with which a message should be delivered. Here the key is the objective of the programme – if you are seeking to develop positive long-term images of the store/organization/product it would seem sensible to space out the messages. Conversely, political parties who seek to influence voters on a specific date tend to bunch their communications and aim for a 'media blitz' immediately prior to polling day.

This leads us on to consider *extinction*. If repetition or reinforcement is removed, then people are likely to forget the product or message. If we overdo it, then people get bored or otherwise alienated from the product. However, the advantage from the point of view of the advertiser is that not advertising does not involve direct costs and the evidence of spontaneous recovery suggests that what has been lost may be quickly recovered.

The rate of extinction appears to be inversely related to the strength of the original learning. In other words, the more repetition, the stronger the imagery, the more reinforcement, the more important the content, the more resistant is the learning to extinction. So the marketer has another balancing act to perform – early, strong learning followed by occasional top-up versus a steady medium level of input.

Think – What examples can you identify of campaigns which have gone for 'strong' learning followed by lower levels of top-up advertising?
– What examples can you identify of steady, medium-level campaigns?

Higher order conditioning. This effect centred on getting Pavlov's dogs to associate the reward of food with stimuli such as showing a card before sounding the buzzer prior to the reinforcement. It gives rise to the notion of a chain of associations which may be quite extensive and in many ways similar to the shaping processes described above. In marketing terms, the associations may be between the product and desirable social status – convenience foods are shown being consumed in luxury surroundings, cars pull up in front of desirable Georgian houses, instant coffee passes muster in an expensive restaurant. The examples are many and various but none the less important, as they enable the product to be linked to potent subjective (and possibly subconscious) desirable outcomes.

Elaboration. Earlier we commented that the more mental processing that was gone through, the greater was the learning. This is an aspect which is receiving increasing attention from marketers. If we can get the individual 'hooked' on our message, the process of elaboration seems likely to produce repetitions within the person's mind for which we do not pay. Hence its attraction to advertisers. For some years the John Player cigarette company ran a series of advertisements which played word games based on their distinctive black packaging. Punning messages such as 'Black to the future', 'Black to front', etc. involved the observer in the decoding of the message and, in many cases, actually led people to start making up their own slogans – very efficient marketing!

The phenomenon of closure discussed under the heading of perception falls into a similar category, with people becoming actively involved in spotting the Benson and Hedges gold cigarette packet or recognizing the latest Silk Cut advertisement.

The wordplay approach emerged again recently, with Holsten Pils running a series of advertisements which were based on anagrams of the letters making up the product name. Once the consumer is seduced into playing such games, the imprinting of the product becomes very much stronger.

Peugeot Cars recently produced a campaign with several linked characteristics. They ran an advertising article about the advantages of diesel engines and Peugeot developments. In the same magazine they had a separate free draw in which a 405 diesel was the prize. To enter the draw the reader had to answer a number of questions, the answers to which were in the article. Finally, an 'I would go for diesel because...' tiebreaker was to be completed. This multi-level approach demanded considerable elaboration – and all for partial/intermittent reinforcement!

Observational learning. This suggests that we can learn at second hand by observing what happens to other people. Here the examples might be negative reinforcement – people will be offended and cause you to be ostracized if you suffer from unpleasant body odour. The solution (which encompasses a degree of insight learning) is to use the advertised deodorant. Similarly, soft drinks are sometimes portrayed as making the consumer more socially popular.

Latent learning applies to many of the advertisements which appeal to the more expensive, one-off purchases. It is unlikely that readers will rush out and refit their kitchens because they have seen an advertisement. Here the aim is to lodge the product in the consumer's cognitive map/awareness set so that the product is positively viewed at the time that kitchen refurbishment is being considered.

Experiential learning. The Kolb cycle of activity, reflection, theorizing and testing fits in well with any of our sampling approaches to marketing and, to some extent, subsumes many of the principles of operant, insight and latent learning. Offering free cheese or paté 'tasters' as customers come into the supermarket, test drives for potential car buyers, free samples pushed through letter boxes all allow the potential consumer to try out the product or service and hence build brand awareness.

Involvement is a concept which we introduced in the introductory chapter and covers several of the ideas expressed above. It seems sensible to differentiate between consumer decisions which are of low significance and those which may hold high importance for the individual. In other words, it is not unreasonable to think that buying a tin of beans is of less significance than purchasing a new hi-fi system, and the mental processing and learning is therefore likely to be different. Cost is likely to be a major factor, but even here we are not able to analyse this in absolute terms. Buying a car may be one of the biggest purchasing decisions of our lives for the majority of the population – but for others it is purely a pipe dream, while for the very rich it may be far less significant.

This concept, which is closely related to elaboration and cognitive processes, provides a useful way to illustrate some of the major theories discussed in this chapter.

Another final concept associated with learning and which is of value to marketers is that of memory.

Memory

There is an obvious link between learning and memory. Most authorities draw a distinction between short-term memory (STM) and long-term memory (LTM). This is an area of interest to both the marketing specialist and students. Marketers want their product to remain in the consumer's memory, while the students are concerned with their ability to recall learned material under examination conditions.

A common representation of the memory process makes an analogy with computer systems (Figure 11.2).

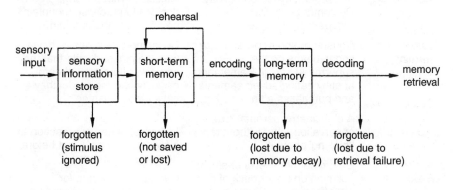

Figure 11.2

The *sensory store* or *sensory information store* (SIS) is believed to be a memory system of extremely short duration. Immediately after the removal of a stimulus input, there appears to be a sensory representation of the stimulus which is held in the mind for a brief time – perhaps one or two seconds only. The

Table 11.1   Learning theories, marketing and involvement

Theory	Examples of low involvement	Examples of high involvement
Trial and error learning	Free sample of hair shampoo delivered through front door and stored in bathroom. When usual shampoo run outs, trial pack is used, found acceptable and purchased (or not).	Faced with mounting debts, individual responds to advertisement offering to solve the problems with a single loan. Learns the costs of borrowing from loan sharks.
Classical conditioning	A positive emotional response is generated by the use of a particular pop tune. This becomes associated with a product, even though the person does not consciously pay attention to the advertising.	The generation of high-order conditioning allows the customer to have positive feelings about a product which may be more expensive than alternatives, e.g. luxury goods.
Operant conditioning	A common brand of baked bean is purchased. They taste 'OK'. The consumer continues to purchase that brand.	Clothes purchased and worn give rise to numerous compliments. Further clothes of the same label are bought.
Iconic rote learning	An individual learns that Amstrad make personal computers without ever consciously focusing on PCs or Amstrad advertisements.	Keen cooks learn about various makes of kitchen knives by careful reading of advertisements which they find enjoyable.
Insight learning	*The Guardian* unavailable at newsagents when on holiday. Customer buys *The Independent* instead.	Commuter, distressed by daily difficulties with parking, decides to purchase mountain bike to solve the problem.
Latent learning	Consumer spots 'low salt, low sugar' beans on the supermarket shelf. Remembers healthy eating advertisements and purchases a tin.	Consumers as a family, having won the pools, decide that they can now afford their 'dream car'. Choose the model they have always wanted.
Vicarious learning	A child learns parental roles by observation – but without really 'thinking' about it.	Individual observers reaction to a friend's new-style suit before deciding to purchase.
Experiential learning	Commuter finds level of smoke pollution on upper deck of bus too offensive to tolerate and decides to travel on the lower deck.	Car taken to garage for service. Customer offered new higher powered model to use for the day. Impressed by the car, the consumer decides to move up the range when the time comes to change car.

capacity of this SIS is limited to that which the individual is aware of. Thus our earlier references to attention and sensory input under the heading of perception become significant once more. Material is assumed to be 'lost' from this part of the system by a process of decay which occurs very rapidly unless the information is processed to the next stage of memory.

Short-term memory (STM) appears to be a limited capacity storage system which is capable of holding only a small amount of information for a short time. To keep information in the STM it is necessary to concentrate hard on the material continually, often repeating it over and over in our mind. In this sense it is possible to consider STM as our 'working memory', with items being held and retained solely for the task in hand and being replaced as soon as the activity changes.

A good example of STM as our 'working memory' lies in looking up a telephone number, retaining it long enough to dial (often rehearsing it by silent repetition) and then forgetting it.

Long-term memory (LTM) is exactly what the name implies. We normally do not say that something has been learned until the material can be recalled at will after a period of days, weeks or months. When this occurs, it is clear that the material has been retrieved from our LTM. The LTM has a much larger capacity than the STM and is able to store very large amounts of material. It is widely believed that STM is translated into LTM through a process which is called *consolidation*.

The mechanisms of memory are not clearly understood – but the analogy that is often made is with the computer. The STM is the equivalent of the on-screen data input which is then saved on disk (roughly equivalent to the LTM). Perhaps the area which is least understood is the process by which we decide which items to transfer from STM to LTM and the mechanism by which this happens.

Another key element in the memory process is *decoding*. This is 'the other end' of the process, and may be one of the most crucial in terms of making our memories work effectively. It is a common experience to have a memory failure ('I know it, I know it, it's on the tip of my tongue…') which is rectified at some later point in time, often when you are not consciously making an effort to recall the data. This experience suggests that the brain continues subconsciously to process information and seek solutions to problems even when the problem has been 'dropped' by our conscious brain. All too often, it seems that there is little doubt that you have the information – the real knack is to extract it from the long-term store on demand. Once again, the code used for storage is likely to be significant, as the associations with existing information are important to the whole retrieval process. Organizing cues for retrieval is important for students. Mnemonic devices are very popular as examinations approach.

Rehearsal seems to be another important element – the repetition or playing with the idea or information appears to help imprint the material in the LTM. In this way we might explain why some material seems to 'stick' without effort, while other material seems to need a great deal of work by reference to our interests. Things in which we are interested may be rehearsed many times because we are already mentally involved and do not perceive this rehearsal as memorizing in a formal sense. We also rehearse by linking the information to other items. This has the advantage of 'protecting' it against other, competing incoming data.

Elaboration is another aspect of the memory and rehearsal processes, where we use comparisons with previous experiences, values, attitudes and beliefs to evaluate information in our working (short-term) memory. It is also the process by which we add to relevant previously stored information. Elaborative activities such as rehearsal serve also to redefine or add new elements to memory. The greater the amount of elaboration or mental processing that is involved, the greater the number of linkages that are forged with existing knowledge. This increases the number of avenues or paths by which the information can be retrieved. Many of the popular 'memory systems' are based on this principle – the classic party trick of memorizing random information is often achieved by processing or elaborating to make associations with existing knowledge, or surreal links are forged between the items to aid recall.

Forgetting is an important factor, as it highlights that, for all the miracles of the human brain, the processes of memory are far from perfect. Figure 11.2 suggests that forgetting may occur at any of four stages in the overall process.

Another source of memory problems is that of *interference*, which can take two main forms:

1 *Retroactive inhibition* or interference occurs when material that has been learned later prevents the recall of the target material.

> **Think** – Can you remember your telephone extension in your
> previous office?
> – The registration number of your previous car?
> – The postcode of your previous address?

If you have difficulties in remembering any of these things, it is likely that it is because the new information has taken precedence over the old.

2 *Proactive inhibition* or interference is when prior learning hinders the learning and retrieval of new information. This is the opposite phenomenon to retroactive inhibition. In this case the existence of the old material prevents the learning of the new information.

> **Think** – Have you ever had the embarrassment of referring to
> the partner of a friend by the name of their previous
> partner?
> – Have you had trouble recalling your new phone
> number after moving?
> – Or the registration number of a new vehicle?

These experiences stem from existing information inhibiting the recall of new data.

Other factors which reduce our capacity for recall fall into the broad category of *personality inhibitions*.

Emotion can cause problems for the memory process. Indeed, it could easily be classified under interference. It is, however, slightly more complex in that strong positive emotions may aid retrieval by creating the phenomenon sometimes called 'total recall'. More commonly, we find that heightened anxiety or other negative emotions cause interference and inhibit recall and memory. It is depressing to realize that we commonly measure recall in examination situations, where the level of anxiety is often very high.

Hint – Before an examination, practice relaxation exercises such as deep breathing, and avoid contact with other class members who are likely to induce hysteria by talking about how well/badly their revision has gone!

Repression, one of the defence mechanisms described earlier, can also interfere with the process of recall. As you will remember, it occurs where people subconsciously avoid retrieving material that they may find disturbing or threatening. The extreme form is sometimes called *amnesia*, where a loss of memory follows a traumatic experience. While not a common phenomenon, it has formed the basis for many a film and TV thriller.

Our review of memory needs little linking to marketing activities, as the need for the consumer to remember the product name, personality and characteristics is, hopefully, self-evident. It is perhaps worth commenting on the possible marketing applications of forgetting.

Think – Under what conditions might you wish consumers to forget?

It is possible to imagine that your product has received some undesirable publicity – the contamination of Perrier Water would be a classic example. Here the problem is to speed up the forgetting of the bad news and the reintroduction of positive images.

Think – Given the information we have reviewed so far, how would you tackle such a problem?

Review exercise – What examples in current advertising/marketing campaigns can you find of the following:

General principles of learning

- Association..
- Positive reinforcement...
- Negative reinforcement..
- Motivation..

Behaviourist approaches

- Classical conditioning...
- Operant conditioning..
- Stimulus generalization..
- Higher order conditioning.....................................

Cognitive approaches

- Insight learning...
- Latent learning..

Other learning theories

- Observational learning..
- Experiential learning...

Memory

- Short-term memory...
- Long-term memory..

Forgetting

- Retroactive inhibition..
- Proactive inhibition...
- Emotional factors..
- Repression...

Associated processes

- Rehearsal...
- Elaboration...

Think – Which of these elements have been used in this chapter?

12 'Segments? – I don't even like grapefruit!'

Segmentation

Introduction

As we noted in Chapter 1, the advent of the mass market posed problems about whether universal messages and products were appropriate. The idea rapidly developed of segmenting the market so that marketing communications can be efficiently targeted and tailored specifically to satisfy the consumer's needs. So marketing has an increasing need to be able to 'standardize' or categorize people into segments in order to utilize their resources effectively.

Market segmentation involves the breakdown of the total broad and varied market into groups, and, in order to be useful, the groups should have the following characteristics:

- *Homogeneous* – the constituent members should have characteristics and needs in common
- *Different* – from other segments of the population
- *Accessible* – the marketer must be able to reach the members of the group with the marketing message
- *Stable* – at least stable enough for communication to be made
- *Large* – enough to make marketing worthwhile and profitable.

In addition to the original idea of targeting marketing messages, it is also possible to look at segmentation as a process by which, if we have found a segment with the above characteristics, we could develop modified products (or even design new products/services) to fit that segment. Examples could include plasters for Afro-Caribbeans which were not made in a 'European pink' colour.

Our segments will also be the focus of our marketing research activity as described in Chapter 8. In some cases we will be researching to define the needs, wants and aspirations of the segment; in other cases we may well be investigating in order to identify the segment in the first place.

There are a number of different approaches to the segmentation problem – some of which are well established, others which are newer. The ideas underlying segmentation are based on work discussed in earlier chapters – so this section is, in many ways, a revisiting of the material discussed earlier in the book.

Inevitably, the appropriateness of the different criteria used will vary from product group to product group.

We will look at some of the possible segmentation systems currently in use. One of the simplest and most obvious is that of gender segmentation.

Gender segmentation

It is perhaps self-evident that some products are gender-specific. The examples quoted elsewhere in this book will suffice (shaving soap for men and sanitary protection for women). In such cases the segmentation largely takes care of itself.

However, where such an approach could prove additionally useful is when an organization marketing a product which has historically been associated with one sex wishes to extend the market by targeting the other gender. One can think of sports which started off as male, but in which women now take part. The Daewoo approach to selling cars has been to research women's feelings and attitudes about the car-buying process and to design a whole marketing strategy on the results. Both of these examples demonstrate marketers taking advantage of the growing independence and economic activity of women in UK society. Recently the media have carried stories suggesting that young males were not enamoured of consuming Diet Cola – the implication being that this was a 'girls drink'. It has been suggested that the same product was repackaged specifically to appeal to the action and excitement-orientated young males. The reader may be able to fill in the appropriate product names....

Another simple segmentation device is age segmentation.

Age segmentation

Here we return to the notion of things such as the 'youth' micro-culture and the idea that age grouping is likely to be a determinant of buying behaviour. One of the most obviously segmented markets is that of holidays, where companies such as '18–30' and 'Saga' Holidays have specialized in very clearly identified age groups. Other products, such as baby food, teenage magazines, etc., are also highly age-specific.

A more sophisticated version of age segmentation stems from our study of the family as a purchasing unit in Chapter 5, and is commonly referred to as life stage segmentation.

Life stage segmentation

The concept of the nuclear family gives rise to a very important idea in marketing – that of the family life cycle. This takes the idea of the family as a consuming unit which progresses through a series of stages. It considers aspects of consumer behaviour such as the focus of interest and the probable levels of disposable/discretionary income. It has been a seminal idea in the area of market segmentation.

Traditional family life cycles and buying behaviour

Stage 1 – Single/Bachelor/Young Unmarrieds

Despite earning power often being relatively low, this section of the community are subject to few rigid demands – so they may typically have a high disposable income. Likely focus of spending may be a car, furnishing and equipping the first home of their own, fashion and recreation, alcohol and eating out, holidays, hi-fi, leisure pursuits and other activities which are likely to centre on obtaining a partner.

Stage 2 – Newly Marrieds

Commonly, two incomes with no children to support gives even more disposable income. Again, cars, clothing, holidays feature in their buying patterns, but this group also has a very high rate of purchasing durable goods, furniture and appliances in this important 'nest building' stage.

Stage 3 – Full Nest 1

With the arrival of the first child, it is assumed that the mother will cease working. The family income declines sharply at the same time as the young child creates a new focus for family expenditure. Moving into a new home, buying furniture and furnishings for the child, purchase of washing machines, tumble dryers and such reflect changing needs. Similarly, day-to-day expenditure on children's food, toys and activities increases. This stage commonly places the family under financial pressure, reducing savings and often creating dissatisfaction with the financial situation.

Stage 4 – Full Nest 2

At this stage the youngest child is aged 6 or over. The general assumption is that the husband's income has increased and the wife may well have restarted work, possibly on a part-time basis to begin with. Hence the financial pressures ease. Expenditure tends to be heavily influenced by the children and their needs, including some relatively expensive items such as bicycles, fashion clothing, music lessons, etc.

Stage 5 – Full Nest 3

As the children grow older, it is assumed that the family will experience a further improvement in finances due to both the wife's improved earnings and the possibility of children getting some part-time or occasional employment. At this stage the family may well replace ageing furniture, buy a better car and/or purchase some luxury items (or items which, until then, had been considered as luxuries – e.g. dishwashers, etc.).

Stage 6 – Empty Nest 1

The couple's joint incomes continue to increase, while the children have left home and are no longer financially dependent on the parents. The combination of these two factors gives perhaps the highest level of disposable income. Expenditure may focus on higher-cost items such as home improvements, luxury goods, holidays and travel.

Stage 7 – Empty Nest 2

Retirement brings a sharp drop in income. Expenditure becomes more health-orientated and may involve moving house to a smaller dwelling, perhaps in a more agreeable climate.

Stage 8 – Solitary Survivor

One partner has died. If still working, the solitary survivor still enjoys a good income and may well move house and spend on holidays, travel, etc. as in Empty Nest 1.

Stage 9 – Retired Solitary Survivor

Similar to the category above, but with a lower income due to retirement. The emphasis of expenditure may well be similar so long as the individual remains active – but, as the person becomes less independent, more may be spent on purchasing the personal services necessary for survival.

The family life cycle is commonly represented as the steady progression illustrated in Figure 12.1.

Think – Identify current advertising campaigns which appear to be targeted at specific stages in the family life cycle.
– How many different targeted stages can you think of?

As we saw in Chapter 5, there have been changes in family life, centring on rising divorce rates and a tendency for growing numbers of partnerships to delay getting married. A more complex 'map' of possible relationships was developed, but we also commented that, despite these changes, the institution of marriage and the family remained strong.

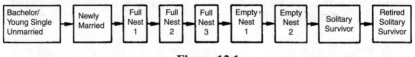

Figure 12.1

The Family Policy Studies Centre report (1985) emphasized this continuity in that it claimed that in the UK:

- nine out of ten people will marry at some time in their lives
- nine out of ten married couples will have children
- two in every three marriages are likely to be ended by death rather than divorce
- eight out of ten people live in households headed by a married couple.

It did, however, identify some changes – the most significant from our viewpoint being an increasing tendency for people *not* to go through all the phases of the traditional family life cycle within one family. This may not matter too much, as the family life cycle is essentially used as a cross-sectional analysis for market segmentation purposes.

In an important article, Lawson (1988), following an analysis of the changing demographic patterns in the UK, suggested that the stages themselves have altered in both length and importance. He claims that in general:

- Full Nest stages are shorter due to lower birth rates and children being born closer together in time
- Bachelor and Empty Nest stages have grown in length and size.

What is important is that, whatever model of the family life cycle is used, it must reflect as accurately as possible the demography of the society.

Lawson presents a 'modernized' family life cycle which, he claims, encompasses over 80 per cent of the population. His data, based on the 1981 census, is set out in Figure 12.2.

The exceptions (the remaining 18.69 per cent) are households with more than one family, those with other residents besides family, and young people living in joint households.

Social class segmentation

BSkyB utilized this approach for focusing its marketing effort. This organization was particularly successful in penetrating the C1, C2 groupings. The communications were tailored to the beliefs, values and perceived needs of those social groups. We have also seen that, in marketing research sampling, organizations commonly use social class as a way of ensuring the validity of their findings.

We can examine some other popular systems for market segmentation, based on class and status. This has long been a recognized method of segmentation. The classification system by social class is usually defined by the A, B, C system. This

Stage	Percentage of households
Bachelor	1.42
Newly married couple	3.11
Full nest 1 (with pre-school children)	11.91
Full nest 1 (lone parent)	1.26
Middle-aged (no children)	1.19
Full nest 2 (school-age children)	16.97
Full nest 2 (lone parent)	1.92
Launching families (with non-dependent children)	6.30
Launching families (one parent)	1.45
Empty nest 1 (childless, aged 45–54)	9.45
Empty nest 2 (retired)	9.51
Solitary survivor under 65	2.66
Solitary survivor (retired)	14.17
Total	81.31

Figure 12.2

takes into account individual's general standing in the population measured by housing, earnings, job, social background, etc.

This is shown in Figure 12.3.

The Registrar General's Scale uses a five-class grouping which is very similar. However, in this case the classes are referred to as I (= A), II (= B), etc. In this system there is a similar distinction between III1 (= C1) and III2 (= C2). The

Social Grade	Social Status	Occupations	Examples
A	Upper middle class	Higher managerial/ professional	Directors, doctors, lawyers, professors
B	Middle class	Intermediate managerial	Managers, teachers, computer programmers
C_1	Lower middle	Junior managerial, supervisory, clerical, administrative	Foremen, shop assistants, office workers
C_2	Skilled working class	Skilled manual labour	Electricians, mechanics, plumbers and other crafts
D	Working class	Semi- and unskilled manual labour	Machine operators, assembly, cleaning
E	Subsistence	None	Pensioners, casual workers, unemployed, students

Figure 12.3   The Jicnar social grade definitions

Jicnar group D is subdivided into IV (= semi-skilled manual labour) and V (= unskilled). The Registrar General does not have a subsistence/unemployed/ pensioner category.

As stated above, the aim is to offer a segment of the population products associated with the class (or group) one higher than themselves. Thus the C2s are supposed to aspire to the lifestyle of the C1s, and offering them a product with white-collar, C1 characteristics should make it attractive to them.

While these approaches have much to commend them, and many marketing students will be familiar with the systems from studying market research, they do suffer from some significant shortcomings:

1 The definitions of class and status are neither clear nor consistent. Most people believe themselves to be of a different class to that which is defined by such schemes – they may see themselves as being of a higher class, or, alternatively, may be clinging to a perception of themselves as (e.g.) 'working class' when the objective data suggests otherwise.

Think – Having read the categories of the Jicnar/Registrar General's Scale how accurate was your description of your social class in Chapter 4?
– If it was 'wrong', why?

---

2 The categories are defined by the occupation of the 'head of the household'. But, as we have seen, changes are taking place in the model of the 'typical' family. The existence of UK law protecting employment rights for women following maternity leave has meant that an increasing number of women are able to return to work earlier than in the past. This affects both the family income and is likely to alter the balance of the decision processes within the family.
3 In practice, the classes do not necessarily command disposable income in the same order as the grades would suggest. Most of us know C2s (such as plumbers, television repair specialists, electricians and the like) who earn a great deal more than the foremen, supervisors and clerical staff with (or for) whom they work. Indeed, many may earn more than the Bs (teachers and middle managers), who are theoretically two categories above them.
4 Improved access to education has made the barriers between classes less distinct. Many graduates now come from working-class backgrounds, and, in the light of our comments on socialization and learning processes, it seems naive to assume that they will abandon the values of their early upbringing.
5 Given the lack of job security that has become common in the UK, we may face the anomaly that a middle-class (B) manager who is made redundant immediately drops to grade E, despite the fact that disposable income could have risen due to redundancy payments. Clearly, people do not change their values, attitudes and buying behaviour so dramatically and quickly.
6 There is considerable doubt as to whether it is class which produces the similarity in lifestyles, or lifestyles which produce the phenomenon of class.

Thus, class and status may only be useful for particular products, services or ideas.

One additional observation is that both the Jicnar and Registrar General systems attempt to objectively categorize the population by class. However, both use labelling schemes (A–E, I–V) which imply hierarchy and have strong connotations regarding status as well. Such inferences were not intended when the systems were created, but have now become deeply embedded in our thinking about class and status.

Geographic segmentation

Another simple device for splitting up the market into manageable segments is by geography. Examples would be the marketing of 'regional' beers, such as Tetley in England or Guinness worldwide. Some food markets are claimed to have regional variations, such as Scotland consuming significantly higher levels of salt than other parts of the UK. Periodically we find marketing data hitting the 'Trivial Pursuits' elements of the national press when short articles appear, pointing out the different purchasing patterns of items as various as fish and chips and black underwear in different parts of the country.

It is also not uncommon for products to be launched/trialled in a single area before being rolled out to cover the whole country. In the light of our earlier discussion about experiments and the validity of information and inferences drawn from them, we may need to exercise caution in our interpretation.

Cultural segmentation

As we saw in Chapter 4, cultures can have an all-pervading influence on people, their behaviour and purchasing patterns. So issues of language, religion, values, etc. can segment a market quite specifically. In that chapter we also introduced the notion of mini- and micro-cultures – once again, this could be a powerful device for identifying significant, different and identifiable groupings.

Geo-demographic segmentation

Another, more concrete, system for segmentation links two previous approaches, and is based on the notion that where people live is a good predictor of their class and status. It also has the advantage that housing is not mobile, and, as residential areas rise or fall in terms of their 'desirability', areas, and even specific postcodes, can easily be reclassified.

The best known of such systems is ACORN (A Classification Of Residential Neighbourhoods) which is another A,B,C system. The ACORN groups are:

A Agricultural areas
B Modern family housing, higher incomes
C Older housing of intermediate status

D Poor-quality older terraces
E Better-off council estates
F Less well-off council estates
G Poorest council estates
H Multi-racial areas
I High-status non-family areas
J Affluent suburban housing
K Better-off retirement areas
U Unclassified.

These broad categories are subdivided to give a total of 38 ACORN types. For instance, the B group (Modern family housing, higher incomes) is split up into five subsets:

- Cheap modern private housing (B3)
- Recent private housing, young families (B4)
- Modern private housing, older families (B5)
- New detached housing, young families (B6)
- Military bases, mixed owner-occupied (B7).

This type of system is of obvious applicability to direct-mail marketing, and is of particular value when analysing catchment areas, especially when organizations are deciding where to site retail stores.

These segmentation systems are sometimes called *demographics,* as they are based on relatively hard evidence – gender, age, geography, marital status, income, occupation and education. These are all 'facts', and it will be seen that accurate census data lies at the root of most of these approaches. However, there has been some speculation about the decreasing accuracy of this database following the 'disenfranchisement' of many people who sought to avoid (or protest against) the so-called 'poll tax' in the UK. Statisticians expressed some concern at the number of people who appeared to have been 'lost' during this period, although there are some signs that they may now be 'returning' to the published statistics.

Lifestyle and psychographic segmentation

This is based more on the 'personality' of the target market – their activities, outlook on life, attitudes and beliefs. There is less emphasis placed on the demographic groupings and hard, factual data of the previous systems, it is targeted more at the motives, values and desires of what might be considered a 'group self-concept'. The concept has received a great deal of publicity via the media and has become part of the common language, with most people being comfortable with expressions such as 'Yuppie' (young, upwardly mobile), 'Twinkie' (two incomes, no kids), etc.

> **Example** – A recent television advertisement for sherry appeared at first to be aimed at a 'younger' audience, which made it seem that the compa\ was aiming for a new market segment. Howeve\ research had shown that the self-concept of its current customers (who were generally in the 45–55 age group) was that they were still as vigorous and youthful as ever! Thus the advertisement managed to target new customers, while reinforcing the self-image of its existing customers. Very neat!

We discussed in Chapter 6 the notion that attitudes are linked to ideas of self-image and the way we see ourselves. Motivation theory also suggests that we may be motivated by our image of ourselves. Thus it may be useful to visit a few concepts associated with self-image and personality.

Personality

Personality is a part of the way in which we perceive other people.

> **Exercise** – How would you describe your Prime Minister to me?
> Jot down some of that person's characteristics on a piece of paper.

In doing this, you will have used some dimensions of personality according to your view of character or temperament.

> **Think** – Which characteristics did you use?
> – How many did you use?

In everyday usage we commonly describe people using a single characteristic, e.g. 'an outgoing person', 'a blunt individual', 'an aggressive so-and-so'. This is an interesting example of selectivity, as we choose to use only a limited number of the facets that make up the person. Even if we are looking at the same person we may choose different aspects to emphasize – You may pick out their honesty while I might highlight their cheerfulness. We have potential problems with the process called *stereotyping* – generalizing and simplifying characteristics to make a tidy 'package' that we can handle. In the exercise above, a person who you are unlikely to know personally was chosen. It highlights the fact that we can make these judgements based on very little first-hand knowledge, using evidence from the media, much of which may have been carefully rehearsed and edited. In real life, we seem to have no problems in 'summing up' a person within seconds of meeting him or her. It is something that we all do every time we meet someone new, as the assessment is important in determining how we respond.

Think   – What example can you think of of situations where
                your first impressions of a person were proved right?
      – What examples can you think of where they were
                wrong?

We often use a single characteristic and build a complete personality around that solitary element. However, people are much more complicated than that, and examples abound of charming criminals, morose comedians and so forth. It is claimed that Hitler loved both Mozart and dogs, both characteristics of 'good' people, according to many. However, as we have seen, our behaviour is, to a greater or lesser extent, limited by the roles we are playing and the situation in which we find ourselves.

Think   – What is your 'personality' when you are at work?
      – With your parents?
      – With your grandparents?
      – Out with your friends?
      – At college?

Whatever our response to these questions, it implies that there is a certain consistency or stability in our behaviour; we recognize in ourselves and in others the tendency to behave in particular ways in given situations. It is this distinctive tendency which we commonly identify as the personality of an individual.

Hollander has put forward a model which may help clarify some of the issues, and this is shown in Figure 12.4. According to this model, the psychological core is a central feature of what we may call personality while accepting the interactive nature of behaviour with respect to the person, the role, the environment and some concept such as the 'real' self.

Freud was one of the father-figures of the study of personality, and gave us the notion of a subconscious element to our make-up. He proposed a tripartite set-up, with the Id being the wholly subconscious, intuitive bit of us – working on the pleasure principle, dominated by sexual drive and being subjective and gratification-seeking. The Ego is wholly conscious and deals with reality, and is the bit that helps us develop interactive skills. It is also the element that includes our self-image. The Super-Ego deals with morality, and corresponds roughly to the idea of a conscience acting as the umpire between the pleasure-seeking Id and the reality-based Ego. See Figure 12.5.

One of the central ideas in this theoretical framework is that the eventual goal of all human behaviour is pleasure and that the Id is the basic source of energy,

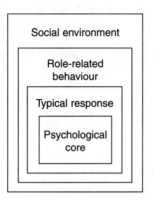

Figure 12.4

drive and motivation. As this source is subconscious, it is the basis of motivational research which seeks to determine the underlying perceptions of products and needs, as we saw in Chapter 8.

In advertising terms, Freud provides fruitful grounds for image making which may suggest that product use will make the individual more popular, interesting or sexually attractive.

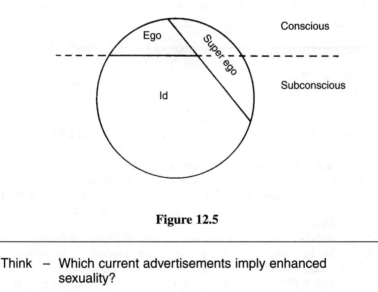

Figure 12.5

Think – Which current advertisements imply enhanced sexuality?

Freud, in identifying the importance of the Super-ego or conscience, has a part to play in making some of the more extreme images socially acceptable. Many people might find the idea of enhanced sexuality uncomfortable to cope with, and this could cause the message to be rejected. In one famous advertisement for condoms a couple were pictured at a party. The sexual attraction was clearly portrayed, they rush from the party to consummate their lust.... The punchline comes with the realization that they are married. In this way the use of condoms is made acceptable by presenting it as being responsible rather than an incitement to immorality. In Freudian terms, the Id is stimulated by the implied sexuality, while the Super-ego is satisfied by the couple being married.

Psychoanalytical theories of human personality such as Freud's are often criticized for :

- subjectivity and a lack of scientific rigour
- their lack of satisfactory definitions of important concepts
- the fact that, being based on an assumption that the root of most behaviour is subconscious, there is a lack of testable predictions and measurable, objective data.

Further criticism has stemmed from what many people see as an over-emphasis on sexual motivation – although Freudian psychologists might argue that this is evidence of defence mechanisms at work.

On the other hand, Freud's ideas reflect many people's experiences and offer explanation of some well-recognized life crises. The acceptance of the subconscious nature of many motives is of great importance to the development of marketing, and there is some face validity in the notion that purchasing behaviour may be an extension of personality.

Think   – How good an explanation of human personality do you
            think psychoanalytical theories offer?
          – Why?

Trait approaches

Traits are characteristics which are common to many, but the strength of any characteristic will vary between individuals; hence a person can be defined by the profile of his or her traits. Traits are relatively stable, are assumed to influence behaviour and are therefore able to be inferred from consistencies observed in the behaviour of individuals.

Cattell (1989) is perhaps the best known of the supporters of the trait approach to personality. He used the technique of *factor analysis* to identify what he believed to be the principal factors of personality, as set out in Figure 12.6.

Trait theories perhaps come close to describing the structure of personality in the way that we use the term in everyday language. It uses words such as shy, tense, controlled, anxious, extrovert, which we can recognize and use to describe people we know. However, it does assume that these traits represent predispositions to behave in particular ways in a wide variety of situations. There is a general assumption that stable, underlying personality traits can be used to explain people's behaviour. At the level of face validity, it seems highly plausible that personality traits should have some effect on purchasing behaviour.

Cool	A	Warm
Concrete-thinking	B	Abstract-thinking
Affected by feelings	C	Emotionally stable
Submissive	E	Dominant
Sober	F	Enthusiastic
Expedient	G	Conscientious
Shy	H	Bold
Tough-minded	I	Tender-minded
Trusting	L	Suspicious
Practical	M	Imaginative
Forthright	N	Shrewd
Self-assured	O	Apprehensive
Conservative	Q_1	Experimenting
Group-oriented	Q_2	Self-sufficient
Undisciplined self-conflict	Q_3	Controlled
Relaxed	Q_4	Tense

Figure 12.6   Cattell's 16 principal factors (16PF)

Think – How useful is the trait approach to understanding personality? – Why?

Clearly, one significant part of our personal construct system is the way in which we see ourselves. This is the basis of self-concept theories.

Self-concept theories

Freud's notion of the Ego as the conscious part of us which deals with reality implies that each individual has some concept of who he or she is, and our general emphasis on perception suggests that our perception of ourselves may be a key element of our personality.

Mead argues that the self has two elements which are, in a way, the private and public faces of the personality. He identifies:

- the 'I' component – unique, individual, conscious and impulsive aspect (the personal, private, individual 'I')
- the 'Me' component – internalized, learned and accepted norms and values (the socially acceptable 'Me').

Rogers makes a similar distinction between the way 'I' see myself and the way others see 'Me'.

Newcomb takes these ideas and has started an interesting approach based on the idea of self-concept as a major determinant of behaviour and hence personality.

In marketing terms, the self-concept approach to personality has a number of attractions. First, it can be hypothesized that people will purchase products which are compatible with their self-concept and may be particularly attracted to products which enhance their 'ideal self' image. In addition, they may be specifically drawn to products which will confirm and support their longer-term 'aspirational' image of themselves.

Thus marketers may have a powerful tool for identifying their products with personality characteristics which are considered to be desirable by the consumers. However, the notion of 'the ideal' may be influenced by social factors. Advertisers' continuing emphasis on slim females causes distress to some observers who claim that it may lead to the development of unreasonable 'ideal selves' and expectations for impressionable young women who aspire to a shape they can never physically attain. The plus side is that the 'ideal' may be amenable to change which will allow still further 'aspirational' imagery.

This approach suggests that characteristics are not directly comparable, that we are all socially conscious, we all have our own self-image and, as learning organisms, we can learn and modify our personality.

However, there is little reason to assume that

- the way people see themselves
- the way others see them and
- the way they would like to be

should be the same.

Luft and Ingham (1955) developed an interesting model of interpersonal perception known as the Johari Window. This focuses on the differences between our self-perceptions and others' perceptions of us. It is usually displayed in the form shown in Figure 12.7.

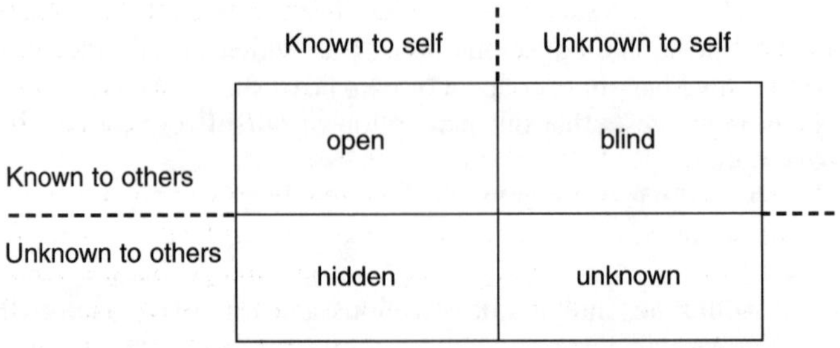

Figure 12.7

The Open quadrant illustrates the facets of ourselves (attitudes, behaviour and personality) which are known to us and which are also apparent to others.

The Hidden area represents those elements which we keep to ourselves and do not disclose to others.

These two areas are centred on those parts of our personality of which we are aware – which are part of our consciousness – and so they would seem to relate to the Freudian notion of the Ego.

The Unknown describes those parts of us which are unknown to both ourselves and to others, but which do influence our behaviour.

The Blind quadrant encompasses those aspects which are evident to other people, but of which we are unaware.

These two areas centre on those parts of our personality of which we are unaware. They are part of our subconscious, and the Unknown quadrant in particular would seem to correspond to Freud's idea of the Id. The Blind quadrant is interesting in that it contains things unknown to me but known to others. This could incorporate two well recognizable states:

- *paranoia* – the delusion that we are more unpopular than we really are
- *pronoia* – the delusion of popularity stemming from an ignorance of what people really think about us.

> **Think** – How do you see yourself?
> – How would you like to be?
> – How do others see you?
> – How do you know?
> – How much agreement is there between the three views?
> – How does this self-concept affect your buying behaviour?

From personal experience, it would seem to be a characteristic of being human that the three different aspects of self-image (how we see ourselves, how others see us and how we would like to be) differ to a greater or lesser extent. Individuals also vary in the robustness of their characters – some are more confident than others. This idea of self-esteem is an interesting one in terms of interpersonal perception – too little, and we perceive a person who 'does themselves down' and who is commonly depressive; too much, and we see someone who is conceited, 'big headed' and in need of being brought down a peg or two.

It can also be argued that the degree to which the three self-concepts agree or overlap gives a working measure of what we commonly call *adjustment*. We normally behave in ways which are consistent with our self-image, but inevitably, from time to time, life does not pan out in the way we would wish. Things go wrong. We experience feelings which are not consistent with our image of ourselves. Sometimes our actions are misinterpreted.

Freud suggested that, in such circumstances, our self-concept (ego) is threatened and, subconsciously, we will adopt various stratagems to relieve the dissonance. He described these behaviours as *ego defence mechanisms*. Here are pen pictures of some of the best known:

- *Repression* is the mental process used to protect the individual from memories, ideas and impulses which would produce emotional discomfort in the sense of apprehension, anxiety or guilt. The notion is that we suppress, censor and exclude disturbing thoughts from our conscious mind.
- *Rationalization* is the application of logic to a situation primarily to avoid facing up to the true motivation for one's actions. In other words, it is rather like a subconscious version of the more conscious process of 'making excuses' – 'I've been too busy at work to revise adequately for this examination', etc.
- *Projection* refers to the process whereby we will sometimes ascribe our own emotions and motivations to other people. It is normally associated with the individuals denying their own feelings or tendencies, and may often be linked with criticizing those characteristics in others – it is sometimes suggested that those students who worry most about others cheating in examinations are the ones who have been tempted themselves.
- *Sublimation* is the term used to describe the process whereby people will sometimes redirect energy from the socially unacceptable (often libidinous and sexually driven) to the socially acceptable. It can also refer to displacing personally undesirable behaviour by less threatening activities – students often 'revise' what they already know rather than face up to the reality of the inadequacy of their knowledge in other areas.
- *Identification* is the process we may adopt in attributing to ourselves, either consciously or unconsciously, the characteristics of another person or group. This is clearly used in many marketing situations, where it is hoped that the endorsement of a product by a successful personality will enhance the chances of the consumer identifying with that personality and hence using the product. Obviously the identification process will vary from individual to individual and will cause great effort to be expended to find the 'right' personality to promote any given product. This is examined in a little more detail in Chapter 13, where the process of attitude change is considered.
- *Fantasy* can sometimes be used as a pleasant escape from reality. Most of us have had the experience of daydreaming during boring classes or suffering from attacks of 'mind wandering' when revising!

The notions of 'displacement', 'fight or flight', aggression (both positive and negative) as coping devices all fit more or less comfortably into this section.

Think – Which of these defence mechanisms can you recognize in your own behaviour?

Defence mechanisms are subconscious processes and are mechanisms to provide desired outcomes for the individual – primarily the reduction of dissonance between our self image and the feedback from life.

Lifestyle may be seen as the individual's attempt to achieve his or her desired self-concept, given the constraints of the real world, and psychographics are the main way in which lifestyle analysis has been made available to the marketing specialist. It is an approach which seeks to describe the lifestyle of a segment of consumers, and focuses primarily on:

- *Activities* – usually observable and measurable. They could include items such as exposure to various media, visits to cinemas or theatres, shopping at specified shopping centres, holiday patterns, club memberships and so forth
- *Interests* – defined both in terms of an object, topic, event or subject and the level of excitement and attention that accompanies either short-term or long-term interest in it
- *Opinions* – the expectations, evaluations and interpretations about objects, topics, events, people or subjects.

For this reason, it is sometimes called *AIO analysis*. However, marketers commonly add some extra dimensions, such as:

- *Demographics* – factors such as age, income, occupation, gender, education, location
- *Attitudes* – collection of data on orientation to places, ideas and so forth
- *Values* – beliefs as to what is acceptable and/or desirable
- *Personality traits*
- *Usage rates* – consumption within a specific product category (e.g. heavy/light users).

Thus it is a potent mixture of factual, 'hard' information, identifying aspects such as disposable income, and 'soft', qualitative data, coming from motivational research techniques and aiming to ascertain the hidden and perhaps subconscious motivations described in our discussion of Freudian theory above.

It offers a number of attractions to the marketer:

- It accepts that consumer behaviour is affected by other factors as well as status and class and includes the important variable of individual personality
- The notion of lifestyle, by definition, encompasses purchasing decisions
- Markets can be segmented by lifestyle
- Appropriate communication channels may be part of the lifestyle and can be relatively well defined and hence exploited
- Campaigns can present brand personalities designed to appeal to specific lifestyles/AIO groups.

The notion of lifestyle has led some marketers to suggest that a significant sector for potential exploitation is the gay community. Clearly, they could be considered as a micro-culture within the larger society. While they are unlikely to fit into the family life cycle as portrayed above, they are likely to enjoy considerable disposable income, without many of the associated costs of children. Some authors and journalists have described this segmentation as the search for the 'pink pound'.

More sophisticated approaches to segmentation

Systems are being developed which incorporate more than one of these 'simple' approaches to segmentation. One of the most impressive and widely used is called MOSAIC, which identifies 58 separate classification types.

In this system the basic classification is done via:

- housing data, similar to the ACORN system described above, but input also comes from
- demographics (interestingly identifying factors such as people who have moved house in the last year and length of time at the address)
- census data focusing on the number and ages of residents
- census data concerned with ownership, facilities and size of household (giving an indication of lifestyle)
- socio-economic census data, e.g. occupation and car ownership
- financial data from sources such as lists of county court judgments and finance house/credit card searches.

The possibility of adding more detailed lifestyle/AIO layers to such a model could offer exciting new tools for segmentation to marketers.

A further development has been possible due to computer technology. Stores such as Tesco and Sainsbury in the UK have introduced 'club cards', which are 'sold' to the public as a means of accumulating discounts or cash back. The card, which is electronically 'swiped' through a machine at the checkout, records all of the individual's purchases – thus enabling the credits to be stored and saved. From the store's viewpoint, it records *actual* purchasing behaviour and detailed records can be accumulated of both patterns and frequency of purchasing.

As the store obtained the full address of the customer when the card was initially issued, the information is now personalized and this enables it to track changes in behaviour (including a 'lack of loyalty') and to target 'suitable' individuals for special promotions and offers. The stores claim that this is in the customer's interest. On a recent television programme a spokesperson claimed that if, for instance, they find patterns of purchasing which indicate an interest in (say) Italian food, that customer could be sent details of new promotions for pasta, sauces, wine, etc. On the other hand, critics suggest that purchasing a home pregnancy test kit at the pharmacy section could result in the arrival of post containing maternity wear and children's goods offers.

Think – How do you feel about a store keeping this information on your behaviour?
– Is it ethical for it to do so without seeking your permission?

Benefit segmentation

One final approach that is of interest is to segment a market in terms of benefits sought from a product. Here a simple example could be distinguishing between people who ride bicycles as

- a cheap means of transport in town
- a means of 'off road' recreation
- a means of exercising
- an excuse to wear lycra shorts.

Summary

There is no universally appropriate segmentation system which is 'right' for all product groups.

In today's marketplace the most useful segmentation tool for some products is likely to be that of lifestyle. The other methods are based on demographics and lack flexibility. For instance, it could be argued that class no longer predicts accurately the disposable income of a group but, on the other hand, class has the advantage that it does discriminate consistently between groups and the basic demographic data is available.

Life stage is clearly relevant. It relates fairly easily to disposable income and, interestingly, may well be highly applicable across different cultures as the family-raising focus applies worldwide. The data is again readily available and investigation is less likely to be perceived as being intrusive.

Lifestyle cuts across the previous two categories by focusing on interests, values, hobbies, etc. The power of this as a marketing tool is that it centres immediately on what is likely to be purchased when there is disposable income.

It is, however, possible to argue that some segmentation methods are better suited to certain products/services than others.

It is also possible to envisage segmentation by using a combination of all three – Class B, Empty Nest 1, 'liberal, *Guardian* readers', who may be prime targets for holidays in India or Africa (e.g. Page and Moy).

As ever, the answer may be 'horses for courses'.

Think – Which approach to market segmentation (or combinations) do you feel is most appropriate for the following products/services?

- Lawnmowers
- Banking services
- Newspapers
- Sun tan lotion
- Satellite dishes and decoders
- 4 x 4 'off road' vehicles
- Washing-up liquid

- Pork-flavoured crisps
- Incontinence pads
- Open-top sports cars
- Top-of-the-range running shoes
- Denture fixatives
- Motor scooters.

13 'So how can we make it work...?'

Attitude change

Introduction

If we accept our earlier proposition that attitudes and behaviour are linked, then, as marketers, we will be very concerned with the process of changing attitudes. Usually we will be concerned with enhancing positive views of our own product, although there could be examples where we may be more interested in down-grading attitudes towards competitors or 'the opposition'.

Think – What examples can you think of of negative attitude change as an objective of the marketer/advertiser?

Earlier in the chapter the inter-relation of the cognitive, affective and conative elements of attitude was discussed. This can be a useful framework for looking at change strategies, as it is possible to initiate change through attending to any one of the three components.

Attitude change via cognitions

Here we focus on the beliefs about the attributes of the product. We may aim to:

a) change these beliefs and/or
b) change the relative importance of existing beliefs and/or
c) develop new beliefs and/or
d) change the beliefs regarding the attributes of the 'ideal'.

The UK government has published a number of reports on diet and health over the last decade and is attempting to change attitudes through what we might call 'cognitive restructuring' of our attitudes towards what we eat. Some years ago it was commonly believed that potatoes and pasta were fattening. This belief has been 'attacked' by the message that carbohydrates are 'energy food' for athletes. Similarly, the relative importance of fibre in the diet has been emphasized. New beliefs about sources of protein and other essentials have been developed so that (e.g.) vegetarianism is becoming both more widespread and more acceptable. Lastly, our image of the 'ideal' is being manipulated. Women have suffered for years from the 'thin is beautiful' message – men are now being pushed to 'fight the flab', women too feel guilty about having 'chubby hubbies' and athletes such as Linford Christie are promoting semi-skimmed milk.

While we may start with cognitions, the aim is to change the overall attitude. We hope for possible sequences, as in Figure 13.1.

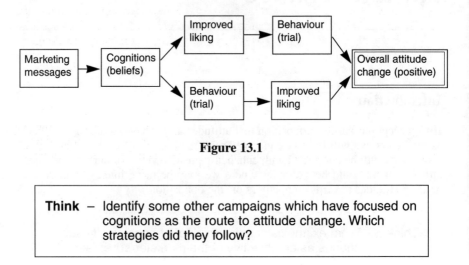

Figure 13.1

> **Think** – Identify some other campaigns which have focused on cognitions as the route to attitude change. Which strategies did they follow?

Attitude change via effects

It is quite feasible to attempt to influence consumers' liking of a product without directly impacting either their beliefs or their behaviour. Here the logic is that increased liking will lead to more positive beliefs which might lead to product purchase. Alternatively, increased liking may lead to purchase. This, in turn, will alter the consumer's experience base and may lead to more positive beliefs about the product. Diagrammatically this can be represented by Figure 13.2.

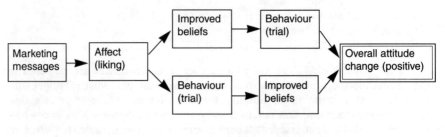

Figure 13.2

Engel, Blackwell and Miniard use the term 'transformational' to describe advertising aimed at 'making the experience of using the product richer, warmer, more exciting, and/or more enjoyable than that obtained solely from an objective description of the advertised brand'. The advertisements 'transform' the value derived from product consumption by influencing consumers' perceptions of the product's emotional and symbolic features.

There are a number of approaches possible when aiming for effect change – classical conditioning, effect towards the advertisement, and repetition/exposure.

Classical conditioning. It is possible to use the classical conditioning methods (see Chapter 11) by consistently pairing the brand name with a stimulus that the subject likes. Several examples use music as the positive stimulus (Hamlet cigars linked with the tranquillity of a Bach aria, Vauxhall Cars with the Eric Clapton 'Layla' melody, etc.). The assumption is that, over a period of time, the positive feelings associated with the established stimuli will transfer to the product.

Effect towards the advertisement. Producing an advertisement which is liked in its own right is thought to increase the tendency to like the product. A note of caution needs to be struck, however, as there is evidence that 'cult' adverts sometimes fail to make the linkage with the product. The use of humour, celebrities and emotion are all discussed later in the chapter.

Repetition/exposure. There is some evidence to suggest that mere exposure on a regular basis may, in itself, be enough to improve affect or liking, although this seems to be most appropriate for low-involvement products.

The implications for the advertiser of adopting an attitude change via effect approach are of some interest:

● Classical conditioning approaches give the most appropriate guidelines
● Attitudes towards the advertisement itself seem to be important
● The advertisements need not contain any factual/cognitive information
● Repetition is critical
● New measures of advertisement effectiveness may need to be developed.

Think – Identify some other campaigns which have focused on effects as the route to attitude change.
– Which strategies did they follow?

Attitude change via behaviour

It is quite possible for purchase to precede the development of either cognition or effect, particularly low-cost, low-involvement products – the process is often one of active experimentation on the part of the consumer ('I'll try this'). In this instance the actions are very much as described under operant conditioning in Chapter 11, so the first problem for the marketer is to induce the individual to purchase or try the product. Free samples, point-of-sale displays, coupons, price reductions and special promotions are the main techniques used for inducing trial. This time the process may look like Figure 13.3.

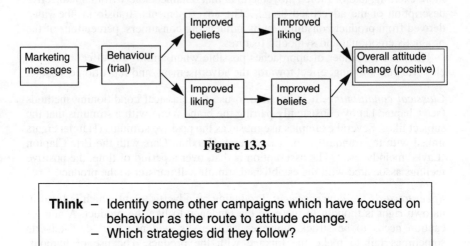

Figure 13.3

> **Think** – Identify some other campaigns which have focused on behaviour as the route to attitude change.
> – Which strategies did they follow?

Factors affecting attitude change

There are six broad categories of factor which influence the ease or difficulty of changing attitudes. They are:

1 Existing attitudes
2 Source factors
3 Message features
4 Channel of communication
5 Receiver attributes
6 Product characteristics.

We shall examine each of these in turn.

Existing attitudes

The process of attitude formation is based primarily on either *primary* (first-hand), or *secondary* experience (passed on from advertisers, parents, friends, etc.). The presence of pre-existing attitudes makes the process of change rather more difficult due to the commitment of the individual to the existing attitude. Generally the higher the commitment and the more strongly held the attitude, the harder becomes the task of attitude change.

We saw, when we reviewed Osgood and Tannenbaum's congruity theory, that where there is a conflict between two attitudes, the resultant attitude tends to have moved more in the direction of the stronger held attitude. This may in part be a reason why it is hard to get people to stop smoking – if they have a lot of self-image invested in the activity it will be difficult to get them to change attitude. Festinger's Theory of Cognitive Dissonance also focuses on this same issue, and most of the discussion in the preceding section is directly relevant to the change process.

Attitudes held due to product experience will also be harder to change than those based on secondary experience (e.g. advertising).

It is interesting to consider the processes involved in political attitudes changing as elections draw near. All parties realize that the chances of winning over the voter who is deeply committed to another party are very slight. The committed Tory is unimpressed by Labour's arguments and vice versa. All parties aim to persuade the 'floating voter' – the person who does not have strongly held attitudes.

Think – Which of your attitudes might be most amenable to change?
– Which might be least?

Source factors

The source of a message is a very important factor in determining how influential the communication is. It is becoming commonplace to find celebrities endorsing products (often for huge fees) – rock stars such as Michael Jackson and Tina Turner appear in Cola commercials, sports stars such as Daley Thompson and John Barnes endorse Lucozade. Sometimes the celebrity explicitly says that the product is great, sometimes implicitly just by appearing (association).

The degree of influence of such appearances appears to be a function of both expertness and trustworthiness – i.e. sports stars should be expert on energy replacement for high levels of performance but, in order to be influential, they should be characters who are trustworthy in the eyes of the consumer (a perception that 'they're only doing it for the money' would tend to discredit the message). Despite this apparently confident and self-evident statement, we might be even more impressed by an untrustworthy source arguing against 'own best interest' (e.g. a convicted murderer expressing the opinion that the death penalty should be reintroduced).

Credible sources generally aid persuasion. Level of knowledge and relevant expertise are both important, but trustworthiness is a key concept – if the source is perceived as being untrustworthy, then expertise/knowledge becomes irrelevant and the message tends to be rejected.

Generally, evidence suggests that the message becomes more persuasive when the source is:

● physically attractive. Attractiveness may also be a function of liking the source. A number of studies have suggested that liking the source is an important factor in the persuasiveness of a message – we are more likely to be

persuaded by those we like than those we dislike
- a celebrity, or
- similar to the target audience.

Finding one or two issues of commonality before attempting to change the third has also been found effective on the grounds that the commonality creates some sort of bonding between source and receiver which makes the area of difference harder to sustain. This coincides neatly with Heider's Balance Theory, reviewed earlier. This particular approach seems most important when consumers do not engage in high levels of elaboration or mental/cognitive processing activity.

Credibility may also be a function of expectation. Several experiments have reported the duping of subjects when the source was introduced authoritatively and appeared as expected (scientists wear white laboratory coats, doctors also have white coats but with a stethoscope, lecturers often have 'high foreheads' and wear glasses, and so on).

Group affiliation may be a follow-on from this point. For change agents to be effective they must be perceived as being a significant member of the group – the person being influenced should see the change agent as 'one of us'. As we will see, groups can exert enormous influence over individuals, both in their behaviour and their attitudes.

Think – Which attitudes have you 'modified' in order to be more comfortable within a group or with friends?

Message features

Messages which are perceived by the receiver as being 'strong' appear to inhibit negative thoughts and encourage positive ones, and vice versa for weak claims and arguments.

Strength in this context depends on the message being seen as both:

- relevant to the receiver's situation
- objective, i.e. factual as opposed to subjective. Generally we have a problem of interpretation – the price of a product may appear high to one consumer and low to another, so giving the factual price may allow the receivers to make their own judgements. People usually see facts as being open to being checked (even if they do not always check themselves) and evaluated. Facts are also seen as being more believable if they can be verified, and under these conditions they create more favourable attitudes.

Early studies found evidence to suggest that significantly greater opinion or attitude change resulted when larger changes were advocated (this may well match with Osgood's Congruity theory). However, there is more recent evidence to suggest that, if the change suggested is so extreme as to run counter to the receiver's self-image/concept (and is hence highly involving to the individual), then a move apart may occur. This is in line with what might be expected from our earlier observations on ego-defence mechanisms and perceptual defence.

Claims

Many advertising messages make claims about the product they are promoting. It is interesting to consider briefly the different types of claims that can be made:

- *Search claims* ('you'll not find anything cheaper') can be tested before purchase
- *Experience claims* ('using this product will change your life') can only be fully evaluated after purchase
- *Credence claims* ('I believe this is the route to peace and prosperity') may be impossible to evaluate.

Petty and Cacioppo (1987) found that making numerous claims was more important under low elaboration/involvement, but did not matter under high involvement where one 'good' argument could swing the decision/attitude.

One-sided/Two-sided

Two-sided messages – putting the downside as well as the upside of a product or decision ('you may find cheaper, but you'll not find better') – is perceived as being more truthful than simple one-sided messages. This finding appears to hold good even when the downside argument is relatively weak.

Threat

Karlins and Abelson (1970) conducted an elegant study of attitudes towards tetanus. Different groups were given written descriptions with differing levels of threat/fear inbuilt. Some were told that the disease was 'difficult to control, but relatively easy to cure'; others were told that it was 'easy to contract and difficult to cure'. The high-fear group was given coloured photographs and descriptions of death. The effectiveness of inoculation against tetanus was also given. Some were given to understand that injections gave an 'almost perfect' guarantee against tetanus, while others were told that inoculations were generally effective but did not eliminate the possibility of contracting the disease. Some were told that the injection was very painful; others were given no hint of discomfort.

The subjects were later asked about attitudes towards tetanus and inoculation. They were not influenced by evidence of effectiveness or painfulness, but they were influenced by fear-arousal. Those who received the high-fear material were more likely both to see the benefits of the vaccine and to have the inoculation.

This study suggests that strong, credible fear messages seem to work!

However, Karlins and Abelson also suggested that situational factors may influence the effectiveness of fear as a change agent. They suggest that a strong fear appeal is superior to a mild one in changing attitude when it:

- poses a threat to the individual's loved ones
- is presented by a highly credible source
- deals with topics relatively unfamiliar to the individual
- aims at the subjects with a high degree of self-esteem and/or low perceived vulnerability to danger.

Conversely, the importance of the subject's initial concern with the issue may be significant. If there is a high initial concern, a fear-arousing communication may overwhelm the individual with anxiety, producing a reduction in the effectiveness of the message, perhaps linked with defence mechanisms such as repression and selective perception.

Executional elements

By executional elements advertising specialists refer to the visual image, sounds, colours, pace, etc. used in the advertisement.

It is believed that advertisements which are liked can be effective in changing attitudes and that those which are disliked can lower consumer evaluations of the product. First-hand experience casts a few doubts over these assumptions, as the author has found that some advertising campaigns which were perceived as being 'irritating' have worked in as much as brand awareness has certainly been achieved!!

This observation might be supported by returning to our comments on the successful marketing of Radion washing powder. Here the brand name has the potential for negative associations – radon (a gas associated with the development of cancer), radium (also linked with cancer), radioactive, are all similar-sounding words. The manufacturers have done little to suppress such connections – as we have already observed, they have utilized lurid colours on the packaging and posters and linked the product to 'hard' slogans.

Repetition

The importance of repetition has already been mentioned in the chapter on learning and the earlier section of this chapter dealing with effects as the route to attitude change. While repetition is clearly a crucial element in conditioning approaches to attitude change and development, it is not without its drawbacks. Early repetitions can allow better evaluation of the message, but there is evidence to suggest that this reaches a peak and then repetition can become tedious and counter-productive. This does seem to be one of the limitations of using humour in advertisements – few things pall as quickly as the repeated joke!

The distinction appears to be between repetition, which enhances the impact of the message, and repetitiveness, which is counter-productive. The point at which one turns into the other and tedium sets in appears to depend on the degree of mental processing that has gone on and the amount of evaluation that has taken place.

Channel of communication

Some channels of communication are perceived as being more authoritative than others; reports carried in some newspapers carry more weight than those published in less prestigious ones.

It has been interesting over the years to see the way in which ITN has 'come from behind' so that it is currently not perceived as being any less authoritative than BBC news.

Similarly, some people see the written word as carrying more authority than the spoken word. Television, with its ability to present words, images and written material, is hence one of the most potent and versatile of the advertising media.

Receiver attributes

Motivation

This has been dealt with extensively in Chapter 6. It may also help to think in terms of utilitarian or hedonic motives, with the obvious implications for sending utilitarian or hedonic messages. Needless to say, it is not a simple either/or choice – many products have both characteristics, and the advertising for products such as cars and houses reflects themes of both motives.

Arousal

Here we are revisiting some of our earlier work on awareness and attention from Chapter 2. Clearly, people will be unlikely to be much influenced by messages which they do not even recognize. Conversely, high levels of arousal or excitement can distort perception considerably. This gives rise to a situation which may be best represented by Figure 13.4.

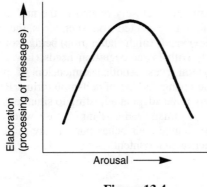

Figure 13.4

This inverted 'U' highlights the need for enough arousal to make it work and the avoidance of high levels of arousal which may lead to an inability to concentrate on the message.

As we might expect, elaboration is highest at moderate levels of arousal. High arousal consumers appear to be more affected by the celebrity of the source.

The advertisement itself can affect the level of arousal – affective messages catch the attention quite well and may, in this way, lead to arousal (or, in the case of adverts such as Hamlet cigars, lower arousal).

This whole area has some interesting implications for advertisement placement – buying television advertising space during sports events may catch a high number of potential consumers, but the nature of the message may need to be considered if the audience is likely to be in a high state of excitement.

Knowledge

Engel, Blackwell and Miniard argue that knowledgeable consumers are better able to evaluate technical messages (and, in the process, to be more influenced by them). They also suggest that consumer knowledge allows sounder judgment of the strengths and weaknesses of the claims.

Mood

There is some evidence to suggest that the mood in which a consumer receives a message affects the likelihood of change. The suggestion is that being in a 'favourable' mood can help/enhance persuasion, while 'unfavourable' moods inhibit persuasion. We also have the notion of arousal (see above). The main messages for the marketer seem to be either the creation of appropriate moods to go with the message or, alternatively, placing your advertisement in an appropriate context (e.g. choice of magazine, or placing a TV commercial in the middle of a specific play, soap, sporting event, etc.).

Personality traits

The need for cognition seems to be closely related to the notion of elaboration developed above, and, as might be expected from such ideas, the evidence points to persons with high cognition needs (high elaboration) being more influenced by message claims. Individuals with lower cognition needs (low elaboration) are more influenced by peripheral cues. Another dimension of personality that appears to influence attitude change is that of self-monitoring. Persons who are high on such scales are likely to be adept at adjusting to situations and tend to be more influenced by 'style' or 'image' advertising. Those who are low on the dimension are less likely to change their behaviour and are more influenced by quality messages with higher factual content.

Product characteristics

Stage in product life cycle is clearly of relevance where new products focus on awareness and trial. Brand image becomes the focus during growth, while maintenance of 'good' attitudes is the objective at maturity.

Similarly, *awareness set analysis* (see Chapter 2) may highlight the need to make the consumer aware of the organization/product. If the product is in the evoked set, then maintenance of positive attitudes becomes the target, while placement in the inept set signals the need for attitude change approaches.

Product experience may well exert more influence than advertising.

Product positioning – the image desired for the product will determine, to a great extent, the nature of the attitude change attempted and the type of message that is appropriate (e.g. the cut price, good value product will use different messages from those of the status symbol).

Relative performance (relative to competitors) may define appropriate messages – if your product is superior, then use the facts as the message; if not, alternative strategies need to be employed. More fuzzy, subjective, affective advertising copy may need to be used.

This can be summarized by Figure 13.5.

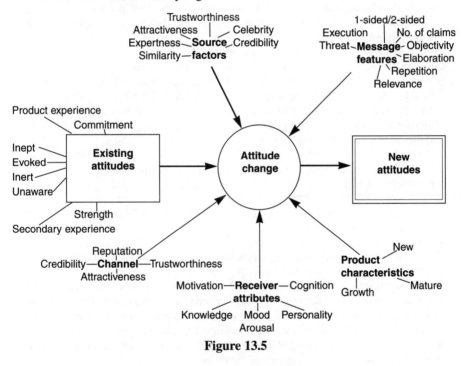

Figure 13.5

Personality and predicting consumer behaviour

We have mentioned on a number of occasions that it seems plausible to suppose that there is a link between personality and buying behaviour. However, the evidence to support this view is less than convincing. One famous attempt to determine the personality characteristics of Ford and Chevrolet owners in 1959 found few statistically significant differences. In fact, the study was only able to predict ownership in 63 per cent of cases, which, given that there were only two choices, is little better than the 50 per cent that could be expected from random chance. The conclusion was that personality was of relatively little value in predicting brand ownership of cars. Several other studies at that time found equally inconclusive results.

The problem may lie in our initial assumption that personality should be a prime factor in determining brand choice. Engel, Blackwell and Miniard point out that personality is only one variable in the process of consumer decision making and that intention might be a better correlate. They continue their argument by proposing that if personality traits were found to be valid predictors of intentions (or even behaviour), they would only be useful as a means of market segmentation if:

- people with common personality traits were similar in terms of demographic factors such as age, income and locality. This is necessary if they are to be reached economically through the mass media. If they do not have these common demographic characteristics there will be no practical means of reaching them as a unique market segment
- the personality measures used are demonstrably reliable and valid
- the differences identified reflect clear-cut variations in buyer activity and preferences. If this is not true, then consumers can show different personality profiles while referring essentially the same product attributes
- any grouping identified is of sufficient size to make a marketing initiative worthwhile. The recognition that 'every individual is unique' is not helpful in terms of market segmentation.

The evidence to date does not support the notion that personality is linked to demographics because:

- personality measurement has numerous problems of reliability and validity, as described above
- personality is not a significant factor in most consumer decisions, and
- the creation of larger groupings tends to dilute the clarity of market segments.

It is therefore not surprising that Engel, Blackwell and Miniard conclude that 'the evidence to date falls short of these criteria, and personality has not been demonstrated convincingly as a useful means of market segmentation'.

The relative failure of personality measures in predicting consumer behaviour has led to the development of alternative approaches in more recent times. The first is the exploration of the notion of brand personality.

Brand personality

Peter and Olson (1990) suggest that we can look at a brand as a series of 'bundles'. They recognize that consumers will see a product as a bundle of attributes (physical characteristics, which could be abstract concepts such as 'quality' or more concrete and tangible aspects), a bundle of benefits (these could be functional benefits or social/psychological payoffs) and a bundle of value satisfactions (possibly short-term instrumental values or longer-term terminal values). This gives rise to the interesting notion of the product or brand possessing a personality. One can think of examples where specific personalities have been created for products – the perfume which is young, fun-loving and a bit rebellious, compared with the perfume which has the image of being more mature, sophisticated and upper-class.

Think – What is the brand personality of:

- Levi jeans?
- Coca Cola?
- BMW cars?
- Swatch watches?
- Carling Black Label?

In the USA Anheuser-Busch created four separate 'personalities' for four new brands of beer. They developed commercials for each brand aimed at different 'drinker personalities'- e.g. one commercial portrayed a 'social drinker' (charact-erized in one account as a typical campus guzzler), another as an 'indulgent drinker' (a male who perceives himself as a total failure), yet another showed a 'reparative drinker' (middle-aged and one who had made sacrifices of personal objectives to help others – drink was the reward!).

Two hundred and fifty beer drinkers watched the commercials and sampled all four beers. They were then asked to state their preferences and to complete a questionnaire which measured their own 'drinker personality'. The results indic-ated that a majority of the respondents preferred the brand that matched their own reported drinker personality. Most consumers also felt strongly enough to respond that at least one brand of beer was not fit to drink.

Unknown to the 250 respondents, all four brands were the same beer!

This evidence links well with the self-concept approaches to personality described above. However, it might be useful to reflect that, while consumers are likely to be attracted to a product personality which enhances or matches up with their 'ideal self', this may be subject to all the reservations we have expressed regarding personality measurement in general. Thus it may be more prudent to suggest that the brand personality may complement, rather than match, that of the consumer.

Communication systems and patterns of influence

In Chapter 2 we looked at some aspects of communication – in that section the focus was very much on the processes associated with perception. We noted that the perception of the receiver defined whether the communication was successful or not. Earlier in this chapter we came back to communication when we looked at the characteristics of influential messages and the way in which they could change attitudes.

Both of these approaches had an implicit assumption that the communication was a single message passed from the sender to the receiver. This is called *one-step communication*, and is shown diagrammatically in Figure 13.6.

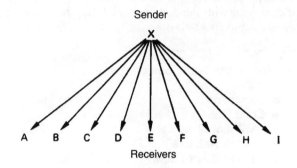

Figure 13.6

This is a common view of marketing communication – the sender transmits a message to each receiver (the targeted potential consumer) and it is then assumed that the individual will respond by purchasing the product or service (or not, as the individual decides). This approach gives us yet another way of segmenting the market – the message and the medium can be chosen to appeal to specific target groups. However, while this is both a very common and common-sense approach to marketing communication, it is not without its limitations:

1 First, there may well be grave doubts as to whether the message actually reaches every receiver. There is considerable evidence to suggest that many commercial breaks on television are used by viewers to stretch their legs, make cups of tea, answer the call of nature, look at the newspaper to see what is on other channels and so forth. These are the very times when advertisers have paid large sums of money to communicate with them. In the work situation, organizations such as the Industrial Society have found that company newspapers and newsletters are rarely read in any detail, while newspaper advertisements are commonly skipped over in the rush to find the part of the paper which is of direct interest to the reader.

2 Secondly, receivers do not, in reality, respond as independent, isolated individuals – much of the material covered in earlier chapters has emphasized the importance of groups and other social interactions in determining behaviour, both in general terms and, more specifically, in purchasing.

One attempt to describe the process more accurately is the idea of *two-step communication*. This may be represented diagrammatically as shown in Figure 13.7.

Here receiver E is seen as an influencer of others. These persons are referred to as *opinion leaders* and are those individuals who reinforce the marketing messages sent, and to whom other receivers look for information, advice and opinions. As shown in the diagram, it is also suggested that, under such a system, the opinion leader will also communicate the message to those receivers who may have missed the original message (G, H, I as shown). The early versions of two-step theory assumed most receivers to be relatively passive in terms of information search and exposure to the mass media, and the opinion leaders were active in disseminating the messages.

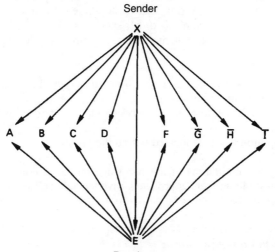

Sender

Receivers

Figure 13.7

The follow-up work on this approach suggested that opinion leaders tended to:

- be of similar social class to the other receivers (or influencers), but may be of higher social status within that class
- be more self-confident
- be more outgoing and socially active
- be more orientated towards innovation
- have greater knowledge and interest in the area of influence
- have greater exposure to relevant mass media than non-leaders.

At first sight this looks like the marketing specialist's dream – an individual who will promote the product, on the ground, free! It is not surprising that considerable effort has gone into trying to identify such people. Several approaches can be taken – for instance, analysis of mailing lists drawn up from coupon replies will identify those who have specific interests and exposure to the mass media; analysis of appropriate organizations' membership lists could show those with the potential to be opinion leaders; while comparison of subscription mailing lists may indicate those who take more than one publication and thus satisfy the sixth point above. More personalized approaches could include *sociometric techniques* (asking people who they go to for advice) or *self-designation* (asking people the extent to which their advice is sought).

The potential excitement at the idea of an elite group of opinion leaders who may be 'recruited' to aid the marketing effort had to be tempered when it was found that the sphere of influence of any individual was rather limited. Common sense suggests that it is rare to heed the advice of a single person on a wide range of topics. Experience would indicate that we are more likely to choose our adviser on the basis of our perception of his or her specialism.

Katz, in 1957, suggested that the degree of influence that is possible will depend on:

● who the opinion leader is – those who are seen as typical of a group may be in a position to exert more influence
● what the opinion leader knows – the advice of the most expert is likely to carry most weight
● where the opinion leader is located within the group.

So gradually the limitations of the two-stage model of communication have become apparent. More recent approaches have tended to describe the process as one of multi-stage interactions.

Word-of-mouth communication

This form of communication is particularly significant and important because it occurs in the highly influential reference groups, as described in Chapter 5. It is relatively informal, and is difficult to manage because it does not involve the marketer directly. It would seem to be powerful specifically because of this 'neutrality' and the enhanced credibility of the messages.

Engel, Blackwell and Miniard call the transmitters of word-of-mouth communication of this sort *influentials*. In contrast to the original two-step model, these influentials are commonly sought out by the receivers rather than acting as active initiators of the messages. They identify seven conditions, one or more of which need to be present if 'opinion leadership' is likely to occur:

1 The consumer lacks sufficient information to make an adequately informed choice.
2 The product is complex and difficult to evaluate using objective criteria. Hence the experience of others serves as the basis for vicarious learning.
3 The person lacks the ability to evaluate the product or service, no matter how the information is disseminated and presented.
4 Other sources are perceived as having low credibility.
5 An influential person is more accessible than other sources and thus can be consulted more easily.
6 Strong social ties exist between transmitter and receiver.
7 The individual has a high need for social approval.

They also argue that the motivations that drive interpersonal discussions which involve product information fall into one or more of five broad categories:

1 *Product involvement.* Here the tendency to initiate conversation is directly proportional to the extent of the interest or involvement in the topic under discussion. The first person within a group of peers to have the new 32-bit, high-resolution personal computer with the new software package is likely to tell others as an outlet for the pleasure or excitement generated by its purchase and use.

Think – What examples of your own behaviour can you identify when you have behaved in this manner with other people?
– What examples of other people's behaviour can you identify when they have behaved in this manner with you?

---

2 *Self-Enhancement.* This is when the motivation to initiate the transaction is to gain attention, show what Engel, Blackwell and Miniard call 'connoisseurship', suggest status, assert superiority or otherwise 'show off'. It is fairly common for this to include the idea of 'insider information', in the way that people will often tell you how they have 'just found the most marvellous recipe for stuffed mushrooms'.

Think – Have you ever done this?
– How did the recipients react?
– Have you ever had this done to you?
– How did you react to the message?

---

3 *Concern for others.* The conversation may simply be aimed at helping a friend or relative to make a better purchase decision. This is particularly common when social or family ties are strong.

Think – What experience of this sort have you had of giving and taking advice from family and friends?
– Do you think the motivation was genuine altruism?

---

4 *Message intrigue.* The need to talk about advertisements or selling appeals. Jokes are often made using the language and imagery of advertisements, and the recent spate of 'mini-soap' adverts seems to be aimed at getting people to talk about the advertisement itself.

> **Think** – Can you think of recent examples where this has happened?

5 *Dissonance reduction.* As we discussed in Chapter 6, cognitive dissonance (worry or doubts) often follow a significant, high-involvement purchase decision. Dissatisfied or worried customers can be a dangerous source of negative information if they vent their anger (a defence mechanism) by 'bad mouthing' the product.

Perhaps this multi-stage approach differs most significantly from the more traditional views in its acceptance that a great deal of the communication is initiated by the person seeking the information, rather than by the influential opinion leader. Here we return to the crucial notion of the credibility of the transmitter. It is reasonable to think that messages will be most influential when somebody seeks the information, and there is a common assumption that, in comparison with other media, another consumer has less ulterior or commercial motive for sharing the information.

Another interesting aspect is the evidence which suggests that we pay more attention, and give higher priority, to negative information. This may be because we expect marketers to emphasize positive aspects and we are particularly alert for any counterbalancing messages. There are also suggestions that the dissatisfied customer is more motivated to share 'bad news' than the satisfied customer is to share 'good news'.

Clearly, positive word-of-mouth can be one of the marketer's most potent assets, and, given the comments in the preceding paragraph, negative word-of-mouth is to be avoided if humanly possible. The marketing specialist cannot control these processes directly, but they can be stimulated, channelled and influenced.

Negative messages can be minimized by dealing with complaints as swiftly and efficiently as possible. Disgruntled consumers can spread the word very quickly, so every effort should be made to remove the source of the irritation.

Influentials can be identified and wooed. As discussed earlier, identifying these people is particularly difficult because one of their key characteristics is their similarity to those they influence. Thus it is not easy to view them as a distinct market segment. The only times when this might be possible is when the expertise is identifiable and thus certain professional groups can be targeted as being likely opinion leaders (doctors for medical products might be one obvious example, while teachers, sports coaches, vicars might provide others). Another option is to use mass media, in the full knowledge that there will be wastage and a degree of inefficiency.

New products – success/failure

It is a common assertion that 90 per cent of new products fail. On the other hand, innovation is the lifeblood of the market. In this section we will examine some of the reasons why some ideas/products/services 'take off' and others 'die the death'.

One of the key thinkers in this field has been Everett Rogers, who defined *diffusion* as the process by which an innovation (any new idea, product or service) is communicated over time among the members of a social system. Out of the mass of research in this area four key elements emerge as being significant to the diffusion process. They are:

- the innovation itself
- the communication processes and channels used
- the time at which individuals decide to adopt the product
- the social systems involved.

The field also classifies people into *adopter* and *non-adopter* categories, and later we will look at the ways in which people may change from non-adopter status to that of adopter – our target!

We will define an *innovation* as any idea or product which is perceived by the potential adopter to be new. This is essentially a subjective definition and, as such, most of our work from Chapter 2 and the study of perception becomes highly significant. While at first the use of such a definition looks to be evasive, it does avoid many of the problems associated with defining newness.

One framework for examining innovation distinguishes between:

- *Continuous innovation* – the modification of an existing product rather than the establishment of a completely new one. It causes the least disruption to established patterns of behaviour.
- *Dynamically continuous innovation* – the creation of either a new, or the alteration of an existing, product, but one which does not alter significantly the patterns of consumer buying or product use.
- *Discontinuous innovation* – the introduction of a totally new product which causes consumers to alter their behaviour patterns significantly.

Think – In which category would you place the introduction of:

- a new coloured toothpaste?
- an electric town car?
- toothpaste with added fluoride?
- the microwave oven?
- the launch of a 'new' model of an existing car?
- the Mars ice-cream?
- the introduction of 24-hour cash dispensers at banks?
- the introduction of 24-hour banking?
- the compact disc?
- wholefoods?
- laser printers to replace dot matrix printers for computers?
- 'virtual reality' machines?

Another potentially useful way of looking at innovation is to recognize that products may have both *hardware* (physical) aspects and *software* (information) elements. The language of the computer is not accidental, as it can highlight the importance of the overall package. As with computers, the most advanced hardware is of little use if the instruction manual is inadequate. Similarly, it is not uncommon for the emphasis at the product development stage to be on the hardware, while the informational and attitudinal elements may be neglected.

It is also widely accepted, following the original work of Rogers, that there are five characteristics which are associated with the success of new products. We will examine them in turn.

Relative advantage

This is essentially another perceptual phenomenon – it is the extent to which a consumer perceives the product to have an advantage over the product it supersedes. Clearly, the logic suggests that the greater the perceived advantage, the greater the probability of adoption.

Compatibility

This refers to the degree to which the product is consistent with existing values and past experiences of the potential consumers. Here the assumption is that the less compatible a product is with the consumer values, the longer it will take to be adopted. In the previous exercise it might be interesting to think of the relative problems associated with introducing a toothpaste which was yellow, or dark red, or black.

Complexity

This is the degree to which the new product is perceived to be difficult to understand and use. The more difficult it is perceived to be, the harder it will be for the product to be accepted. Once more, the key is the perception of the consumer – many people perceive the operation of a personal computer as being complex, yet they have mastered the more difficult skill of driving a motor car.

Trialability

It is believed that new products are more likely to be adopted when consumers can try them out on an experimental basis. This is relatively simple with low-cost items – food product samples are commonly given to shoppers as they enter supermarkets and, in a similar vein, we used the example of free trial sachets of shampoo when we looked at behaviour change as the trigger for attitude change above. However, trialling can be rather more difficult with more expensive, high-involvement products. Leasing can be one solution to this problem which can reduce the perceived risk for consumers, and earlier we used the idea of sampling new models of cars when existing models are taken in for service.

Observability

This characteristic is a measure of the degree to which adoption of the product, or the results of using the product, are visible to friends, neighbours and colleagues. This seems to affect the diffusion process by allowing potential consumers to see the benefits of the product and thus increase (or even create) a 'want' for themselves. The process can be given additional impetus if the visible product is seen to be used by celebrities or other role models. Examples of this are designer labels on clothing which are clearly visible, so we have the LaCoste alligator or the Pringle lion (both of which were both visible and worn by sporting celebrities). Some products are, by their very nature, highly visible – people who buy a new car are unlikely to keep it a secret from their neighbours; most fashion items are clearly observable. Another highly observable innovation which was rapidly adopted was the Sony 'Walkman'. However, some products are very non-observable – few people could tell you the make of dental floss used by even their very best friends.

Think – How do advertisers make us aware of their 'private' products such as toilet paper, toothbrushes, or underwear?

Using the product innovations listed in the earlier exercise:

Think – How well do these products fit the five characteristics of innovation:

- a new coloured toothpaste?
- an electric town car?
- toothpaste with added fluoride?
- the microwave oven?
- the launch of a 'new' model of an existing car?
- the Mars ice-cream?
- the introduction of 24-hour cash dispensers at banks?
- the introduction of 24-hour banking?
- the compact disc?
- wholefoods?
- laser printers to replace dot matrix printers for computers?
- 'virtual reality' machines?

Another question for the reader is:

> **Think** – What successful innovations can you identify which do
> not possess these characteristics?

And again:

> **Think** – What new product failures can you identify?
> – How do they fit with the 'required' characteristics?

It may be that some other characteristics have arisen from your analysis of success and failure – there may well be additional factors such as the time lag before consumers experience the desired benefits (the prediction would be that the greater the delay in gratification, the less the chance of trying out the product). The symbolism of the product for the consumer seems to be another important factor – how else can we explain the dominance of Levi jeans when they are so very similar to most other jeans?

Another issue which deserves some attention is *speed of diffusion*. While the importance of word-of-mouth has been emphasized, it does have a significant drawback in that it is largely outside the marketer's control. The thing that the marketer can control is the marketing strategy to be adopted and, again, this is likely to be a significant determinant of the speed of diffusion. Promotion is often used to create a favourable image for the brand by pairing it with suitably positive images. The aim is to boost the symbolism of the product – in many markets where the products are essentially very similar, symbolism may be the only relative advantage that an organization has to offer. Price can also create brand image as well as an immediate relative advantage. Generally, high prices denote quality, low prices, low quality. Price can also be used to position a product as 'good value for the money'. Once established, economies of scale can sometimes allow a sustained price advantage for a product. Another important element of the marketing mix is distribution – good site locations and a large number of outlets will obviously help the diffusion process.

Another factor may well be what Engel, Blackwell and Miniard refer to as *competitive intensity*. Here they are suggesting that some organizations are more highly competitive than others, follow more aggressive strategies and allocate greater resources to the launch of new products. The suggestion is (perhaps not surprisingly) that such organizations' innovations diffuse more quickly.

The reputation of the organization can also be a helping influence. It is often asserted that IBM computers are not as technically advanced as many of their competitors, but their products continue to dominate the market because of the reputation the company holds and the fact that, to many people, computers mean IBM.

In many fields, diffusion will be helped when there is a standardized technology. At the time of writing, doubt is being expressed about the viability of a new television channel in the UK due to the fact that existing frequencies will need to be changed and millions of video recorders may need to be retuned. The problems of agreeing common international standards for things like the technology for high-resolution television have, it is claimed, held up the diffusion process for a period of years.

One final set of factors centres on interest rates, the state of the economy and the notion of consumer confidence. Such things are often the lifeblood of day-to-day politics, but their impact on consumer behaviour cannot be denied, particularly in the case of high-involvement, high-cost items. High interest rates will affect the real price paid by the customer, and the level of consumer confidence seems likely to determine an individual's willingness to commit himself to expensive, long-term payments. When watching the news, it sometimes sounds as if consumers are concerned about the exchange rate and similar economic indicators, whereas the reality is more likely to be both more personal and more immediate. Purchasing behaviour is more likely to be affected by individuals' perceptions as to whether they are likely to receive their performance-related bonus – or even whether they will still have a job in six months' time.

Think – What experience have you had of putting off a purchase until things had 'picked up'?

Consumers in the diffusion process

An important element of the diffusion process is the consumer and the acceptance that different types of consumers may adopt a new product at different times in the product's life cycle. Rogers' classic work identified five categories of adopter, and is often described pictorially in terms of either a normal distribution curve (Figure 13.8) or an 'S' curve (Figure 13.9).

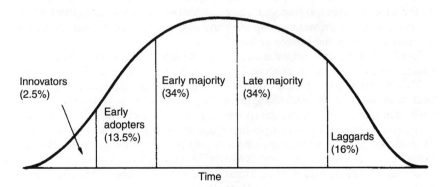

Figure 13.8

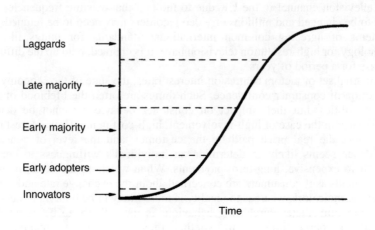

Figure 13.9

Innovators are venturesome individuals who are willing to take risks.

Early Adopters are often viewed as more respectable, but are quick to take up new ideas which they have seen 'piloted' by the Innovators. They also seem to act as some sort of role models and opinion leaders for the

Early Majority, who, typically, may seek to avoid risks and who are relatively deliberate in their purchasing behaviour, while the

Late Majority are sceptical and cautious about new ideas and the

Laggards are very traditional and set in their ways.

The time dimension is important, as the model suggests that each group learns by observing the previous group's behaviours and then, after the 'vicarious learning', adopting the behaviour itself.

If this is correct, the importance of the innovators cannot be overstated. The whole process will stall if someone does not make the first purchases.

The characteristics of these consumer groups have been the focus of a great deal of research. The results suggest that innovativeness is often most clearly marked in people who are of high social status, upwardly mobile, educated and/or literate, and young. But, not surprisingly, one of the key determinants is income. High-income people not only have the ability to buy more new products, they also have the ability to risk trying new products. This factor is likely to be of extreme importance when dealing with high-cost items, but the linkage when considering low-cost, low-involvement goods is less clear.

Some research has indicated personality variables – innovators are more likely to be risk takers. Other research has proposed a possible link between innovation and the cognitive style of problem solving – innovators being individuals who tend to produce different ways of organizing, deciding and behaving which may involve significant change and the undertaking of new activities.

Communication patterns also appear to link with innovation. Earlier adopters seem to use both mass media and interpersonal sources more than later adopters. There is some evidence to suggest that the gay community (mentioned as a possible market segment in the previous chapter) may possess many of the key characteristics required for innovators and early adopters, and could therefore be a useful segment to target. However, such an approach is not without its dangers, as other groups in society could come to see the product as being associated with gays and become less willing to adopt a product which they see as being part of a dissociative group lifestyle. On the other hand, it is not at all unusual to find elements of gay fashion being happily absorbed into the mainstream.

Loyalty

One of the prime aims of marketing is to satisfy the customer and ensure repeat business. The issue of customer loyalty has become big business over recent years, and it can be viewed as part and parcel of the very processes we have been considering in the foregoing chapters. However, competition and computer technology have now pushed customer loyalty centre stage.

In the past we have had promotional devices such as stamps – these were collected and eventually exchanged for goods. This has developed further through special offers (collect the tokens and claim your tomato soup bowl) to Air Miles on your credit card.

The large grocery retailers have embarked on a fierce campaign aimed at market share and consumer loyalty. In addition to special offers, cut price petrol is offered if your bill is over a certain amount; vouchers for good causes are given for using your own plastic carrier bags; cash rebates are available via the loyalty card such as the Tesco Clubcard and Sainsbury Reward Card schemes mentioned earlier.

However, the technology now available gives most of these 'normal' marketing devices added impetus because, as we noted, it allows the retailer to track individual household expenditure. Patterns of buying can be determined and variations acted upon. Stories are currently circulating that the purchase of a home pregnancy testing kit, for instance, can trigger mailshots of what are considered suitable follow-up offers.

It is also possible to identify when a customer has failed to shop for a week or two. This may involve the notion of switching retailer – and the computer can be programmed to respond by sending out encouraging flyers to tempt the wanderer to return. This does give rise to the idea that the customer might be able to play off one superstore against another.

It is also common in some industries, such as bingo clubs, for attendance to be monitored and absentees specifically targeted.

It becomes a daunting prospect if we are unable not to go shopping without being spotted!

14 'Pass me my crystal ball...'

Forecasting, change and the future

Very old joke
'The meeting of the Clairvoyants' Society has had to be cancelled due to unforeseen circumstances'.

The CIM defines marketing as 'the management process responsible for identifying, anticipating and satisfying consumers' requirements profitably'. The verbs 'identifying' and 'anticipating' imply forecasting.

In the modern organization, the idea of market forecasting is particularly relevant – especially for those in competitive markets. Organizations which trade are concerned with the level of demand, as this will determine the amount of cash coming into the organization from sales revenue. Even organizations which are not 'traders' are concerned, as they will need to make a case for their budgets, or predict the levels of service possible under different budgetary limits.

The forecast demand levels are, in fact, central to many organizational decisions – they are often the basis for strategic decisions about issues such as:

- purchase/stock levels of raw materials
- staffing levels
- training needs
- planning production
- distribution options
- securing finance.

There is a case for revisiting the ideas on control discussed earlier when we explored the idea of management being a process of reducing uncertainty – the forecast (in this case, market forecasts) being at the very core of the thinking.

Different situations, different problems

In broad terms, there would seem to be three separate situations in which we may be involved. They are:

1 Where we are operating with existing products/brands/services in an existing market. This situation is characterized by the existence of historical sales data – in all probability this data will be available for our competitors as well as for our own organization. It implies a ready access to sales reports, customer satisfaction surveys, 'reality-based' attitude research and the rest of the customer care package.
2 In this case we may be introducing a new brand into an existing market. Here we will have a different database, as there will be no information on the new brand – but we may well have extensive knowledge of the market, the target customers and the relative performances of the competing brands in that market.
3 The third case is where we have a new product which is creating a new market. Here we will have little in the way of hard, historical data and may well have to rely on information gathered via marketing research. It may be recalled that we thought that this was a situation in which there was the greatest uncertainty and hence the most risk in marketing and business terms.

In addition, we may identify two different environmental states:

1 *Stable* – in which little is likely to change either in the market, technology or demand.
2 *Dynamic* – in which extensive change is likely.

When looking at the process of forecasting it is important to recognize that there are some overlapping and potentially confusing concepts in this area and it may be useful, before we go much further, to borrow from Foster and Davis (1994), who make a distinction between:

● *Projections* – these stem from using simple averaging techniques to find trends and seasonality in historical data, and using these to produce estimates of future movements – on the basis of 'all things being equal'.
● *Predictions* – these are the result of using more powerful statistical analysis to identify factors which are linked with historical movements, and developing estimates making appropriate assumptions about each factor.
● *Forecasts* – these result from merging the statistical projections or predictions with market knowledge, to provide what is agreed to be the best current estimate of future movements.

So we might conclude that forecasting is a mixture of both 'science' (statistical analysis) and 'art' (market knowledge, predicting future developments, etc.). It is this very mixture of the quantified and the intuitive which makes the process of forecasting difficult – in fact, the only thing one can be sure of is that any forecast we make will be proven wrong sooner or later. The only debate is likely to be by how much and when. In real terms, the difference between a 'good' forecast and a 'bad' forecast is that the 'good' will be less wrong than the 'bad'.

Many of the difficulties inherent in the forecasting process have been discussed elsewhere in this text, e.g. the problems of controlling unpredictable factors, the sheer number of factors which may influence a given market, the difficulties of environmental screening, the hazards of operating within an economy which may be driven by forces outside the control of the government, let alone a marketing manager, etc.

On the other hand, we may be able to think of cases where the market remains relatively stable, so that forecasting sales for next month is relatively simple. We may also have a situation where sudden fluctuations are rare and the seasonal variations seem to be fixed in a clear and identifiable pattern. In such cases it does not require much skill to add a percentage to last year's figures to produce a workable forecast for the coming year.

So:

Think – If we are going to be wrong, why bother to forecast?

The paradox seems to be that when forecasts are easy to produce they are of least value, and when they are most difficult to produce they are of most strategic importance.

The general justification is that those who have understood their markets in calmer times may have a baseline from which to understand any changes occurring. The underlying assumption is that plans made on the basis of analysis and understanding are much more likely to be of use than those based on 'gut feeling' or, even worse, wishful thinking.

In the marketing context forecasting should:

- give a clear idea of likely weekly, monthly or yearly sales
- contribute to an understanding of how a market operates – both in terms of our own marketing mix decisions and also predicting the impact of competitors' strategic decisions
- help us with 'what if' scenario planning
- give warnings of threats/opportunities occurring within a market.

Timescales

One common and useful framework for looking at forecasting is to draw a distinction between:

- short-term
- medium-term
- long-term

forecasts. We are all used to this when we consider weather forecasts – the short-term is usually given in the evening and is concerned with whether it will rain tomorrow; the medium-term is the forecast for the coming week; the long-term is usually concerned with either a 'hard winter/hot summer' or global warming.

Needless to say, the timescales will vary according to the industry/situation we are considering. For electricity supply, for instance, we may well define short-term as being the next day, but the medium-term may well be looked at in terms of the next five years; long-term could be stretching as far as the next fifty years. These forecasts could be used for very different purposes. Short-term forecasts will be concerned with loading and ensuring supply at peak demand times, and so may be looking at factors such as predicted weather and temperatures, specific events (such as Bank Holidays or the Cup Final). Medium-term forecasts will be focused on the need to predict maintenance demands as well as the demand for the product, and so may well be looking at factors such as age of equipment, new factory openings, football clubs planning to instal floodlighting, etc. Long-term forecasts are likely to be centring on issues such as the need to design and build new facilities for electricity generation, plans to extend/contract the National Grid and so forth. In all of these cases the capacity for error is considerable – due to factors such as an unexpected drop in temperature, the withdrawal of a company planning to move into an area, the discovery of new technology which may allow alternative generation opportunities. All this is not to mention the predictable uncertainties of government changes and political realignments.

At this point it is also worth pointing out that there are other significant dimensions to forecasting in addition to timescale. The principal ones are:

- *Geographic area* – we may wish to develop forecasts for different parts of the country, continent or globe
- *Products* – we may wish to introduce a new product to our range, and forecasts may be needed for such an eventuality
- *Brands* – the introduction of a new brand would require appropriate forecasts.

In each case we may need short-, medium- and long-term forecasts – so the number of individual forecasts can escalate rapidly.

Whatever type of forecast we are concerned with, the very process is intimately tied to the guesses we make about what is likely to happen – i.e. the assumptions we make.

Assumptions

As we commented in our earlier discussion on perception, we often 'see what we expect/want to see', so the importance of assumptions becomes clear – the assumptions are likely to affect our perceptions and hence the decisions we make. We also suggested that many jokes are based on the process of leading the listener to a particular set of assumptions and then changing the mindset with the punchline.

Another very old joke

Man telephoning doctor: 'Doctor, come quickly, my wife has appendicitis – she has stomach cramps and is in pain'.
Doctor: 'Give her an aspirin, and tell her to sleep it off'.
Man: 'Why won't you come – she has appendicitis'.
Doctor: 'You are assuming that it is appendicitis – but I know that I removed your wife's appendix seven years ago'.
Man: 'Come at once – you are assuming that I only have one wife'.

As we are dealing with an uncertain future when forecasting, it can be argued that the most important task is to *identify*, *recognize* and *record* the assumptions that underpin the forecast made. The advantage of doing this as a relatively formalized process is that, if the circumstances do not occur as we predicted (i.e. the assumptions prove to be wrong), we will know *why* the forecast went awry, we may then be able to switch to an alternative set of assumptions and may be able to learn from the experience and improve our forecasting in the future. We might even coin the expression *'aftcasting'* for this process of looking backwards to improve our future predictions.

This process of 'aftcasting' will also help to determine the level of confidence that we might hold regarding any particular forecast. If we look back to previous predictions and forecasts and find that they have been largely right, then we are more likely to give credence to the current forecast. On the other hand, if history shows that we have been mostly wrong, we are likely to have less confidence.

History, statistics and data

In the previous section we looked at the presentation and interpretation of data. In this section we now revisit to see how we can use these techniques to help us in the important forecasting process.

Our historical data may be any number of things:

- Sales
- Revenue
- Market share
- Profitability
- Size of market, etc.

We may find it of value to plot graphs of one against another with a view to ascertaining whether there is any significant correlation between the two factors.

Correlation measures the strength of the relationship between two variables and is usually expressed in terms of a *correlation coefficient*. The value of the correlation coefficient, when calculated, always lies between +1 and –1. A value of +1 means that the two variables are perfectly correlated and if we have a value close to +1 then it indicates that the two variables move in the same direction together – i.e. as one increases, so does the other. This would show on a scattergram as in Figure 14.1.

If we obtain a correlation coefficient of –1, this indicates that the two variables

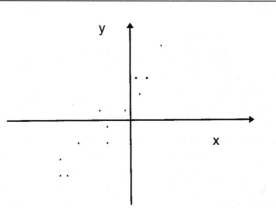

Figure 14.1   Scattergram showing positive correlation between x and y

are perfectly correlated in a negative sense – i.e. if we have a value close to –1 it means that as x increases, so y decreases. Again, this could be shown by a scattergram (Figure 14.2).

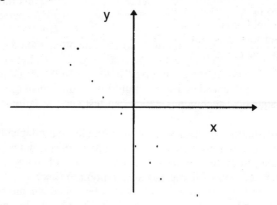

Figure 14.2   Scattergram showing negative correlation between x and y

Values which come out as close to zero suggest that there is no linear relationship between the two variables. This would show on a scattergram as in Figure 14.3.

We could use correlation calculation to establish the price elasticity of our product – i.e. get a measure of how price-sensitive it is by correlating sales volume with price.

As mentioned in the introduction to this section, we will not go into the arithmetical calculations on the grounds that these are time-consuming, depressing for many students and relatively simple to handle given an appropriate computer program. However, it is important to ensure that we do not over-interpret our correlations.

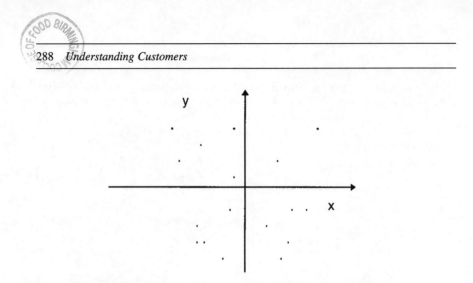

Figure 14.3   Scattergram showing no correlation between x and y

Some reasons for caution

1 A high correlation figure can emerge by accident – in other words, by a statistical freak. If we run the statistics between many disparate variables we may come across things which correlate highly – *but which are not linked*. Examples of this emerge from time to time – one often quoted example was the figures in the 1930s showing a strong positive correlation between suicides and the number of radios in the community. In the post-war period there was a time when cancer rates correlated quite highly with the consumption of bananas. There are statistical techniques which can test such 'relationships', but these are beyond the scope of this text.
2 A high figure may also occur when both variables are independently related to a third. We might find that the price of refrigerators correlates closely with the price of cars. The 'third variable' might be the cost of living (indicated by the inflation rate and cost of living index) at a point in time.
3 Another possibility is that the variables may be linked *via* another variable. An example could be that motorcycle accidents are negatively correlated to age. The reason may well be that more young people ride motorbikes than older persons – and age may well be associated with a more cautious and conservative riding style.
4 Yet another possibility is that we may get a zero correlation figure because the two variables are not linked linearly. They may have a clear relationship, but if it shows on a graph as in Figure 14.4, the correlation coefficient is likely to be close to zero.

Regression analysis

This is the technique which allows us to describe the relationship between variables using a mathematical equation.

If we have significantly high correlation (either positive or negative) we may wish to explore the relationship in more detail. For statisticians, this is often concerned with finding the 'line of best fit' and, in some cases, identifying the equation of this line. The reason for this is that more detailed calculations, based on the relationship, can then be carried out and projections derived by the process called *extrapolation*.

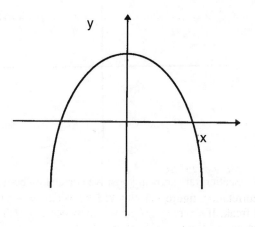

Figure 14.4

One very simple method of finding the line of best fit does not involve calculations at all. It involves plotting the data on a scattergram and then drawing the line of best fit by eye! The easy access to clear plastic rulers makes this even easier. If we use our earlier example (Figure 14.1).

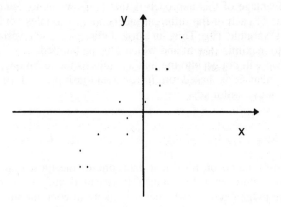

Figure 14.5 Scattergram showing positive correlation between x and y

we can use our ruler to draw what looks like a 'line of best fit' – it may well be as useful as going through complicated calculations (Figure 14.6).

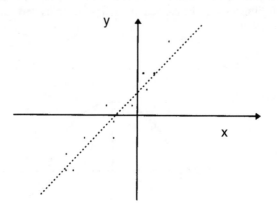

Figure 14.6 Scattergram showing positive correlation between x and y and also a 'line of best fit'

Once again, there are now many computer packages which allow you to carry out regression analysis to determine the line of best fit. This is the line on which (all things being equal) we will base our projection.

Additionally there is a technique called *multiple regression* in which the calculations are even more complex) which allows the y variable (the dependent variable) to be related to a number of different x variables (independent variables) – i.e. whereas the original approach measured the relationship between y and a single x variable, this can explore the relationship between y and more than one x. The advantage of this approach is that it allows us to determine the relative importance of each of the different independent variables (x) in influencing the dependent variable (y). This, in turn, indicates which variables need to be included to maximize the fit and which may be omitted.

While we will not go into the mathematics of the technique, it is important to remember that it is based on *linear* relationships, and so the reservations identified above still hold.

Time series

In forecasting based on historical data, one of the most important activities is looking for patterns in historical data. If we can identify a pattern we may be able to exercise judgment as to whether it is likely to continue into the future – thus helping us considerably in the forecasting process. We construct a time series by plotting the dependent variable (e.g. sales, revenue, expenses, etc.) against time as the independent variable (x). In order to understand the structure of such a time series we need to consider four elements:

1 Trends
2 Cyclical movements
3 Seasonal movements
4 Irregular movements.

Trends
If we follow normal procedure we obtain a graph in which time is expressed on the x-axis and the dependent variable is the y axis.

Here are four basic formulations:

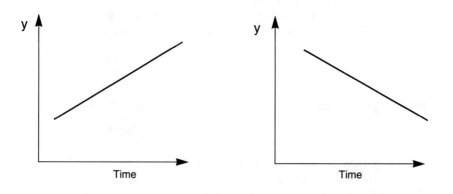

Figure 14.7   Increasing linear trend   **Figure 14.8**   Decreasing linear trend

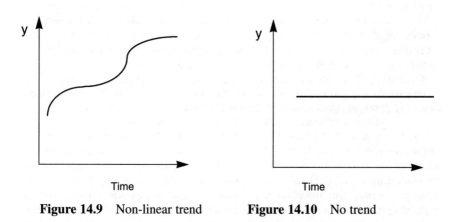

Figure 14.9   Non-linear trend   **Figure 14.10**   No trend

The increasing linear trend shows that the dependent variable has increased over time, and such an extended period of steady increase is likely to be the result of an expanding market if we were using sales volume as the dependent variable.

Conversely, the decreasing linear trend could reflect a decreasing market.

The non-linear trend shows that there is a variation in the sales – sometimes increasing, then levelling out and finally increasing again. Such a pattern could result from advertising and promotion campaigns, which have an effect while they are running but which do not continue to increase sales once they have ended.

The no trend series suggests that this could be a staple product where there is a constant demand which is unaffected over time.

These examples are simplistic, but show the ways in which such graphs might be interpreted. However, we can only determine that there is a trend – we do not necessarily know *why* the trend occurs.

In Figure 14.11 we have plotted sales by year. Obviously we may wish to express other data against different timescales – sometimes it may be appropriate to log things by hours, sometimes against days, while other data may be more appropriately examined monthly, quarterly or at even longer intervals.

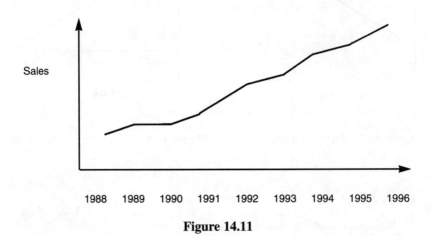

Figure 14.11

Here we clearly have a *time trend* – overall sales have risen over the nine years and if we were to apply our correlation programme we would find quite high positive correlation between the two variables sales and time.

But, as we have just pointed out, we may need extra work to determine the reason for the linkage. It may be due to factors which are *internal* to the organization, such as having an active marketing department which manipulates the marketing mix effectively. If, on the other hand, the product were to be incontinence pads, the 'improvement' could be due to an expanding market owing to increasing numbers of elderly persons in the community, i.e. an *external* factor.

We could also apply our regression analysis programme (or use our clear plastic ruler) to determine the line of best fit. This may then help us to project the likely sales figures for 1997, 1998, 1999, etc.

Cyclical movements
Sometimes we construct our time series graph and discover that we have a trend overall, but in addition we have a regular pattern of readings above and below the trend line. When the pattern lasts longer than a year, we call it *cyclical*. Figure 14.12 would be an example of a cycle, and it is the sort of thing we identified earlier in the book when we were looking at the economic cycle of depression, recovery, boom, recession.

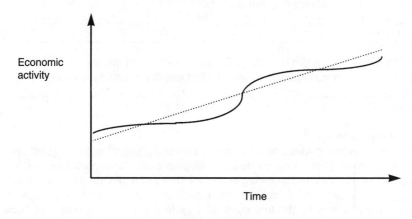

Figure 14.12

The regularity of the pattern allows us to forecast what is likely to happen next, and, within limits, when it is likely to occur.

Seasonal movements
These are exactly as described above, but the expression *seasonal* applies when the period of the repeated pattern is one year or less.

Obviously we are most comfortable when the seasonal pattern is annual (the common meaning of the word seasonal) – but statisticians use the word for shorter periods when repetitive patterns exist. So consumption of electrical power will show regular patterns over a 24-hour period (and also a weekly pattern), and these will both be called seasonal as well as the more obvious annual one when we consume more electricity during the cold winter months and less in the warmer summer months. Traffic flow may be another example of 24-hour and weekly patterns imposed upon a bigger annual seasonal usage.

Once again, we may only have identified a pattern – the important stage is to understand the reason for the pattern. In some cases it may be related directly to the calendar – the sale of Christmas cards and presents, or package holidays linked to school holidays, would be good examples. In other cases, such as the sale of sunglasses, ice-cream, or the consumption of water, the link may be to temperature or sunniness.

Having identified both the pattern and the underlying cause, we are now in a stronger position to predict future demand. We may also be in a position to make strategic marketing decisions to help reduce the impact of seasonality.

Example – Walls, the ice-cream manufacturer, found, not surprisingly, that sales were highly seasonal, so the decision was taken to 'diversify' into sausages – another seasonal product but one which allowed all-year-round activity.

Think – What other examples can you think of where organizations have levelled out their activity levels?

Irregular movements
This is the movement which does not fit into the trend, cyclical or seasonal patterns described above. These movements are analogous to the 'unexpected factors' we talked about when we were looking at control theory and may represent a random variability in the series caused by unanticipated, non-recurring factors. Alternatively, it may be the first signs of a cyclical pattern which has not been previously identified – think about the arguments as to whether a couple of good summers represent the signs of global warming or whether they are just part of the 'normal' variety we might expect.

Smoothing methods

These are the statistical techniques used to smooth out the irregular element of time series and give more accurate forecasts. Clearly, if we have a value which looks to be an 'oddity', we are faced with the problem of how much weight to attach to what may be a single rogue value.

The simplest approach is to calculate a *moving average*. We do this by calculating the mean of (say) the most recent four values. When the next reading comes in, we recalculate the mean using the new value, but dropping the one which came at the very beginning (i.e. still using the four most recent values).

It is useful to plot the moving average on the same graph as the original time series to see how well this technique eliminates the more extreme variations and gives a better (perhaps) easier line to extrapolate for our forecast.

A similar approach can be taken with seasonal fluctuations. Here it would be sensible to take a moving average of the overall series, but it is also useful to take a moving average of (say) Quarter 1 values, Quarter 2 values and so forth. This approach is the basis of *seasonal adjustment*, and it allows more sensitive and realistic forecasts to be made which include both the overall trend and the cyclical/seasonal elements in our projections.

In this section we have looked at a number of approaches to examining historical data to help us make better projections and predictions. Our forecasts will involve these calculations and techniques combined with our wider knowledge of the market within which we are operating (as considered in our discussions of marketing research) and the application of that most rare of commodities, common sense.

However, we may only have got half of the story. To date we have looked at historical data and evidence relating to the market concerned. This is, in effect, a static snapshot which is passive and does not take any account of the influence which the actions of the organization itself might have on the situation. If we return to our definition of marketing, we will see that it is an essentially *proactive* activity which is aimed at influencing and affecting the market and the consumers. So we will need to consider the likely impact of the marketing decisions and strategies which we may adopt.

Most of the approaches discussed apply primarily to short- and medium-term forecasting. The issues and data for long-term forecasts are slightly different.

Longer-term forecasts

It is perhaps self-evident that the further ahead one attempts to forecast, the greater the chance of error. Yet, as we have seen earlier, some business decisions have such a long lead time that we are forced to look ten, twenty or even fifty years ahead – and our forecasts about the market at that time are likely to be of even greater significance as the long-term projects are often the most important and expensive for the enterprise.

When looking further ahead, we can place much less reliance on our techniques which are based on historical data. It also demands a greater concern with external factors. We are likely to need assumptions about the size and make-up of the population, levels of economic activity, patterns of employment and wealth, education levels, inflation, competition, political alliances, etc. – and these are only some of the socio-political and economic factors. We will also need, in many cases, to predict future technologies, materials and processes.

Inevitably, the number of assumptions renders the outcomes rather more speculative than we might wish, and differing assumptions usually account for different forecasts emerging from different government and private 'think tanks'.

At the furthest end of the long-range forecast lies *scenario writing*. It is not uncommon for a number of scenarios to be developed – optimistic, pessimistic and one central view. Overall, such an approach is better suited to generating thought about the general circumstances likely to prevail rather than identifying specific predictions or forecasts about demand levels. Such scenario planning may help in planning how a company might remain competitive in the longer term, or how it might extricate itself from a market in a relatively orderly fashion, and is worth undertaking periodically, even on a very informal basis.

Review

Forecasting is a fundamental activity for proactive marketing management and can be conducted as short-term, medium-term or long-term, allowing short-, medium- and long-term decisions to be made. Statistical techniques can be employed to aid the process of analysing historical data with a view to establishing relationships or identifying time trends. In effect, we will use forecasting as a means of developing our own models and understanding of the world and markets in which we are operating.

An important element is the process which involves checking whether the assumptions we have made turned out to be correct and the model used accurate. We coined the expression 'aftcasting' to highlight an important step in learning and developing our understanding. We can also focus on our assumptions to engage in a useful process of playing 'what if...' and examining possible outcomes and contingencies.

The importance of expert knowledge and opinion must never be overlooked. Opinions can be gathered from both within and outside the organization. The formalized version of this is sometimes referred to as the *Delphi technique*, which seeks predictions and forecasts in a variety of areas from the experts. The results are then collated and summarized and the findings returned to the panel for review. This allows for assumptions to be modified and/or adapted in the light of other predictions. These are then reviewed and collated and another summary circulated. The process continues until all the experts have reached a degree of agreement and many of the assumptions have been tested and justified and their implications absorbed.

Even in relatively simple cases the development of such models can become complex. If we were to consider the demand for ice lollies we might draw up a model which focused on just three variables – price charged, temperature and competitor's price. If we use a very simplistic format and allow three classifications for each – high, medium or low – we rapidly discover that we already have twenty-seven possible configurations to consider. The advent of easily accessed computer programs is a great help in the whole process, but the overwhelming imperative must be that of understanding the market, not simply inputting data, pressing the button and believing the printout.

It seems highly plausible that the type of forecasting activity required will be a function of the environment in which we are operating:

- Simple linear forecasting is appropriate when the situation is straightforwardly progressive or predictable (e.g. council tax revenues, traffic flows, etc.)
- More complex scenario planning is appropriate in more dynamic environments
- Combinations of scenarios, modelling and linear forecasting may be appropriate in complex environments such as the oil industry.

It may also be a function of our perceived purpose. It is claimed that the Pentagon in America produced six future scenarios – all of which were predicated on the assumption of war. There is no Pentagon scenario based on the likelihood of universal peace!

A look into the crystal ball

We live in a world that is changing rapidly. In writing this book the author has been only too aware of the changing nature of marketing and advertising – the happenings of the past three years since the first edition have shown up the capacity of the world to throw up new problems and issues.

Still, as they say, 'nothing ventured, nothing gained'.

It may be worth attempting to make some more prophesies about social and behavioural factors which could affect the processes and practice of marketing as well as the general world of work. We may examine some of these possible changes, in no particular order.

Marketing and business issues

The indications are that the world move towards open, competitive markets will continue – and with it the move towards globalization in marketing and strategic terms. The competitive element leads to speculation on the problems facing organizations who operate in a saturated market. There are a number of options open to the enterprise in such a situation:

- It can 'invade' foreign markets with existing products to expand the potential market
- It can create alternative uses for current products with the aim of 'breaking through' natural saturation limits
- It can create extended products for alternative uses
- It can aim to increase the rate of innovation to decrease the time to replacement
- It can aim to meet customer needs more closely – i.e. increase the amount of variety or customization – to gain a larger share of new and replacement business.

Example – Mars reached saturation level in the US sweet market in the late 1980s (it had reached about 19 lb per person per year).
Mars response was to increase the variety in its products.
It introduced more new products in 1990 than it had in the previous twenty-five years.

Think – What other examples can you think of where organizations have adopted (or are adopting) such strategies?

In Chapter 1 we sketched out a history of the marketing function, and comment was passed that we may be at the start of a new phase which we called mass customization, so it is natural to examine this idea in a little more detail. This is part of the move towards 'getting close to the customer' which allows the organization to know exactly what the customer wants and aims to satisfy that specific need. The original approach to this was the custom-built product, which always attracted premium prices and was beyond the reach of all but a tiny handful of very rich individuals. The current objective is to provide a 'customized' service to customers without the penalty of high cost – but with all the benefits of tying the buyer ever closer to the organization.

Six strategies to mass-customizing products and services are emerging:

1 *Component sharing*. Here the same component is used across many products. Komatsu found its costs rising due to product variety in the 1970s driven mainly by its expansion into international markets. The company responded by producing a standardized core module which could be shared across all product models.
2 *Component swapping*. In this operation different components are paired with the same basic product, thus creating as many products as there are components to swap. T-shirts or Swatch watches would be examples of this approach.
3 *Cut-to-fit*. Here one or more components is continually variable within preset or practical limits. Some jeans' manufacturers are already working with this idea and, indeed, it has been common for many years in the 'customizing' of men's suits. Another example is the National Bicycle Industrial Co (part of Matsushita), which can produce 11,231,862 variations on eighteen models of bikes in 199 colour patterns and an infinite number of sizes!
4 *Mix*. Components are mixed together to such an extent that the end product is unrecognizable. Here paint colours, fertiliser, breakfast cereals would be examples. This approach can work with anything that has a recipe, so the potential for (say) vended customized drinks could be considerable.
5 *Bus*. Here we have a standard structure that can attach different fittings and components. Camera manufacturers have done this for years and it is a very profitable way to extend product life, but other examples could include products such as track lighting or regional magazines.
6 *Sectional*. Here we can have a configuration of any number of differing components in arbitrary ways, so long as each component is connected to another at standard interfaces. Older examples would be Lego or Meccano, but modern digital news retrieval systems would also fall into this category.

Another example of mass customization which will be interesting to watch is the Nissan 'five any's' – Any volume, Any time, Anybody, Anywhere and Anything. Here the objective is to create a system to produce low-volume, special niche vehicles at reasonable cost. This implies very fast development and start-up. The underlying assumption is that the final assembly of cars will be from large modules, which would be brought together and finally 'coated' with the body panels.

The design element would involve the customer (Nissan has gone so far as to name this new role the *Automotive prosumer*), who chooses the combination of body structure, drive train components, suspension, etc. The system will check for safety aspects which may be problematic in some combinations. At the more cosmetic level it is planned that the prosumer will be able to define the seat contours, instrument panel layout, trim, sound systems, etc. It is even hoped to continue the process by developing suspension systems which can be modified while the vehicle is in use. The aim is to allow this design process to take place at a workstation in the dealership.

All of which seems admirable – *the punchline is that Nissan is planning to make the lead time from specification to delivery three days*!

It has even been suggested that final assembly could be done at the dealership – that really would be getting close to the customer.

All of these ideas are part of the new movement of relationship market-ing which centres on reducing the 'distance' between seller and buyer. The development of the computerized tracking systems linked to supermarket checkouts which allow individualized purchasing patterns to be identified is a similar approach. The signs are that we will see more of it in a wider range of contexts.

Macro issues affecting people at work

The workforce are subject to broader issues in just the same way as the popu-lation at large – indeed, they are the population at large. The 'demographic downturn' has led to a shortage of school-leavers in the mid-1990s. This is likely to create problems for organizations who have traditionally recruited young persons as trainees (the National Health Service being a typical example which will need new sources of trainee nurses if targets are to be met). The knock-on effect of shortages could distort rates of pay and create problems of comparisons and career progression. Organizations may need to seek alternative sources of labour – women returners and the newly retired are the sources most quoted, although government actions such as raising the retirement age could also diminish the impact somewhat.

The legal requirements for equal opportunities for women, ethnic minorities, the disabled, etc. could also be significantly enhanced by market forces in the changed labour market.

The emergence of a single European market will mean mobility of labour as well as increased markets and competition. The need for improved language training for all levels of the organization seems imminent – not just overseas reps and senior management, but also first-line supervisors, telephonists, etc.

One significant factor which we may need to consider is the state of the economy – both nationally and worldwide. The 1980s and early 1990s saw a growing number of people unemployed and with markedly less job security than had been common over the previous forty years. Some writers, such as Handy and Hutton, have speculated that we may be approaching the 40–30–30 society. In this scenario only 40 per cent of the population have secure permanent employment, 30 per cent are in insecure or temporary jobs and 30 per cent are unemployed or casual, marginalized workers. If this were to come about, the impact on the marketing field would be considerable – with disposable income focused in a relatively small group and the opportunity for a 'new' form of market segmentation emerging.

Another crucial fact is that the political and social values of a society will permeate all organizations. The political colouring of future governments will determine many of the problems faced by managers and marketers.

The development of mass communication systems

We already have satellite TV links and there is a growing market for dishes and decoders. It seems likely that the penetration of satellite and cable TV will continue as these channels recognize and realize their economic power in buying up major events (particularly sport) for 'resale' via their particular systems. It could also emerge that the 'media moguls' capitalize on their position and seek economies of scale by standardizing their product over large areas of the globe. The result could be the development of, say, some form of 'Euroculture'. An alternative could be an even more pervasive worldwide American culture.

The speed of worldwide communication suggests that fashions may spread ever more rapidly. The marketing opportunities offered by this increasing ability to reach very large proportions of the population very quickly afford great opportunities for marketers. If this were to happen, the downside would be a tendency for fashions to last even shorter periods of time before they are swamped by the next wave. In such market sectors, the diffusion process would be speeded up across the whole range.

A counter-prediction could be the likelihood of the development of many more local communication systems which would focus very much on more immediate issues relevant to much more limited geographical areas. The probability is that both scenarios may be true so that, overall, the range of communication media will increase, thus offering significant choices and opportunities to the marketer.

High technology

In many ways the future is already with us – in the shape of computers, robots, fax machines and so forth. The future looks set to expand the utilization of such technology.

This could result in changing patterns of working – the advent of computers and modems means that working from home may be a real possibility for many people. The impact on sales jobs could be great, in that representatives may need to visit base only rarely as most contact could be via computer links and teleconferencing facilities.

Another prediction is that the rising importance of electronic communication will render many of our traditional skills obsolete. One which may become markedly less important is book reading. One could easily see the time when material such as that included in this text would be transmitted by means other than a book. This raises the interesting possibility that this volume could become a collector's item! More significant for the marketer is the development of the Internet and the growing number of homes connected to cable systems. The opportunities for communication – both ways – is enormous and seems likely to become a significant shopping medium for many markets.

Continuing this train of thought leads on to the impact on the education system. As we learn more about the ways in which people learn, and link this with the advances in technology, it seems likely that we will see the growth of new forms of education – much smaller groups being taught via electronic (TV) media. The implications of such an idea could be quite significant – schools as we know them could be a thing of the past and this, in turn, would have a dramatic effect on the socialization process (remember, school was described as a major part of the socialization process).

Other developments which could have important implications would centre on the effect of improving technology on the health of the population. Some predictions suggest that we may all live very much longer in the future, which would have a significant effect on the already problematic population and demographic profile of society.

The development of exciting new systems currently referred to as 'virtual reality' seem to have the potential to change our lives dramatically. For instance, if it becomes possible to 'experience' luxury overseas holidays without travel, in the privacy of one's own home, the impact on the leisure industry could be spectacular as well as disastrous.

Environmental issues

The rise of the 'green' consumer has been a well documented feature of the late 1980s and early 1990s. Environmental consciousness has made an impact on marketing practice through the emphasis on the use of recycled and bio-degradable packaging, and the development of environmentally friendly products. Despite some cynicism that the fad has passed, it would seem probable that this trend will continue with more companies developing products which can be sold under a 'green' banner, although future scientific findings will no doubt influence which part of the green movement will take the high ground. To some extent, such issues are the concerns of the relatively affluent and developed societies; it could prove difficult to sell the message to societies which can see the luxuries of the developed world, aspire to such benefits for themselves, but do not have the resources to pay the 'green premium'. One potential danger is companies overplaying the 'green card' by claiming environmental sanctity when it is not justified. This could lead to a sceptical consumer backlash.

Social changes

Within the UK there are suggestions that we will see a change in the political systems – less centralization and more regional structures. The implications for our party political system are significant.

Others predict the decline of class differentiation. What does seem even more probable is that, due to the changes in the demographic profile, a decline in gender role differentiation and dramatic changes in notions of what constitutes 'womens work' will emerge.

The signs of a continuing erosion of ideas such as the Welfare State seem clear. This, in turn, suggests a rapid increase in private medicine, private education and private social services.

At the time of writing, the movement towards a more integrated Europe continues. The growth of the EC as a trading and economic unit is highly significant, especially in the context of the new nations seeking membership. The move of Eastern bloc countries towards the free market system is clearly a marketing opportunity of immense proportions. Paradoxically, the break-up of the USSR could weaken the moves towards a larger unified Europe – nothing unites a group more than a common enemy. Once again, the future could embrace both the moves towards larger and smaller units by encouraging more relatively small countries to join together into 'federal' trading coalitions.

Taking an even broader perspective, worldwide predictions focus on the increasing expectations of people throughout the world (largely due to the improvements in communications) and the likelihood of a growing lack of tolerance of northern wealth by the inhabitants of the poorer southern hemisphere.

The indications are that we may well see an increase in political extremism.

Demographics

As already mentioned, the dominant features in the UK are:

- the impact of the low birth rate in the 1970s on the labour market is the key factor – the reduction in the number of school-leavers, with all that it implies for employment patterns and career paths, and
- the ageing population – the number of pensioners aged 60+ is marked.

The predicted advances in medical research and improvements in health care are likely to make the problem even worse.

This could see the end of the 'youth culture', which many say has dominated our society since the 1960s, and the associated rise in 'middle-age' numbers and values. There will also be a genuine growth of 'grey power' in terms of both markets and politics.

This also has implications for the 'non-greys'. There could develop a tension between the (relatively) small number of young, economically active souls attempting to care for a population which has become top-heavy in terms of pensioners, the retired and, potentially, an overwhelming need for geriatric care.

On the other hand, BSE/CJD, contaminated water, epidemics of antibiotic-resistant viruses, wars over diminishing water supplies, may make all of this speculation irrelevant.

As mentioned above, one of the worst problems may be attempting to run a system in the absence of economic growth, with worldwide population explosions and the expectation of the populace at large as major issues for us all to manage.

Most of the 'futurology' literature is relatively alarmist – books, newspapers, television programmes all trumpet 'the end of the world as we know it' – but it

...y client. Thus, a hungry person is not going to be motivated by consider-
tion of safety or affection, for example, until after his hunger has been satisfied. Maslow
later modified this argument (1968)[6] by stating that there was an exception to the rule in
respect of self-actualisation needs. For this group of needs it seems that satisfaction of a
need gives rise to further needs for realising one's potential.

What little research has been carried out on Maslow's hierarchy concept has proved
somewhat inconclusive. Probably the most frequent criticism that has been made is that
systematic movement up the hierarchy does not seem to be a consistent form of behaviour for many people. Alderfer (1972)[7], for example, argued that individual needs were
better explained as being on a continuum rather than in a hierarchy. He considered that
people were more likely to move up and down the continuum in satisfying needs at
different levels. He concluded that there were really only three major sets of needs –
Existence Needs (ie the basics of life), Relatedness Needs (ie social and interpersonal
needs), and Growth Needs (ie personal development needs). This does provide for a
more dynamic model of human needs. Nevertheless, Maslow's theory has provided a
useful framework for the discussion of the variety of needs that people may experience
work, and the ways in which their motivation can be met by managers.

McGregor – Theory X and Theory Y

Like Schein's classification of managers' assumptions about people, McGregor's Theory
and Theory Y[8] are essentially sets of assumptions about behaviour. In proposing his
ideas, McGregor pointed to the theoretical assumptions of management that underlie its
behaviour. He saw two noticeably different sets of assumptions made by managers
about their employees. The first set of assumptions regards employees as being inher-
ently lazy, requiring coercion and control, avoiding responsibility and only seeking security. This attitude is what McGregor termed 'Theory X'. This is substantially the theory of
scientific management, with its emphasis on controls and extrinsic rewards. Schein's
idea of Rational-Economic Man (see para 5 above) is very similar to that of Theory X.

McGregor's second set of assumptions sees people in a more favourable light. In this
case employees are seen as liking work, which is as natural as rest or play; they do not
have to be controlled and coerced, so long as they are committed to the organisation's
objectives. Under proper conditions they will not only accept but also seek responsibility; more rather than less people are able to exercise imagination and ingenuity at
work. These are the assumptions of 'Theory Y'. They are closely related to Maslow's
higher-level needs and to Schein's concept of Self-actualising Man.

Theory X and Theory Y have made their greatest impact in the managerial world rather
than in the academic world. The two labels have become part of the folklore of 'management style', which will be looked at in the chapter on leadership (Chapter 7). They do
serve to identify extreme forms of management style, but there is a danger that they may
be seen only as polar extremes representing an 'either/or' style. In real life a blend of the
two theories is more likely to provide the best prescription for effective management.

Herzberg's Motivation–Hygiene Theory

Herzberg's studies (1959)[9] concentrated on satisfaction at work. In the initial research
some two hundred engineers and accountants were asked to recall when they had experienced satisfactory and unsatisfactory feelings...

atisfaction, while others led frequently to dissatisfaction (see Figure 5.3). The factors iving rise to satisfaction were called *motivators*. Those giving rise to dissatisfaction were alled *hygiene factors*. These studies were later (1968)[10] extended to include various roups in manual and clerical groups, where the results were claimed to be quite similar.

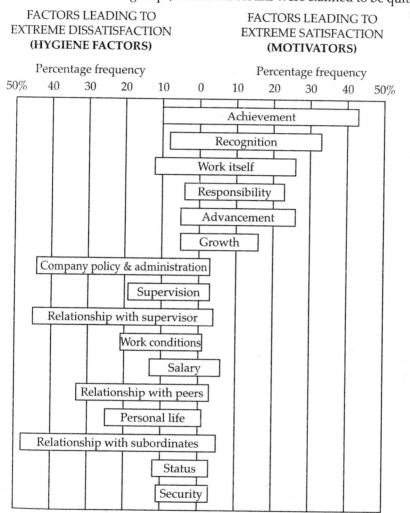

| FACTORS LEADING TO EXTREME DISSATISFACTION **(HYGIENE FACTORS)** | FACTORS LEADING TO EXTREME SATISFACTION **(MOTIVATORS)** |

e: The *length* of each 'box' denotes the frequency with which the factor occurred in the situations ribed by the respondents. The overlap of the boxes across the centre line indicates:

that motivators have their *negative* aspects, eg lack of achievement can lead to dissatisfaction; and

that hygiene factors have their *positive* aspects, eg salary can be a source of satisfaction.

Figure 5.3. Factors affecting job attitudes.

most important motivators, or satisfiers, to emerge were the following:

chievement.

ecognition.

Vork itself.

may be relevant to note that the producers of such material have a vested interest in frightening us, the recipients. Their interest is in selling books and newspapers, getting publicity – we could almost coin the phrase 'Bad news is good news; good news is no news'. As we saw in the chapter on perception, they need to make their predictions ever more terrifying in order to retain attention.

The reality is that, although the rate of change is undoubtedly fast in some spheres of activity, there are other areas which remain relatively stable. As a friend of mine summed it up, 'the speed of product innovation in consumer electronics is not matched by any comparable dynamism in the field of, say, bread, tomato soup, or household plumbing'.

Whatever the future holds, whether it be growth, decline or stagnation, the marketing of products, ideas and values will continue to be a major and significant task. The understanding of consumer behaviour will become ever more important.

A final point...

Forecasts and plans

There is a clear link between forecasts and plans. Generally we develop our plans following a forecasting process. A common depiction of the issues is as shown in Figure 14.13.

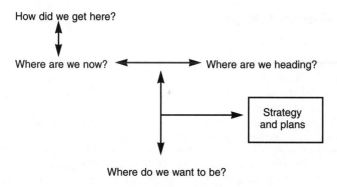

Figure 14.13

The link between the forecast and the plan should be fairly clear – we make our plans based on the conclusions we have reached, i.e.:

Forecast→Plan

However, we do need to be careful and realize that our plans could also affect the forecast. An example might be a plan to reduce the price of a highly price-sensitive product. This would give a different outcome to that forecast on the basis of 'all other things being equal', i.e.:

Plan→Forecast

In reality, of course, 'all other things being equal' is a pretty duff assumption, especially if we are operating in a competitive environment, as all the players in the market will be adjusting their marketing mix strategies hoping to establish a competitive edge.

In an earlier section we examined control theory as a means of explaining some of our actions and philosophy and we classified the causal factors as being *predictable*, *unpredictable* and *unexpected*. In the current context there are some factors which lend themselves to predictions based on historical data – we have already used the example of the changing age distribution of the population of the UK in an earlier explanation and we have already referred to the growing number of elderly persons in several places within the book. This might constitute an example of a factor which was both predictable and *external* to the organization. Similarly, a drop in the birth rate has obvious implications for the education service, the number of schools required and the employment of teachers.

In a competitive environment we face a situation where all of the players in a particular market will be attempting to influence the same body of customers. We therefore move into a world which is much less predictable, and one in which we have a chance of making our own scenarios come true by using our knowledge of behaviour to affect the outcomes. The concepts explored earlier in the book give an insight into the ways in which we, as marketing specialists, may influence the behaviour of the consumers in the marketplace.

Footnote – Forecasting, predicting and influencing – an example

One of the most advanced marketing operations affecting us in our daily lives is the supermarket. In the previous chapter we passed comment on the tracking methods now being developed which remove a great deal of speculation from the system – there is little need to conduct research to *ask* what people have bought if the information on their *actual* purchases is already available, along with their postcode, social class and other segmentation variables.

A visit to a supermarket offers an interesting case study (see Chapter 7 for the inherent weaknesses of one-shot anecdotes). Supermarkets are commonly located away from the centre of town and offer plenty of free car parking. It is not recommended to do a full week's shopping on the bus or by bicycle – this gives some indication of the class/status segment of the market they are aiming for. They provide facilities such as toilets, baby-changing facilities, newspaper sales, lottery tickets....' The logic of 'one-stop shopping' is very persuasive in that one often thinks 'I'll get it here while I'm shopping, even though it may be a little more expensive....'

We enter the store wheeling our trolley. The atmosphere is controlled – warm, fairly quiet, but with an encouraging, friendly hum. We are greeted with the sight of the fresh vegetables. These look attractive (often chosen for visual appeal and with some fruit waxed to give a glossy, 'healthy' appearance), aided by special lighting to enhance the colours. There is very little in the way of smell – certainly the vegetable section in the supermarket does not smell like a small local greengrocers. The fruit and vegetables are there to be handled and put into bags.

This gives the shopper a choice – to hand pick, or choose ready-packed (at a premium). The piles of produce make the idea of pre-packed seem quite attractive, as all the fruit and vegetables look very similar.

I then move on to the fish counter – which, interestingly, also does not smell. The products look appetizing, clean, glossy, unstained and bloodless, and are immediately available. Some writers have suggested that the aim of the process is to put the shopper into a light trance – but there is stimulation demanding attention (offers, discounts, 3 for the price of 2, 'as recommended by Delia Smith', etc.) – all preventing the slump into 'zombiedom'.

And yet, as the shopper cruises the aisles, special items leap into their awareness set (often from the 'hot spot' premium-priced shelves 51–53 inches up on the left). The bakery provides a welcome 'real smell' which provokes the purchase of freshly baked bread before a trip down the wine aisle. Again, recommendations are made, and it is often necessary to navigate around the special offer gondolas set in the middle of the wider aisles.

Products are given personalities – and we are classified to match. Supermarket specialists maintain that the population is split into dieters, foodies, economizers, health freaks and comfort eaters, and the various products are packages to fit (can you identify yourself?).

We come to the checkout, help is given to pack away our purchases, we pay by switch card, allowing a painless transaction, and the final elegance comes with the question, 'Do you want any cash back?' Not only a trolley full of shopping – but going home with a full purse! It only remains to fill up the car on the way out and it's all over for another week!

In Chapter 1 we raised the question of how you felt about manipulating the behaviour of other people.

We might finish by enquiring how you feel about being manipulated!

Key learning points from Part Four

- The consumer modelling approach is based on the assumption that we can simplify the consumer buying process and illustrate this in such a way as to portray something useful and meaningful about the phenomenon
- Models can be:
  verbal, algebraic or pictorial
  micro or macro
  descriptive, diagnostic or predictive
  static or dynamic
  qualitative or quantitative
  data based or theory-based
  behavioural or statistical
  generalized or ad hoc
  low-level, medium-level, high-level
- Models are evaluated on their:
  validity
  factual accuracy
  rationality

completeness
simplicity
originality
heuristic power
explanatory power
predictive power
- Models are classified as:
black box
personal variable
decision process
comprehensive or 'grand'
- The Nicosia model includes the firm and its relationship with the consumer and involves feedback
- The Howard–Sheth model is basically a learning model of the buying process
- The Engel, Kollatt and Miniard model is basically a decision-making model
- Learning is a process which can be applied to consumer behaviour
- We learn via association, motivation and reinforcement
- Conditioning approaches develop 'habits'
- Cognitive learning involves problem solution and the idea of 'latent' learning
- We also learn by imitating our role models
- An innovation is an idea or product perceived by the potential innovator as new
- Diffusion is the process by which news of the innovation spreads
- Adoption is the process by which the consumer decides whether or not to accept the innovation
- Opinion leaders are very important in the process of adoption
- Adopter categories:
innovators
early adopters
early majority
late majority
laggards
- Product characteristics which affect adoption:
relative advantage
compatibility
complexity
trialability
observability
- Forecasts are fundamental to marketing planning they encompass projections and predictions short-, medium- and long-term
- Patterns and relationships form the basis for our forecasts correlations, time trends.

References, bibliography and further reading

Argyle, M. (1989) *The Social Psychology of Work* (2nd edn), Penguin.

Baker, M. J. (1985) *Marketing: An Introductory Text* (4th edn), Macmillan.

Bannister, D. and Fransella, F. (1977) *Inquiring Man*, Penguin.

Bartol, K. M. and Martin, D. C. (1991) *Management*, McGraw-Hill.

Bee, R and Bee, F. (1993) *Management Information Systems and Statistics*, Institute of Personnel Management.

Bilton, T. *et al.* (1989) *Introducing Sociology*, Macmillan.

Bloom, B. S. (1956) *Taxonomy of Educational Objectives. Handbook 1: The Cognitive Domain,* Longmans Green.

Boring, E. G. (1923) *'Intelligence as the tests test it', New Republic,* 35.

Bowie, N. E. and Duska, R. F. (1990) *Business Ethics* (2nd edn), Prentice-Hall.

BPP (1995) *Understanding Customers*, BPP.

Buchanan, D. A. and Huczynsk, A. A. (1985) *Organisational Behaviour*, Prentice-Hall.

Cannon, T. (1994) *Corporate Responsibility*, Pitman.

Cattell, H. B. (1989) *The 16 PF: Personality in Depth*, IPAT.

Cattell, R. B., Eber, H. W. and Tatsuoka, M. M. (1988) *Handbook for the 16 PF*, IPAT.

Christensen, L. B. (1988 *Experimental Methodology* (4th edn), Allyn & Bacon.

Drake, R. I. and Smith, P. J. (1973) – *Behavioural Science in Industry*, McGraw-Hill.

Engel, J. F., Blackwell, R. D. and Miniard, P. W. (1990) *Consumer Behaviour* (6th edn), Dryden.

Engler B. (1985) – *Personality Theories* (2nd edn) – Houghton Mifflin.

Entwistle, N. J. (1981) *Styles of Learning and Teaching*, Wiley.

Eysenck, H. J. (1964) *Uses and Abuses of Psychology*, Penguin.

Eysenck, H. J. (1970) *The Structure of Human Personality*, Methuen.

Eysenck, H. J. and Wilson, G. (1978) *Know Your Own Personality*, Pelican.

Foster, D. with Davis, J. (1994) *Mastering Marketing,* Macmillan.

Foxall, G. (1990) *Consumer Psychology in Behavioural Perspective*, Routledge.

Gregory, R. L. (ed) (1987) *The Oxford Companion to the Mind*, Oxford University Press.

Gummesson, E. (1991) *Qualitative methods in Management Research,* Sage.

Hawkins, D. I., Best, R. J. and Coney, K. A. (1989) *Consumer Behaviour: Implications for Marketing Strategy* (4th edn), Irwin.

Helmstadter, G. C. (1970) *Research Concepts in Human Behaviour*, Appleton-Century-Crofts.

Hergenhahn, B. R. (1988) *An Introduction to Theories of Learning* (3rd edn), Prentice-Hall.

Howard, J. A. and Sheth, J. N. (1969) *The Theory of Buyer Behaviour*, Wiley.

Huff, D. (1973) *How to Lie with Statistics*, Penguin.

Jarry, D. and Jarry, J. (1991) *Dictionary of Sociology*, Collins.

Johns, T. (1994) *Perfect Customer Care,* Century.

Kakabadse, A., Ludlow, R. and Vinnicombe, S. (1987) *Working in Organisations*, Penguin.

Karlins, M. and Abelson, H. (1970) *Persuasion*, Crosby Lockwood.

Kolb, D. A. *et al.* (1971) *Organisational Psychology: An Experiential Approach*, Prentice-Hall.

Kotler, P. (1986) *Marketing Management* (3rd ed), Prentice-Hall.

Kotler, P. and Roberto E.L. (1989) *Social Marketing*, Free Press.

Lawson, R. W. (1988) 'The family life cycle: a demographic analysis', *Journal of Marketing Management,* Vol. 4, No. 1, CIM.

Luft, J. and Ingham, H. (1955) *The Johari Window: A Graphic Model of Interpersonal Awareness*, UCLA.

McDaniel, C. and Gates, R (1993) *Contemporary Marketing Research* (2nd edn), West.

McDonald, M. (1992) *Strategic Marketing Planning,* Kogan Page.

McGregor, D. (1960) *The Human Side of Enterprise,* McGraw-Hill.

Maxwell, A. E. (1970) *Basic Statistics in Behavioural Research* – Penguin.

Mehrabian, A. (1968) *An Analysis of Personality Theories*, Prentice-Hall.

Narayana, C. L. and Markin, R. J. (1995) 'Consumer behaviour and product performance: an alternative conceptualization', *Journal of Marketing*, 39.

Ohmae, T. (1990) *The Borderless World*, Fontana.

Oppenheim, A. N. (1966) *Questionnaire Design and Attitude Measurement*, Heinemann.

Osgood, C. E., Suci, G. J. and Tannenbaum, P. H. (1957) *The Measurement of Meaning*, University of Illinois Press.

Packard, V. (1957) *The Hidden Persuaders*, Penguin.

Peter, J. P. and Olson, J. C. (1990) *Consumer Behaviour and Marketing Strategy* (2nd edn), Irwin.

Peters, T. J. and Austin, N. (1985) *A Passion for Excellence*, Random House.

Peters, T J. and Waterman, R. H. (1982) *In Seach of Excellence,* Harper & Row.

Pettinger, R (1994) *Management* – Macmillan.

Petty, R. E. and Cacioppo, J. T. (1987) 'The effects of involvement on responses to argument quantity and quality,' *Journal of Consumer Research*, 14.

Reber, A. S. (1985) *Dictionary of Psychology*, Penguin.

Reeves, T. K., and Harper, D. (1981) *Surveys at Work: a Practitioner's Guide,* McGraw-Hill.

Robertson, I. T. and Cooper, C. L. (1983) *Human Behaviour in Organisations*, Macdonald and Evans.

Robson, C. (1973) *Experiment, Design and Statistics in Psychology*, Penguin.

Schein, E. H. (1970) *Organisational Psychology* (2nd edn), Prentice-Hall.

Thouless, R. H. (1953) *Straight and Crooked Thinking*, English Universities Press.

Turton, R. (1991) *Behaviour in a Business Context*, Chapman & Hall.

Watson, T. J. (1986) *Management, Organisation and Employment Strategy*, Routledge & Keegan Paul.

Williams, K. C. (1981) *Behavioural Aspects of Marketing*, Butterworth-Heinemann.

Williams, R. (1976) *Keywords*, Fontana.

Wilson, D. C. (1992) *A Strategy for Change,* Routledge.

Wilson, R. M. S. and Gilligan, C. with Pearson, D. J. (1992) *Strategic Marketing Management: Planning, Implementation and Control,* Butterworth-Heinemann.

Wright, G. (1984) *Behavioural Decision Theory*, Penguin.

Index